WHEN THE DECLARATION OF INDEPENDENCE WAS NEWS

IN CONGRESS, JULY 4, 1776.

A DECLARATION

BY THE REPRESENTATIVES OF THE

UNITED STATES OF AMERICA,

IN GENERAL CONGRESS ASSEMBLED.

WHEN in the Course of human Events, it becomes necessary for one People to dissolve the Political Bands which have connected them with another, and to assume among the Powers of the Earth, the separate and equal Station to which the Laws of Nature and of Nature's God entitle them, a decent Respect to the Opinions of Mankind requires that they should declare the causes which impel them to the Separation.

We hold these Truths to be self-evident, that all Men are created equal, that they are endowed by their Creator with certain unalienable Rights, that among these are Life, Liberty, and the Pursuit of Happiness—That to secure these Rights, Governments are instituted among Men, deriving their just Powers from the Consent of the Governed, that whenever any Form of Government becomes destructive of these Ends, it is the Right of the People to alter or to abolish it, and to institute new Government, laying its Foundation on such Principles, and organizing its Powers in such Form, as to them shall seem most likely to effect their Safety and Happiness. Prudence, indeed, will dictate that Governments long established should not be changed for light and transient Causes; and accordingly all Experience hath shewn, that Mankind are more disposed to suffer, while Evils are sufferable, than to right themselves by abolishing the Forms to which they are accustomed. But when a long Train of Abuses and Usurpations, pursuing invariably the same Object, evinces a Design to reduce them under absolute Despotism, it is their Right, it is their Duty, to throw off such Government, and to provide new Guards for their future Security. Such has been the patient Sufferance of these Colonies; and such is now the Necessity which constrains them to alter their former Systems of Government. The History of the present King of Great-Britain is a History of repeated Injuries and Usurpations, all having in direct Object the Establishment of an absolute Tyranny over these States. To prove this, let Facts be submitted to a candid World.

He has refused his Assent to Laws, the most wholesome and necessary for the public Good.

He has forbidden his Governors to pass Laws of immediate and pressing Importance, unless suspended in their Operation till his Assent should be obtained; and when so suspended, he has utterly neglected to attend to them.

He has refused to pass other Laws for the Accommodation of large Districts of People, unless those People would relinquish the Right of Representation in the Legislature, a Right inestimable to them, and formidable to Tyrants only.

He has called together Legislative Bodies at Places unusual, uncomfortable, and distant from the Depository of their public Records, for the sole Purpose of fatiguing them into Compliance with his Measures.

He has dissolved Representative Houses repeatedly, for opposing with manly Firmness his Invasions on the Rights of the People.

He has refused for a long Time, after such Dissolutions, to cause others to be elected; whereby the Legislative Powers, incapable of Annihilation, have returned to the People at large for their exercise; the State remaining in the mean time exposed to all the Dangers of Invasion from without, and Convulsions within.

He has endeavoured to prevent the Population of these States; for that Purpose obstructing the Laws for Naturalization of Foreigners; refusing to pass others to encourage their Migrations hither, and raising the Conditions of new Appropriations of Lands.

He has obstructed the Administration of Justice, by refusing his Assent to Laws for establishing Judiciary Powers.

He has made Judges dependent on his Will alone, for the Tenure of their Offices, and the Amount and Payment of their Salaries.

He has erected a Multitude of new Offices, and sent hither Swarms of Officers to harrass our People, and eat out their Substance.

He has kept among us, in Times of Peace, Standing Armies, without the consent of our Legislatures.

He has affected to render the Military independent of and superior to the Civil Power.

He has combined with others to subject us to a Jurisdiction foreign to our Constitution, and unacknowledged by our Laws; giving his Assent to their Acts of pretended Legislation:

For quartering large Bodies of Armed Troops among us:

For protecting them, by a mock Trial, from Punishment for any Murders which they should commit on the Inhabitants of these States:

For cutting off our Trade with all Parts of the World:

For imposing Taxes on us without our Consent:

For depriving us, in many Cases, of the Benefits of Trial by Jury:

For transporting us beyond Seas to be tried for pretended Offences:

For abolishing the free System of English Laws in a neighbouring Province, establishing therein an arbitrary Government, and enlarging its Boundaries, so as to render it at once an Example and fit Instrument for introducing the same absolute Rule into these Colonies:

For taking away our Charters, abolishing our most valuable Laws, and altering fundamentally the Forms of our Governments:

For suspending our own Legislatures, and declaring themselves invested with Power to legislate for us in all Cases whatsoever.

He has abdicated Government here, by declaring us out of his Protection and waging War against us.

He has plundered our Seas, ravaged our Coasts, burnt our Towns, and destroyed the Lives of our People.

He is, at this Time, transporting large Armies of foreign Mercenaries to compleat the Works of Death, Desolation, and Tyranny, already begun with circumstances of Cruelty and Perfidy, scarcely paralleled in the most barbarous Ages, and totally unworthy the Head of a civilized Nation.

He has constrained our fellow Citizens taken Captive on the high Seas to bear Arms against their Country, to become the Executioners of their Friends and Brethren, or to fall themselves by their Hands.

He has excited domestic Insurrections amongst us, and has endeavoured to bring on the Inhabitants of our Frontiers, the merciless Indian Savages, whose known Rule of Warfare, is an undistinguished Destruction, of all Ages, Sexes and Conditions.

In every stage of these Oppressions we have Petitioned for Redress in the most humble Terms: Our repeated Petitions have been answered only by repeated Injury. A Prince, whose Character is thus marked by every act which may define a Tyrant, is unfit to be the Ruler of a free People.

Nor have we been wanting in Attentions to our British Brethren. We have warned them from Time to Time of Attempts by their Legislature to extend an unwarrantable Jurisdiction over us. We have reminded them of the Circumstances of our Emigration and Settlement here. We have appealed to their native Justice and Magnanimity, and we have conjured them by the Ties of our common Kindred to disavow these Usurpations, which, would inevitably interrupt our Connections and Correspondence. They too have been deaf to the Voice of Justice and of Consanguinity. We must, therefore, acquiesce in the Necessity, which denounces our Separation, and hold them, as we hold the rest of Mankind, Enemies in War, in Peace, Friends.

We, therefore, the Representatives of the UNITED STATES OF AMERICA, in GENERAL CONGRESS, Assembled, appealing to the Supreme Judge of the World for the Rectitude of our Intentions, do, in the Name, and by Authority of the good People of these Colonies, solemnly Publish and Declare, That these United Colonies are, and of Right ought to be, FREE AND INDEPENDENT STATES, that they are absolved from all Allegiance to the British Crown, and that all political Connection between them and the State of Great-Britain, is and ought to be totally dissolved; and that as FREE AND INDEPENDENT STATES, they have full Power to levy War, conclude Peace, contract Alliances, establish Commerce, and to do all other Acts and Things which INDEPENDENT STATES may of right do. And for the support of this Declaration, with a firm Reliance on the Protection of divine Providence, we mutually pledge to each other our Lives, our Fortunes, and our sacred Honor.

Signed by ORDER and in BEHALF of the CONGRESS,

JOHN HANCOCK, PRESIDENT.

ATTEST.
CHARLES THOMSON, SECRETARY.

John Dunlap broadside. The New York Public Library.

WHEN THE DECLARATION OF INDEPENDENCE WAS NEWS

EMILY SNEFF

OXFORD
UNIVERSITY PRESS

OXFORD
UNIVERSITY PRESS

Oxford University Press is a department of the University of Oxford.
It furthers the University's objective of excellence in research, scholarship,
and education by publishing worldwide. Oxford is a registered trade mark of
Oxford University Press in the UK and in certain other countries.

Published in the United States of America by Oxford University Press
198 Madison Avenue, New York, NY 10016, United States of America.

© Oxford University Press 2026

CIP data is on file at the Library of Congress.

ISBN 9780197816691

DOI: 10.1093/oso/9780197816691.001.0001

Printed by Marquis Book Printing, Canada

The manufacturer's authorized representative in the EU for product safety is
Oxford University Press España S.A. of Parque Empresarial San Fernando de Henares,
Avenida de Castilla, 2 – 28830 Madrid (www.oup.es/en or product.safety@oup.com).
OUP España S.A. also acts as importer into Spain of products made by the manufacturer.

For Dad

Contents

Acknowledgments

When I eulogized my father, Mark Sneff, in March 2019, I told the people who had gathered to honor his life how sad and frustrated I was that he would never read this book. I miss my dad every day, but as a historian and a writer, I miss him as my reader. This book is dedicated to his love for learning and his love for me. I also want to share my deepest gratitude to my favorite brother and news producer, Michael Sneff, and my biggest supporter, my mother, Sally Sneff.

This book would not exist without the steadfast encouragement of my graduate advisor, Karin Wulf. Josh Piker, Nick Popper, and Zara Anishanslin smoothed the transition from dissertation to book manuscript with their thoughtful suggestions and great enthusiasm for this project. Throughout the writing process, Lindsay Chervinsky, Liz Covart, Jonathan Gienapp, Julian Mortensen, and Rachel Shelden have cheered me on and made me a better historian.

I want to thank Oxford University Press for bringing these stories behind the Declaration to the world. Susan Ferber has been a tremendous support and her deft hand has made my words sing. I am grateful to Nancy Toff, Rada Radojicic, the external reviewers, and everyone at the press who has been a part of this project.

The research in this book received generous funding from the McNeil Center for Early American Studies, the Society for Historians of American Foreign Relations, the Omohundro Institute of Early American History and Culture, and the John Carter Brown Library, as well as the Graduate Studies Advisory Board and the Harrison Ruffin Tyler Department of History at William & Mary. Special thanks to

Diane and Mel Baiada for their love and support. My research would not have been possible without the work of the archivists, conservators, and editors who have preserved and interpreted the copies of the Declaration and other records over the past 250 years.

And for the support of this book, with a firm reliance on their feedback and encouragement, I pledge my thanks to my family, friends, and fellow historians: Joe Adelman, Danielle Allen, David Armitage, Katie Boyce, Jasper Conner, Sara Georgini, Tyler Goldberger, Eliga Gould, Holly Gruntner, Martha King, Karen Kreider, Paula and Jim Lyons, Samantha McClellan, Phil Mead, Cari Meffle, Belinda and Hugh Middleton, Carolyn Pearce, Marie Pellissier, Elizabeth Rodini, Helena Yoo Roth, Mary Jane Sneff, Joan Jockel Stanley, Steve Sarson, Darshan Shah, Hannah Sisk, Will Slauter, Emily Suth, Katy Telling, Dan Twiford, Jeff and Linda Twiford, and Lindsay Tyson.

Introduction

The News of Independence

For two weeks, Polly Palmer waited. The only pieces of paper in her house were blank commissions awaiting a soldier's name and her father's signature. There was nothing suitable for a letter. Finally, on August 4, 1776, clean paper in hand, Palmer sat down to write to an old friend.[1] Her letter was layered with humility. She apologized for the lateness of her response, the imperfections of the last letter she had sent, and how unsuitable a correspondent she was compared to her father. At thirty years old, she signed the letter with the pen name of her teenage years—"Myra"—for the security of anonymity rather than nostalgia. Times had changed. Polly Palmer was writing to thank one of the most powerful men in the United States for sending her the founding document of her new nation.

Every copy of the Declaration of Independence produced in 1776 has a story to tell, including Polly Palmer's. The beautiful and gregarious Mary Palmer, known as Polly, lived in Germantown, now part of Quincy, Massachusetts.[2] She became friends with John Adams while he was courting Abigail Smith.[3] As a teenager, Palmer would take the family horse and chaise and travel the thirteen miles from Germantown to Boston by herself, through the woods and in all sorts of weather, calling on her father's business associates along the way. She often returned after dark and laughed at her mother and sister for worrying about her.[4] In April 1764, when she was eighteen years old, Polly Palmer received her smallpox inoculation with John Adams at his uncle's house in Boston.[5] Her friendship with Adams was fortified by two weeks spent together in close, contagious quarters, waiting for their skin to erupt in pustules. When they were both feeling better, they took in the fresh air together. John Adams wrote to Abigail about sharing chaise rides around town and across the Boston Neck with "Myra."[6]

The following year, Polly Palmer experienced a trauma that affected her mental and physical health for the rest of her life. Family lore has it that one afternoon in 1765, as Palmer sat reading a book, her father boasted about his daughter to a friend. He claimed that nothing could scare her. The friend wagered that he could shake Palmer's nerves, and he fired a gun out the window above her head. That gunshot changed her life. From the age of nineteen, Palmer's nerves overwhelmed her. Every sound, from children playing to thunder rolling, was terrifying. The sound of gunfire made her convulse.[7] Over the next ten years, Joseph Palmer—anguished, according to the family, by the part he played in damaging his daughter's health—served in the Massachusetts Provincial Assembly and as a colonel in the militia. The onset of the American Revolution must have been unsettling for anyone living near Boston. For Polly Palmer, it meant daily audible reminders of her trauma.

The war gave Polly Palmer a reason to write to her friend John Adams on June 15, 1776. "You will wonder at receiving a Letter from one who is very far from being Sufficiently qualified to write to a Member of the Grand Congress," Palmer stated.[8] She claimed that she was "under parental injunctions" to send a report of some skirmishes in Boston Harbor to Adams, because Joseph Palmer was too busy to write. She also knew that one of Adams's sources of news, his wife Abigail, was out of town. So Polly Palmer burdened herself with the responsibility of sending intelligence to a member of the Continental Congress. While she waited for an opportunity to mail her letter, she added a postscript copied directly from her father's notes, listing the numbers of Continental Army soldiers and militiamen involved in these skirmishes. Then Palmer described a fierce fight between a few privateers and two British warships that lasted all day, ending just before midnight. She "never saw such fighting before," and she wrote that "the flashes were almost without Intermission."[9] It was an unnerving reminder that, although the British forces had evacuated Boston, they were not gone for good. Signing this first letter "Polly Palmer," she begged Adams's pardon for the many ink-blots and inaccuracies she saw on the page. Palmer trusted that Adams had "too much good Nature, to expose the faults of an illiterate Girl." But Palmer was not illiterate, and she was no longer a girl.

Polly Palmer's letter reached John Adams in Philadelphia during the momentous first week of July 1776.[10] In his reply, dated July 5, Adams refused to accept Palmer's "modest Apologies."[11] She had written "with a great deal of real Elegance and Perspicuity, a minute and circumstantial Narration." Adams assured Palmer that her letter gave him a better understanding of what had played out in Boston Harbor than any of the other accounts he had seen in newspapers and correspondence. "In Times as turbulent as these, commend me to the Ladies as Historiographers," Adams wrote, in his standard tone of well-meaning condescension toward the women in his life. "The Gentlemen are too much engaged in Action," he claimed. "The Ladies are cooler Spectators." In one of the letters that John Adams wrote to his wife on July 3, he praised Palmer for writing an account that seemed to have come from "the Pen of an accomplished Historian."[12] Adams did not treat people as "Historians" or "Historiographers" lightly or frequently in his corre-spondence.[13] He later complained that "the History of our Revolution will be one continued Lye from one End to the other."[14] But something about Polly Palmer made John Adams think she would make a fine his-torian, and not just because it was the responsibility of "Ladies" to record historical events.

In his July 5 letter to Polly Palmer, John Adams enclosed "a Declaration in which all America is remarkably united."[15] He folded up one of the first broadsides of the Declaration of Independence, printed by John Dunlap hours after the Continental Congress approved the text.[16] Adams did not offer any explanation for the Declaration or any context for what it meant, only that "it compleats a Revolution, which will make as good a Figure in the History of Mankind, as any that has preceeded it."[17] Adams treated Palmer as someone who understood the historical importance of the American Revolution and the Declaration of Independence. Palmer was not a government official, or a military commander, or a clerk, or anyone responsible for spreading the news of independence. She did not need this copy of the Declaration of Independence. Adams could have told Palmer to share the Declaration with her father, but he only sent his "Compliments to Papa, and Mamma and the whole Family," with hope that they would "see more serene Skies" in the new United States. Adams's letter to Palmer was optimistic. He trusted that Boston would be safe, that the Declaration of Independence would invigorate civilians and soldiers alike, and that his friend would continue writing to him.

In Polly Palmer's response to John Adams on August 4—delayed by "an absolute want of Paper" suitable to send to a member of the Continental Congress—she sincerely thanked him for his "Present of the Declaration of independancy."[18] She was overjoyed by this news. But she had no intention of writing any more history. Palmer felt the need to correct a minor error in her June 15 letter, because she was "loth that any misinformation" from her pen "shou'd lead to a false Account." She agreed to write to John Adams whenever "any event of a Public Nature happens," but doubted that she ever could give him a better account than those of Abigail Adams. Polly Palmer signed this letter as "Myra" for fear that, on its way to Philadelphia, it might end up on Staten Island, where the British fleet had assembled in the six weeks since her last letter to Adams.

Despite John Adams's insistence that he wanted to correspond with Polly Palmer, she did not write to him again until November 1789—this time as a librarian rather than a historian. Palmer was living in the Adams family's house at Peacefield, and Adams was the Vice President of the United States.[19] Adams trusted Palmer to help catalog the books in the Peacefield library so that he could decide how much of his personal collection to bring to the nation's capital. Palmer and Adams had searched together for a particular history of New England, and she wrote a short letter to let him know that she had found the book, "unless the same

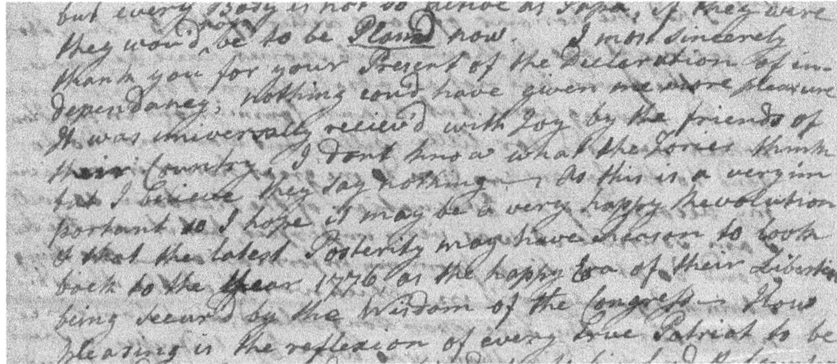

Figure I.1 Letter, Polly Palmer to John Adams, August 4, 1776. Collection of the Massachusetts Historical Society, Boston.

fairy who bro't it has carried it away again."[20] This letter is a reminder that Palmer and Adams connected much more in person, in Braintree, than in writing. Thirteen years of silence in the collected Adams family papers does not mean thirteen years without friendship or conversation. This letter is also a reminder that, as John and Abigail Adams's political power grew, Polly Palmer's health declined.[21] Palmer assured Adams that, "health permitting," she would do her best to clean and organize the books, while one of her cousins wrote out the catalog.[22] But she could only do this library work if the New England winter brought a "warm spell," because she could not "afford a fire in that room." The worry that Palmer had about presenting herself as a correspondent worthy of Adams's time crept back in. Thirteen years after she had apologized for writing to a "Member of the Grand Congress," she asked pardon again for her "boldness in writing to the Vice President." Palmer died at the age of forty-five in 1791, in the middle of Adams's first term in office.

An intimate knowledge of information networks, a clear narrative writing style, and a coincidence of timing brought thirty-year-old Polly Palmer into the founding moment of the United States. She personally received a copy of the Declaration of Independence from one of the men who crafted the text—who praised her skills as a historian—and yet, as recipient, she faded into the background of history. The letter that

John Adams sent to Polly Palmer on July 5, 1776, became a collectible, and the broadside printed by John Dunlap that it originally enclosed either was separated from the letter or does not survive.[23] Palmer is, at most, a footnote in the history of the Declaration of Independence. She is remembered as "poor Aunt Polly" in her niece's memoir, "quite a literary genius" before the trauma she experienced at age nineteen and a "confirmed invalid" afterward.[24] But these letters and the lost Dunlap broadside prove that Palmer was much more than that. Throughout their friendship, Adams trusted that Palmer understood the political and cultural changes that she was living through. When Polly Palmer signed her thank-you note for the Declaration of Independence as "Myra," she proved that she understood perfectly.

❈❈❈

There was a time when the Declaration of Independence was news. Most books written about the Declaration have pursued questions about its precedents and authorship, as well as its legacy.[25] But in 1776, when the Declaration was news, it was part of an ever-changing and circulating amalgam of accurate and inaccurate information, gossip, military intelligence, speculation, and opinion.[26] At approximately 1,320 words, from "When in the Course of human Events" through "our sacred Honor," the Declaration took fewer than ten minutes to read and filled only one or two columns of a typical newspaper.[27] This was a text that could be communicated swiftly. But it was also a text for which the context in which it was communicated mattered. The questions of who experienced the news of independence, and when and how they did so, reveal a critical, overlooked history of the American Revolution.

In 1818, John Adams wrote that the accomplishment of independence "in So short a time and by Such Simple means, was perhaps a Singular Example in the History of Mankind."[28] The eighty-two-year-old remembered that "Thirteen Clocks were made to Strike together." But in the moment, half a lifetime earlier, Adams wrote that "you cant make thirteen Clocks, Strike precisely alike, at the Same Second."[29] The Declaration of Independence claimed the "Consent of the Governed." However, the

Continental Congress did not define who would consent to the founding of the United States. By July 2, 1776, only twelve of the thirteen delegations in the Congress had instructions to vote for independence based on the popular sentiment of their home colonies. After multiple postponements of the vote, only twelve clocks struck at the same time. A thirteenth clang from New York came days later. Popular consent was, at best, complicated.[30] Some people—those who were fiercely loyal to King George III, but also those who just wanted to maintain their life as it was—thought that independence could be reversed or negotiated.

The traditional story of the Declaration of Independence focuses on the delegates in the Continental Congress, particularly the committee of five men tasked with drafting the text, and the fifty-six men who later signed the Declaration. The men at the center of this story had frustratingly foggy memories.[31] In 1776, the author of the Declaration was not a single man or committee, but rather the entire Congress. The only two names that circulated with the text were John Hancock's and Charles Thomson's, as president and secretary of the Continental Congress, respectively. As the years went by, the authorship of the Declaration of Independence mattered more and more to Thomas Jefferson and John Adams, the two longest-lived members of the drafting committee, who both died on July 4, 1826. Weighed down by all their subsequent political and diplomatic accomplishments, as well as the animosity that festered and then faded between them, Jefferson and Adams recounted the drafting of the Declaration in their autobiographies and in letters.[32] They both falsely recalled signing the Declaration on July 4, 1776.[33] True, the signed parchment copy of the Declaration that sits in the rotunda of the National Archives in Washington, DC, is titled "In CONGRESS, July 4, 1776. The Unanimous Declaration of the Thirteen United States of America."[34] But, on July 4, this parchment did not exist, and support for independence was not unanimous. The signatures were added over time and represented a mix of delegates who voted for independence, delegates who voted against independence, and delegates who were not in the Congress on July 4. The parchment is timeless, in the worst sense of the word.

When the Declaration of Independence Was News tells a different story, motivated by straightforward questions: who knew what, where, and when, and why did that knowledge matter? By July 19, 1776, when the Continental Congress decided to create a parchment copy of the Declaration to be signed, thousands of people had learned the news of independence. The Declaration had been carried to most of the thirteen United States, printed in broadsides and newspapers, read aloud, hand-copied by clerks, translated into German, shared with Wolastoqiyik and Mi'kmaq allies, and packed aboard ships crossing the Atlantic. Most of the printed and manuscript copies of the Declaration that were produced in 1776 suffered the same fate as Polly Palmer's Dunlap broadside: they were not preserved. But the copies of the Declaration that do survive, along with letters, diaries, and other records, hold the stories of a cast of characters much more diverse and geographically dispersed than the delegates who signed the parchment in Philadelphia.[35]

According to the final paragraph of the Declaration of Independence, the Continental Congress published the text for two purposes.[36] Within the United States, the Congress wanted to use it to construct a national identity.[37] The Declaration "totally dissolved" the political connection between the united colonies and Great Britain, which needed to be replaced by a political connection among the United States. The Congress also wanted the Declaration to create an international identity. They hoped that the news of independence would compel European powers to recognize the United States as a sovereign confederation, rather than rebel colonies.[38] The delegates were particularly keen to form an alliance with France. The Congress in Philadelphia needed the courts of Europe to know that the United States could "levy War, conclude Peace, contract Alliances, establish Commerce," and "do all other Acts and Things which Independent States may of right do."[39]

One problem with the final paragraph of the Declaration is that the Continental Congress voted to declare independence while plans for confederation and foreign treaties were still incomplete drafts, at a time when people around the Atlantic expected the war would soon end in a British victory.[40] As the delegates in Philadelphia voted for independence,

General George Washington and the Continental Army anxiously watched a massive British fleet bear down on New York, led by the King's Commissioners for Restoring Peace. Once the Declaration of Independence was printed, the Congress had limited power over what people did with it or thought of it. Outside of the Pennsylvania State House—the Congress's meeting place, later renamed Independence Hall—the Declaration was celebrated. But the text was also reprinted, translated, excerpted, decried, critiqued, and interpreted in ways that undermined the United States. The Declaration's audience—the "candid World"—was left with unanswered questions about what the United States would be, whether they could find allies, and whether they could win the war and secure their independence.

Publishing the news of independence to the world was messy work.[41] It is easy to assume that the Declaration of Independence remained the same no matter when, where, or why a new copy was produced. In reality, almost every printed or manuscript copy of the Declaration produced in 1776 varies in format, type size, punctuation, capitalization, and spelling. There was no single authoritative text.[42] Manuscripts were copied from printed editions and vice versa.[43] Errors and omissions are inevitable when someone transcribes a text. Even Timothy Matlack had to fix mistakes he made while inscribing the parchment copy of the Declaration for the Continental Congress.[44] A compositor can make similar errors setting type, especially when preparing text for a narrow newspaper column. Copies of the Declaration were made to be distributed, and as they traveled through the mail, changes to the text—whether deliberate choices or mistakes—were reproduced in other places. Translation of the Declaration from English into other languages further transformed the text. The clarity of the translation depended on the goals, skills, and location of the translator. The Congress did not supervise the translation of the Declaration into French, even though it was the language of diplomacy, not to mention the language of the United States' anticipated ally.[45] Each moment of transcription, typesetting, translation, and transmission widened the gap between a new version of the Declaration of Independence and the first printed version, the

Dunlap broadsides. Each of these steps also took time, which meant that the Declaration circulated around the Atlantic for months.[46]

The Continental Congress declared independence, but the work of spreading that news involved printers, post riders, ship captains, civic leaders, soldiers, clerks, orators, preachers, diplomats, and translators. The delegates in Philadelphia left the decision of how the Declaration should be published to state and local governments and military officials. But the ongoing war displaced printers, disrupted mail routes, and caused supply shortages, which impacted when and how the Declaration appeared in print.[47] Some of the people tasked with reading the Declaration aloud refused, and the political beliefs they had held privately were made public. From the middle of August through the fall, the Declaration was news in Europe—printed under the heading "London," because the Declaration traveled to the imperial capital through the correspondence of British officers who landed on Staten Island in the days following July 4. The Continental Congress failed to share the news of independence with the much hoped-for ally, France, until later in the fall.

As news, the Declaration of Independence was malleable, easily combined with other pieces of information and misinformation, or overshadowed by other stories. A soldier at Fort Ticonderoga heard a reading of the Declaration and wrote that "it made a little Buze; but was soon forgotten."[48] Readers of a newspaper printed in Dublin, Ireland, saw the Declaration of Independence in their Thursday issue. The following Saturday, they read an extract of a fabricated letter from Philadelphia that claimed that, after declaring independence, the Continental Congress had placed a crown on a bible, which they prayed over and broke into thirteen parts, one for each colony.[49] The Declaration also could be suppressed. A complaint in a Boston newspaper claimed that the royal governor of Nova Scotia "would not permit the poor Dupe of a Printer" in Halifax to publish more than the last paragraph of the Declaration in his newspaper.[50] The Declaration of Independence encountered unique contexts everywhere it went, from smallpox outbreaks to military victories. It was entrusted to communications networks that were under constant threat, and it was often preceded by salacious rumors. It was proclaimed to soldiers who would die weeks later. And, it was printed on thin sheets of paper that were not meant to last for very long. All this fragility and unpredictability in 1776 has been forgotten because, ultimately, the United States survived.[51]

The Declaration of Independence traveled farther in 1776 than historians will ever have enough evidence to trace. The ubiquity of newspapers on board all types of ships—including ships carrying human cargo—means that any number of newspaper printings of the Declaration could have circulated through North American, Caribbean, European, and even African ports. The printers whose names can be found at the bottom of a broadside or in the masthead of a newspaper were assisted in their work by unnamed men and women, from family members to apprentices to enslaved laborers. Almost all the surviving evidence of people engaging with the Declaration of Independence in 1776—the records of who attended public readings, who subscribed to newspapers, who purchased broadsides, and who sent copies of the Declaration through the mail—tells the stories of white men with some amount of political power. But there were also all sorts of people standing within earshot of public readings, walking past broadsides posted up in public spaces and newspapers lying open on tavern tables, and overhearing conversations among families and neighbors. Not everyone who interacted with the news of independence had the means to record their reaction to it.

When the Declaration of Independence Was News begins in Philadelphia in May 1776 and ends in Baltimore in January 1777. The chapters along the way make stops in Boston, Charleston, Gwynn's Island, Leiden, Lisbon, London, New York, Paris, Providence, Sint Eustatius, and other places where the news of independence traveled in 1776. Chapter 1 focuses on the first resolution issued by the Continental Congress that attributed the colonists' grievances to King George III. The May 15 Resolution was a timely text that reacted to the most recent news in Philadelphia. As the resolution circulated around the Atlantic, it was perceived to be a declaration of independence, until the

(335)

The PENNSYLVANIA EVENING POST.

Price only Two Coppers.   Publiſhed every *Tueſday*, *Thurſday*, and *Saturday* Evenings.

Vol. II.]   SATURDAY, JULY 6, 1776.   [Num. 228.

In CONGRESS, July 4, 1776.
A Declaration by the Repreſentatives
of the United States of America,
in General Congreſs aſſembled.

WHEN, in the courſe of human events, it becomes neceſſary for one people to diſſolve the political bands which have connected them with another, and to aſſume, among the powers of the earth, the ſeparate and equal ſtation to which the laws of nature and of nature's God intitle them, a decent reſpect to the opinions of mankind requires that they ſhould declare the cauſes which impel them to the ſeparation.

We hold theſe truths to be ſelf-evident, That all men are created equal; that they are endowed, by their Creator, with certain unalienable rights; that among theſe are life, liberty, and the purſuit of happineſs. That to ſecure theſe rights, governments are inſtituted among men, deriving their juſt powers from the conſent of the governed; that whenever any form of government becomes deſtructive of theſe ends, it is the right of the people to alter or to aboliſh it, and to inſtitute new government, laying its foundation on ſuch principles, and organizing its powers in ſuch form, as to them ſhall ſeem moſt likely to effect their ſafety and happineſs. Prudence, indeed, will dictate that governments long eſtabliſhed ſhould not be changed for light and tranſient cauſes; and accordingly all experience hath ſhewn, that mankind are more diſpoſed to ſuffer, while evils are ſufferable, than to right themſelves by aboliſhing the forms to which they are accuſtomed. But when a long train of abuſes and uſurpations, purſuing invariably the ſame object, evinces a deſign to reduce them under abſolute deſpotiſm, it is their right, it is their duty, to throw off ſuch government, and to provide new guards for their future ſecurity. Such has been the patient ſufferance of theſe colonies, and ſuch is now the neceſſity which conſtrains them to alter their former ſyſtems of government. The hiſtory of the preſent King of Great-Britain is a hiſtory of repeated injuries and uſurpations, all having in direct object the eſtabliſhment of an abſolute tyranny over theſe ſtates. To prove this, let facts be ſubmitted to a candid world.

He has refuſed his aſſent to laws, the moſt wholeſome and neceſſary for the public good.

He has forbidden his Governors to paſs laws of immediate and preſſing importance, unleſs ſuſpended in their operation till his aſſent ſhould be obtained; and, when ſo ſuſpended, he has utterly neglected to attend to them.

He has refuſed to paſs other laws for the accommodation of large diſtricts of people, unleſs thoſe people would relinquiſh the right of repreſentation in the legiſlature, a right ineſtimable to them, and formidable to tyrants only.

He has called together legiſlative bodies at places unuſual, uncomfortable, and diſtant from the depoſitory of their public records, for the ſole purpoſe of fatiguing them into compliance with his meaſures.

He has diſſolved Repreſentative Houſes repeatedly, for oppoſing with manly firmneſs his invaſions on the rights of the people.

He has refuſed for a long time, after ſuch diſſolutions, to cauſe others to be elected; whereby the legiſlative powers, incapable of annihilation, have returned to the people at large for their exerciſe; the ſtate remaining in the mean time expoſed to all the dangers of invaſion from without, and convulſions within.

He has endeavoured to prevent the population of theſe ſtates; for that purpoſe obſtructing the laws for naturalization of foreigners; refuſing to paſs others to encourage their migrations hither, and raiſing the conditions of new appropriations of lands.

He has obſtructed the adminiſtration of juſtice, by refuſing his aſſent to laws for eſtabliſhing judiciary powers.

He has made Judges dependant on his will alone, for the tenure of their offices, and the amount and payment of their ſalaries.

He has erected a multitude of new offices, and ſent hither ſwarms of officers to harraſs our people, and eat out their ſubſtance.

He has kept among us, in times of peace, ſtanding armies, without the conſent of our legiſlatures.

He has affected to render the military independant of and ſuperior to the civil power.

He has combined with others to ſubject us to a juriſdiction foreign to our conſtitution, and unacknowledged by our laws; giving his aſſent to their acts of pretended legiſlation:

For quartering large bodies of armed troops among us:

For protecting them, by a mock trial, from puniſhment for any murders which they ſhould commit on the inhabitants of theſe ſtates:

For cutting off our trade with all parts of the world:

For impoſing taxes on us without our conſent:

For depriving us, in many caſes, of the benefits of trial by jury:

For tranſporting us beyond ſeas to be tried for pretended offences:

For aboliſhing the free ſyſtem of Engliſh laws in a neighbouring province, eſtabliſhing therein an arbitrary government, and enlarging its boundaries, ſo as to render it at once an example and fit inſtrument for introducing the ſame abſolute rule into theſe colonies:

For taking away our charters, aboliſhing our moſt valuable laws, and altering fundamentally the forms of our governments:

For ſuſpending our own legiſlatures, and declaring themſelves inveſted with power to legiſlate for us in all caſes whatſoever.

He has abdicated government here, by declaring us out of his protection and waging war againſt us.

He has plundered our ſeas, ravaged our coaſts, burnt our towns, and deſtroyed the lives of our people.

He is, at this time, tranſporting large armies of foreign mercenaries to complete the works of death, deſolation, and tyranny, already begun with circumſtances of cruelty and

Figure I.2 *Pennsylvania Evening Post*, July 6, 1776. Museum of the American Revolution, Philadelphia, 2003.00.1167.

news of the Declaration of Independence began to spread. Chapter 2 looks at another resolution issued on May 15, by the Virginia Convention, which instructed the colony's delegates in the Congress to propose independence. These instructions led to the Declaration of Independence, the Articles of Confederation, and the Model Treaty—three interconnected texts that lost their connection because the Declaration of Independence was approved first. This chapter explores the debate on independence, the three-week postponement of the vote, and the drafting of the Declaration of Independence during that time.

In Chapter 3, the Declaration of Independence becomes news. This chapter begins in Philadelphia, where the Declaration was first printed, proclaimed, and translated. Other examples of public readings and broadside and newspaper printings of the Declaration across the United States bore similarities to what happened in Philadelphia and reflected a burgeoning national identity. But there is also evidence of printers and public officials making decisions about publishing the Declaration that reflected their local circumstances, especially in the middle of the war. Chapters 4 and 5 highlight the news of independence in two specific locations: New York and Boston. Chapter 4 contrasts the celebration of the Declaration in Manhattan, the headquarters of General George Washington and the Continental Army, with the disdainful reaction from the British forces assembling on Staten Island. The King's Commissioners for Restoring Peace tried to issue their own declaration, offering pardons to those who had in the commissioners' view been misled by the Congress. This declaration of the commissioners' limited powers influenced the Congress's decision to sign a parchment copy of the Declaration of Independence. Chapter 5 highlights the experiences of Abigail Adams and her children in Boston, where they all were inoculated for smallpox and received the news of independence in the span of a few days. Though the Declaration offered momentary joy to people like the Adamses who were waiting to erupt in pustules, smallpox remained the biggest news story in Boston in July and August 1776.

Chapter 6 shows how the Declaration of Independence was communicated to Native Americans during conferences in Watertown, Massachusetts, and German Flatts, New York. The Declaration arrived in the middle of the proceedings in Watertown, and, after it was translated for the Wolastoqiyik and Mi'kmaq chiefs who were present, Wolastoqiyik Chief Ambrose Bear responded, "we like it well." This marked the first formal acknowledgment of the United States by a foreign power. In German Flatts, the Six Nations presented a wampum belt in recognition of the Declaration of Independence, and they committed to remaining neutral at a time when the delegates in the Continental Congress were deeply concerned about violence on the "Frontiers." Chapter 7 focuses on Anglican ministers' reactions to the Declaration of Independence. King George III was the head of the Church of England, and after July 4, clergymen faced threats and violence as they made the challenging decision to either stop praying for the king or close their churches.

When the news of the Declaration of Independence left the United States, its path was not as straightforward as the Continental Congress might have hoped. Chapter 8 highlights the broadsides of the Declaration that ended up in the National Archives at Kew because they were intercepted by British officials. These copies of the Declaration illuminate a copy that no longer exists: the broadside that the Congress tried to send to Silas Deane, their agent in France, which was thrown overboard to prevent interception by the British. The first copies of the Declaration of Independence reached the British imperial capital in August 1776, and Chapter 9 reveals how London printers changed the Declaration by censoring, excerpting, and manipulating the text and printing it alongside other pieces of news. European newspapers copied the Declaration as it appeared in these London papers and propagated misinformation about the United States. As Chapter 10 shows, Silas Deane became increasingly anxious. Months went by without any word from Philadelphia, while the Declaration of Independence became known through European newspapers. When Deane finally received a copy of the Declaration directly from the Congress in November, he was frustrated that the delegates had not thought to send a more formal copy of the text, appropriate for the courts of Europe.

The Conclusion returns to the Continental Congress in January 1777, when they were meeting in Baltimore for fear that British forces would invade Philadelphia. In this moment of uncertainty, the Congress decided to create a printed version of the Declaration of Independence with the names of the men who had signed the parchment copy by that time. These broadsides were meant to be preserved in the archives of each state. They mark the end of the time when the Declaration of Independence was news.

The Continental Congress wanted the United States to find a place "among the Powers of the Earth," but the delegates did not accomplish this in 1776.[52] With the benefit of hindsight, July 4 marks a rupture, a point of no return, and a national birthday. The Declaration of Independence is remembered as a genre-defining document. But that is only because, eventually, it worked.[53] The United States found foreign allies, won the war, and secured political independence from Great Britain. When Polly Palmer received the news of independence from her friend John Adams, she hoped that "the latest Posterity may have Reason to look back to the Year 1776, as the happy Era of their Liberties being secur'd by the Wisdom of the Congress."[54] Adams himself recognized the "Toil and Blood and Treasure, that it will cost Us to maintain this Declaration, and support and defend these States."[55] But, through "all the Gloom," Adams could "see the Rays of ravishing Light and Glory." Many people experienced the time when the Declaration of Independence was news. But they could see only glimpses of what the future might hold for the Declaration—and for the United States.

I

Short of Independence

The May 15 Resolution

On July 4, 1776, the king of Portugal issued an edict. José I banned ships of the thirteen rebellious British colonies from entering any Portuguese port, and gave any ships that were already in port eight days to leave. One of these ships was the *Rachel*, a brigantine that had sailed from Philadelphia. In fact, it was the arrival of the *Rachel* in the port of Lisbon that had prompted José I's edict. Somewhere among the goods and pieces of mail in the *Rachel*'s cargo was a small piece of paper with two paragraphs printed under the heading, "In CONGRESS, May 15, 1776."[1]

The Continental Congress issued a resolution on May 15 that some people—including the king of Portugal—understood to be a declaration of independence. In the resolution, which the Congress actually agreed to on May 10, the delegates recommended that the "respective Assemblies and Conventions" in each of the thirteen colonies should remove any remnants of British authority.[2] "Where no Government sufficient to the exigencies of their affairs has been hitherto established," they should form new governments, founded on the consent of the governed, so as to ensure "the happiness and safety of their constituents in particular, and America in general."[3] John Adams, always keen to celebrate a victory, remembered the resolution as a "decisive Event."[4] It was the result of a year of work on his part, "through a Scaene and a Series of Anxiety, labour, Study, Argument, and Obloquy."

The Continental Congress appointed John Adams, along with South Carolina delegate Edward Rutledge and Richard Henry Lee of Virginia, to draft a preamble for this resolution. According to Adams, Rutledge and Lee let him take the lead. Adams seized the opportunity to rebuke King George III rather than seek his protection. No one outside of the Congress would have known that the resolution, which passed on May 10, received unanimous support from the delegates, while the preamble would pass on May 15 by only a slim majority. After that vote, a number of delegates in Philadelphia worried about how their words would be received.

⊗⊗⊗

When the Continental Congress convened in Philadelphia in May 1775, just after the Battles of Lexington and Concord, independence was not a foregone conclusion. In July 1775, the Congress offered an olive branch to King George III, a petition addressed to the "Most Gracious Sovereign" from his "faithful subjects."[5] The Olive Branch Petition asked the king to redress the colonists' grievances and effect a "happy and permanent reconciliation" between the thirteen colonies and Great Britain. But George III refused to read the petition. Instead, he proclaimed that the colonies had been "misled by dangerous and ill-designing men"—the delegates in the Congress—and were engaged in an "open and avowed Rebellion."[6] In his speech at the opening session of the British Parliament in October 1775, George III was resolute. Though the "authors and promoters" of the "desperate conspiracy" in the colonies had pretended to want a reconciliation with Great Britain, their real goal always had been to create an "independent empire."[7]

When the news of the king's speech reached Philadelphia on January 8, 1776, Rhode Island delegate Samuel Ward was incensed. He wrote to his daughter, "thus you see my Love your Daddy's Sentiments are confirmed."[8] Whereas the king was convinced that the Congress had always meant to declare independence, Ward and his colleagues were convinced that the king had always "meant to make himself an absolute despotic Tyrant."

The news of the king's speech was printed in Philadelphia in January 1776, the same week that Thomas Paine published his rousing pamphlet *Common Sense*.[9] Writing anonymously, Paine insisted that the time for loyalty to the king had passed. His argument was reinforced by how dismissive of the colonists' concerns the king had been in his speech to Parliament. The cycle of "running three or four thousand miles with a tale or a petition" like the Olive Branch and "waiting four or five months for an answer" was "folly and childishness" to Paine.[10] The Continental Congress needed to move on. The final line of *Common Sense* suggested that, "Until an independence is declared, the Continent will feel itself like a man who continued putting off some unpleasant business from day to day, yet knows it must be done, hates to set about it, wishes it over, and is continually haunted with the thoughts of its necessity."[11]

John Adams agreed with Thomas Paine about independence, but he became increasingly annoyed as people mistakenly attributed *Common Sense* to Adams himself. In Adams's view, Paine had put forward in his pamphlet some "very inadequate Ideas" about government.[12] Adams, on the other hand, had spent a long time thinking about how to replace the royal governments in each colony. He decided to write his own anonymous pamphlet, which would map out his ideas for representative government based on three independent branches with a system of checks and balances.[13] If Paine's *Common Sense* changed the conversation around new governments, Adams's *Thoughts on Government* would be the instruction manual.

While Adams was working on his *Thoughts*, the Continental Congress learned about Great Britain's new "restraining Act, or prohibitory Act, or piratical Act, or plundering Act, or Act of Independency," as Adams described it.[14] Parliament had responded to the king's speech by formally cutting off all trade with the thirteen colonies. Ships from British North America could be seized at will, though the property of loyal subjects could be returned later. This embargo told the world that the colonies were not just rebels—they were the enemies of Great Britain.

John Adams saw the Prohibitory Act as a kind of declaration of independence, suggesting that it might be "fortunate that the Act of

Independency should come from the British Parliament, rather than the American Congress."[15] But some of the delegates in the Congress chose to focus on a glimmer of hope in the language at the conclusion of the act, where Parliament allowed the king to send commissioners to the colonies with the power to grant pardons and bring about a reconciliation with Great Britain. The act did not specify who the commissioners would be, how many there would be, when they would arrive, or what exactly they would have the power to do. Still, the possibility of peace commissioners would haunt the Congress. New York delegate James Duane insisted that, "while Commissioners are daily looked for," the colonists should defend themselves, but do nothing more.[16] Adams felt that Duane and others were being "duped" by the "Phantom" commissioners, whereby Parliament could be using the same trick that Adams had used on his farm in Braintree to catch a horse, "holding out an empty Hat, as if it was full of Corn."[17]

While the Continental Congress waited for the king's commissioners, the delegates sent a representative of their own across the Atlantic. In November 1775, the Congress had appointed a Committee of Secret Correspondence to form covert connections "with our friends in Great Britain, Ireland, and other parts of the world."[18] This predecessor of a foreign-affairs committee had been quietly working to find allies overseas and learn what the rest of the world thought about the united colonies and the war with Great Britain. In March 1776, the committee decided to send Connecticut delegate Silas Deane to Paris, empowered to be a covert agent of the united colonies in France. It was not unusual for Americans to tour Europe, and the committee reasoned that it was "scarce necessary to pretend" that Deane had "any other business at Paris than the gratifying of that curiosity, which draws numbers thither yearly, merely to see so famous a city."[19] But, to be safe, Deane would assume the guise of a merchant.

The Committee of Secret Correspondence expected Silas Deane to keep a record of his conversations with "great personages" and send intelligence back to Philadelphia "by every safe Opportunity."[20] New York delegate John Jay taught Deane how to write with invisible ink, in case he learned information that could only be entrusted to someone who could reveal the message.[21] As soon as Deane arrived in Paris, the committee expected him to connect with the French foreign minister, Charles Gravier, the Comte de Vergennes, and to ask Vergennes an important question: If the Continental Congress declared the colonies to be independent, would France "acknowledge them as such, receive their Ambassadors," and "enter into any Treaty or Alliance with them, for Commerce, or defence, or both?"[22]

On May 10, 1776, the Continental Congress took an important step toward independence by agreeing that each of the thirteen colonies needed to adopt new governments. As John Adams set to work on a preamble for the resolution, delegates came and went. Thomas Jefferson arrived in Philadelphia after being delayed in Virginia by a severe headache.[23] Rhode Islander William Ellery joined the Congress to replace Samuel Ward, who had died of smallpox. John Dickinson of Pennsylvania—arguably the most conscientious delegate, and a longtime advocate for rights but not independence—traveled to Delaware.[24] Without Dickinson in the room, delegates who had been instructed not to support independence were utterly confused when they read Adams's preamble to the resolution about new governments.

John Adams had poured a year's worth of frustration—at both the British king and Parliament and his own sluggish colleagues in the Congress—into his draft. But the preamble was also a text for a specific moment, written with a new sense of urgency and a commitment to change. Still, moderate delegates were left wondering, why now? There were three answers to this question. One was sewn into the clothes of a man named George Merchant, one was cruising the Delaware River, and one was sitting upstairs in the Pennsylvania State House.

A complicated journey had brought George Merchant to Philadelphia in May 1776. Merchant was a Virginia rifleman who had been captured by British forces in Quebec in November 1775 and taken to London. In March 1776, he was released from prison and allowed to travel to Bristol,

England, where he secured passage to Halifax, Nova Scotia. From there, he escaped to Portsmouth, New Hampshire, and made his way to General George Washington in New York and on to the Continental Congress in Philadelphia.[25] Merchant had left England with copies of treaties sewn into his clothes to avoid detection. George III had arranged these treaties with German princes to send soldiers to North America.[26] One of the princes, Frederick, Landgrave of Hesse-Kassel (and George III's cousin and godfather to his newborn daughter, Princess Mary), provided so many soldiers that the entire German force has been remembered as "Hessians," though there were also soldiers from Brunswick, Waldeck, and Hanover.

Careful readers of George III's speech at the opening of Parliament in October 1775 would have noticed that the king had mentioned "friendly offers of foreign assistance."[27] He had said that he would send soldiers from his Hanoverian electorate to the Mediterranean island of Minorca and to Gibraltar, at the southern tip of the Iberian Peninsula. But the movement of soldiers from his own electorate around Europe was different from deploying massive numbers of German soldiers to North America. The decision was perceived as another sign that the king had abandoned his colonists.[28]

On May 6, John Dunlap printed the earliest intelligence of German mercenaries bound for North America in his *Pennsylvania Packet* and added an aside to his readers: "*Oh* GEORGE! *Are these thy commissioners of peace and reconciliation?*"[29] The next day, Dunlap's note was translated in Philadelphia's German newspaper: "O George! Sind dis deine Friedens-boten!"[30]

As Philadelphians first read in their newspapers that tens of thousands of German soldiers were on their way to join the war, the Continental Congress resolved into a Committee of the Whole, chaired by Virginia delegate Benjamin Harrison, to consider "the state of the United Colonies."[31] A considerable number of committees were active at any given moment, tackling specific issues or drafting reports and resolutions, but a Committee of the Whole was special. It was a conversation among all the delegates who were in Philadelphia. The Committee of the Whole met on Monday, May 6, and again on May 8 and 9. The details of who said what were left intentionally unrecorded in Secretary Charles Thomson's official minutes, but these meetings resulted in the Congress's decision on Friday, May 10, to recommend new governments in every colony.[32]

In between these meetings of the Committee of the Whole, two British warships had set off a panic in Philadelphia. A man-of-war, HMS *Roebuck*, had been cruising between Cape May, New Jersey, and Cape Henlopen, Delaware, for a while. Under instructions to the captain, Andrew Snape Hamond, to patrol the entrance to the Delaware River, the *Roebuck* was harassing every ship that tried to sail between the capes, including the *Betsey*, which Silas Deane was taking to Bermuda, where he hoped to find safe passage to France.[33] In early May, Hamond decided to move south and leave the British frigate *Liverpool* to annoy the rebels.[34] But first, on Tuesday, May 7, the *Roebuck* and the *Liverpool* moved up the Delaware River, collecting casks of fresh water. Their presence stoked fears of a British invasion. The Pennsylvania Committee of Safety rushed to defend Philadelphia, dispatching thirteen "gondolas," or armed row-boats, to "attack, take, sink, destroy, or drive off" the British ships.[35] On May 8, the gondolas exchanged cannon fire with the *Roebuck* and the *Liverpool*. Despite being low on ammunition and having to cut up blankets and items of clothing to roll up as cartridges, the Pennsylvanians repeated their barrage on May 9 with "so much spirit and skill" that the *Roebuck* and the *Liverpool* were forced to sail south, with the gondolas in pursuit.[36]

The mood in Philadelphia became anxious, and the Continental Congress witnessed how much terror British ships could cause. No one in the Congress knew yet if the British and German reinforcements were going to target Philadelphia or New York City.[37] They could only rely on intelligence from captains of merchant vessels who sailed alongside the massive, slow-moving fleet of British ships bringing supplies and soldiers across the Atlantic. One of these sympathetic captains claimed that "a large number of Hessians, Brunswickers, and English troops" were "all bound to Philadelphia, in order to disperse...that hornet's nest the

Congress."[38] New York made more sense as a long-term base of operations for the British, but a successful swipe at the "hornet's nest" in Philadelphia could bring a quick and decisive end to the war.

The third pressing concern for the Continental Congress in May 1776 was Pennsylvania politics.[39] The Congress shared the Pennsylvania State House with the provincial assembly. In the first few months of 1776, the delegates were increasingly aware that the decisions they made on the first floor of the State House might be undermined by decisions made by the conservative Pennsylvania Assembly on the second floor.[40] On the first day of May, the Congress took a rare day off so that the State House could host an election for new representatives in the assembly.[41] Choosing between men who supported independence and men who favored reconciliation, the electors stuck with the assemblymen who wanted to reconcile with Great Britain. Not until a few days later did Pennsylvanians learn the news of British ships moving up the Delaware River and the king sending German soldiers to North America. The election might have gone very differently if it had been scheduled a week later.

The preamble to the resolution that the Continental Congress passed on May 10 reflected these dramatic developments. In it John Adams laid out all the reasons why this resolution recommending new governments was necessary at this moment. The king had given "no answer, whatever, to the humble petitions of the colonies for redress of grievances and reconciliation with Great Britain," and was instead sending "the whole force of that kingdom, aided by foreign mercenaries," to subdue the colonists.[42] The resolution recommended governments that made sense for the specific circumstances of each colony. But the preamble argued that "every kind of authority" under the crown of Great Britain "should be totally suppressed, and all the powers of government exerted, under the authority of the people of the colonies, for the preservation of internal peace, virtue, and good order." The colonists' "lives, liberties, and properties" were at stake. Adams had written, in essence, a declaration of independence.[43]

The preamble marked the first time that the Continental Congress would publicly blame the king for turning his back on the united colonies.

It began by asserting that "his Britannic Majesty, in conjunction with the lords and commons of Great Britain," has "excluded the inhabitants of these United Colonies from the protection of his crown."[44] By John Adams's later account, James Duane of New York was the loudest critic of the preamble. "Why all this Haste?" he questioned, "Why this Urging? Why this driving?"[45] The German soldiers were still just rumors, and George Merchant had not reached Philadelphia yet with the treaties that confirmed the news. "If the Facts in this Preamble should prove to be true, there will not be one Voice vs. Independence," Duane insisted. But he still held out hope that the king's commissioners would bring an answer to the Congress's petitions, relief to their grievances, and, ultimately, peace. Samuel Adams, John Adams's cousin and colleague from Massachusetts, reminded Duane that their petitions had been answered with "Fleets and Armies."[46]

Pennsylvania delegate James Wilson had missed the debate about the resolution itself and took the opportunity of debating the preamble to question the Continental Congress's powers. If "all Government originates from the People," then, Wilson argued, the people of the colonies should be consulted.[47] He wondered, "Will the Cause suffer much, if this Preamble is not published at this Time?" The Pennsylvania Assembly was already scheduled to meet the following Monday. Wilson predicted that, if the Congress published this preamble before the assembly meeting, political chaos would ensue inside and outside the Pennsylvania State House, with "an immediate Dissolution of every Kind of Authority." Wilson implored his colleagues, "Before We are prepared to build the new House, why should We pull down the old one, and expose ourselves to all the Inclemencies of the Season."[48] But the vote proceeded, and the Congress approved the preamble on May 15, without unanimity.

As the final May 15 Resolution with its preamble left the Pennsylvania State House to be printed, it was treated as a single text that had received the approval of the whole Congress. Only the delegates knew that it was actually a measured resolution paired with a radical preamble. The Maryland delegates were hesitant to go against the "sacred" instructions from their constituents. They walked out of the State House after the vote on the preamble and immediately sent a copy of the May 15 Resolution to the Maryland Convention.[49] Other delegates also sent copies of the resolution to their home colonies and waited for reactions. Caesar Rodney shared the May 15 Resolution with his younger brother in Delaware and explained that "most of those here who are Termed the Cool Considerate Men think it amounts to a declaration of Independance."[50] Rodney admitted that the preamble "certainly savour's of it," but he told his brother to "See and Judge for Your Self." Thomas Jefferson, eager to help the Virginia Convention form a new government, sent a copy of the May 15 Resolution to Virginia. It would be important and challenging work. Jefferson thought that any colony that established a bad new government might as well have kept "the bad one offered to us from beyond the water without the risk and expense" of the war.[51]

John Adams was quick to call the May 15 Resolution "the most important Resolution, that ever was taken in America."[52] He thought that confederation was important "for our internal Concord," and foreign alliances "for our external Defence," but all that independence required was the suppression of royal authority.[53] Nevertheless, the May 15 Resolution could not be *the* declaration of independence. It was the product of only twelve colonies, because Georgia was left unrepresented until Button Gwinnett and Lyman Hall reached Philadelphia on May 20.[54] The colonies were still called colonies, and the only things binding them together were representation in the Continental Congress and George III's indiscriminate label of "all rebels." Adams later recalled that James Duane had decried the May 15 Resolution as "a Machine for the fabrication of Independence," at which Adams had smiled and replied, "I thought it was independence itself; but We must have it with more formality yet."[55]

It was unclear how many more steps it would take to reach formal independence. Great Britain had taken one step with the king's proclamation of rebellion, another with the king's speech at the opening of Parliament, and yet another with the Prohibitory Act cutting off all trade with the colonies. The Continental Congress had reacted to these moves, and individual colonies had taken their own steps toward political independence. With the May 15 Resolution, the Congress had taken a step that was meant to bring all the colonies into sync with one another and to publicly acknowledge, for the first time, that the king had forced the Congress to move.

✹✹✹

Traveling from Philadelphia to Lisbon, the crew of the merchant ship *Rachel* felt the tension reflected in the Continental Congress's May 15 Resolution. The *Rachel* spent the first two weeks of its six-week journey to Portugal stuck in the Delaware River in a dangerous bottleneck of ships that were trying to avoid the *Roebuck* and the *Liverpool*. When it finally reached open water, the *Rachel* brought the news of the May 15 Resolution to Lisbon. Soon afterward, the Portuguese government would force the ship to leave.

The British envoy in Lisbon, Robert Walpole, immediately recognized the significance of the resolution. He and other European officials who had been looking for a declaration of independence found one in the resolution. On July 2, Robert Walpole sent a letter enclosing a French translation of the May 15 Resolution to the Portuguese king's longtime chief minister, Sebastião José de Carvalho e Melo, the Marquês de Pombal.[56] For decades, Pombal had dictated Portugal's foreign policy. But, in this case, he was being dictated to by Walpole. The British envoy was confident that the Portuguese court would treat the Continental Congress's resolution with indignation. He suggested that Portugal should revoke the privileges of rebel ships until the British colonies reconciled with their king.[57] Pombal quickly shared Walpole's letter and the May 15 Resolution with José I, who ordered the publication of a punitive edict, which Pombal communicated to Walpole.

José I's edict, dated July 4, 1776, claimed that there had been no reason for the Portuguese government to prohibit trade with British-American ships before May 15, but the total suppression of British authority proposed by the Continental Congress was a threat that could not be ignored.[58]

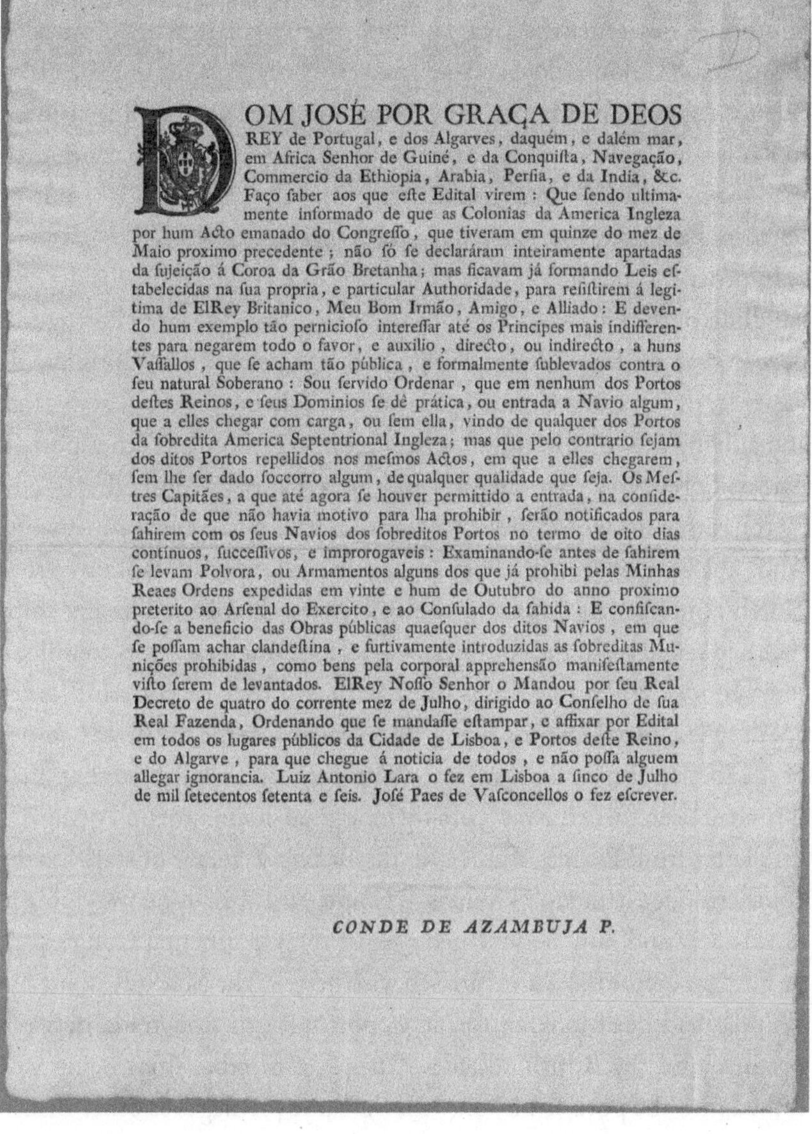

DOM JOSÉ POR GRAÇA DE DEOS REY de Portugal, e dos Algarves, daquém, e dalém mar, em Africa Senhor de Guiné, e da Conquista, Navegação, Commercio da Ethiopia, Arabia, Persia, e da India, &c. Faço saber aos que este Edital virem : Que sendo ultimamente informado de que as Colonias da America Ingleza por hum Acto emanado do Congresso, que tiveram em quinze do mez de Maio proximo precedente ; não só se declaráram inteiramente apartadas da sujeição á Coroa da Grão Bretanha; mas ficavam já formando Leis estabelecidas na sua propria, e particular Authoridade, para resistirem á legitima de ElRey Britanico, Meu Bom Irmão, Amigo, e Alliado : E devendo hum exemplo tão pernicioso interessar até os Principes mais indifferentes para negarem todo o favor, e auxilio, directo, ou indirecto, a huns Vassallos, que se acham tão pública, e formalmente sublevados contra o seu natural Soberano : Sou servido Ordenar, que em nenhum dos Portos destes Reinos, e seus Dominios se dè prática, ou entrada a Navio algum, que a elles chegar com carga, ou sem ella, vindo de qualquer dos Portos da sobredita America Septentrional Ingleza; mas que pelo contrario sejam dos ditos Portos repellidos nos mesmos Actos, em que a elles chegarem, sem lhe ser dado soccorro algum, de qualquer qualidade que seja. Os Mestres Capitães, a que até agora se houver permittido a entrada, na consideração de que não havia motivo para lha prohibir, serão notificados para sahirem com os seus Navios dos sobreditos Portos no termo de oito dias continuos, successivos, e improrogaveis : Examinando-se antes de sahirem se levam Polvora, ou Armamentos alguns dos que já prohibi pelas Minhas Reaes Ordens expedidas em vinte e hum de Outubro do anno proximo preterito ao Arsenal do Exercito, e ao Consulado da sahida : E confiscando-se a beneficio das Obras públicas quaesquer dos ditos Navios, em que se possam achar clandestina, e furtivamente introduzidas as sobreditas Munições prohibidas, como bens pela corporal apprehensão manifestamente visto serem de levantados. ElRey Nosso Senhor o Mandou por seu Real Decreto de quatro do corrente mez de Julho, dirigido ao Conselho de sua Real Fazenda, Ordenando que se mandasse estampar, e affixar por Edital em todos os lugares públicos da Cidade de Lisboa, e Portos deste Reino, e do Algarve, para que chegue á noticia de todos, e não possa alguem allegar ignorancia. Luiz Antonio Lara o fez em Lisboa a sinco de Julho de mil setecentos setenta e seis. José Paes de Vasconcellos o fez escrever.

CONDE DE AZAMBUJA P.

Figure 1.1 Edict issued by Dom José I on July 4, 1776. John Carter Brown Library.

José I could not remain neutral or indifferent when the Congress had attacked "El Rey Britanico, Meu Bom Irmão, Amigo, e Alliado"—the British king, his dear brother, friend, and ally. Great Britain and Portugal had a centuries-old alliance. While the British king was focused on his

North American colonies, the Portuguese king was thinking about South America. Since the Treaty of Paris in 1763, Portugal had controlled the port of Colônia do Sacramento, across the Río de la Plata from Buenos Aires.[59] The Marquês de Pombal and José I were willing to listen to Robert Walpole and ban all trade with the thirteen British colonies so that they could call on Great Britain for help keeping Spain out of Portugal's colonies, especially Colônia do Sacramento.

In order for the ban on American ships to take effect, broadsides and handbills of the king's edict needed to be distributed to every Portuguese port so that no ship captains could plead ignorance.[60] The Conselho da Fazenda, or Treasury Council, was responsible for printing, stamping, and affixing the edict in public spaces around Lisbon and other ports.[61] The edict required participation and surveillance by local officials and merchants who would need to translate the new policy for anyone who was not literate in Portuguese, including ship captains from North America. As copies of the edict were distributed, many ships that had sailed from the colonies were left seeking a safe port to unload their goods. When two ships filled with 250 tons of corn and other goods sailed into the Spanish port of A Coruña, at the northwest corner of the Iberian Peninsula, local merchants there were delighted that these ships had been turned away from their original destination in Portugal.[62]

A letter from Robert Walpole to the British secretary of state for the Southern Department, Thomas Thynne, 3rd Viscount Weymouth, reveals why and how he schemed against the Continental Congress. It seems that, before the *Rachel* arrived with news of the May 15 Resolution, Walpole had been looking for an opportunity to stop trade between Portugal and the British colonies. The sight of rebel ships being welcomed into the port of Lisbon with the same privileges as other British vessels had been "a long time a matter of great dissatisfaction" to the British envoy.[63] Walpole assured Weymouth that he "did not hesitate sending a Translation" of the May 15 Resolution to Pombal. The king and Pombal, in turn, did not hesitate to react. Walpole enclosed José I's July 4 edict in his letter to Weymouth, "persuaded, that this Conduct of the Court of Portugal will be very agreable to His Majesty," George III.

In case the Marquês de Pombal did not do what he wanted, Robert Walpole had a backup plan. On July 2, the same day that he shared a French translation of the May 15 Resolution with Pombal, Walpole also sent a copy of the resolution in English to Sir John Hort, the British consul general in Lisbon. He advised Hort that the officers in his department should not give any assistance to ships from the colonies, since, as of May 15, these vessels had "no right to enjoy the Benefit of His Majesty's Protection in foreign Countries" and should be treated as enemy ships.[64] Hort had known about the *Rachel* and the May 15 Resolution before he received Walpole's message. He agreed that the resolution of "that illegal Assembly"—the Continental Congress—had "put every inhabitant of those Colonies out of the King's protection."[65] But he was not sure whether or how to judge the loyal ships from the disloyal. He wrote his own letter to the Viscount Weymouth, worried that, if British officials in all foreign ports indiscriminately intercepted ships from North America, it might "breed an opinion of public unsteadiness."[66] But before he could send off his letter to Weymouth, Hort heard that José I's edict had been posted at the merchant's exchange in Lisbon. The decision about how to treat ships from the colonies was out of his hands. So he added a short postscript to his letter to let the secretary of state know that, within a week, every American ship would be turned away or confiscated by order of the Portuguese king.

On July 4, 1776, Portugal issued an edict that was, essentially, a declaration of dependence on Great Britain. Though the Marquês de Pombal had no idea that the king's edict would coincide with the Declaration of Independence, even diplomats who were well aware of the weeks that it took for information to cross the Atlantic were suspicious of the timing. The French chargé d'affaires in London became convinced that Pombal must have known that the colonies would declare independence on July 4 and planned the edict for the same date.[67] Meanwhile, Robert Walpole anticipated that the edict would be a model for other European powers.[68] If rebel ships could be turned away from every port they tried to enter, it would be devastating for the Continental Congress and the Continental Army. But Walpole was overlooking two key differences between

Portugal and other countries such as France or Spain. First, Portugal and England had been unbroken allies for 400 years; and second, Portugal did not control any of the Caribbean ports that American merchants and privateers relied on for the circulation of supplies and information. Unfortunately for Walpole, Portugal was the only European nation that would change its commercial policy because of the Continental Congress's May 15 Resolution.

As the *Rachel* sailed into the port of Lisbon, the *Sirena* was sailing into the port of Bristol in southwest England. It had taken thirty days for James Furse, the captain of the *Sirena*, to travel from Boston to Bristol. But Furse had been waiting in Massachusetts for a while before setting sail. On April 11, privateers had seized his old ship, loaded with rum and molasses from the British Caribbean island of Grenada.[69] Furse petitioned the Massachusetts Council to grant him and his crew the liberty to return home to Bristol, but even after purchasing a new ship he was not allowed to leave. On June 1, Furse petitioned the Massachusetts Council again, claiming that he was "far distant from his Connections and his Family" and that he had no intelligence to communicate.[70] Finally, the council agreed to let Furse and his men set sail, while also instructing officials in the port of Cohasset to "pay the Closest Attention" to what was loaded onto the ship.

If anyone in Cohasset searched the *Sirena*'s cargo, then they missed something ubiquitous but highly valuable: a newspaper. When Captain James Furse sailed for Bristol, he brought with him the May 30 issue of the *New-England Chronicle*, printed by Samuel Hall in Boston. At the top of the first column of the front page, under the heading "AMERICAN UNITED COLONIES," was the May 15 Resolution.[71] On reaching Bristol, Furse gave the newspaper to a local printer, who published the resolution in the city gazette on July 3. The news spread to London a few days later and then to newspapers across Great Britain and Europe. But the text printed in these newspapers was not exactly what had been approved in Philadelphia on May 15.[72] It was missing a word: "now." Perhaps the compositor in Bristol missed the small capital letters that Samuel Hall had used to emphasize this word in the *New-England Chronicle*. Whatever the reason, without "now," British newspaper printings of the May 15 Resolution lost some of the urgency that John Adams had infused in the preamble.

The news of the May 15 Resolution traveled across the English Channel to France, where Silas Deane had spent the first week of July traveling from the port of Bordeaux to Paris.[73] In the first volume of communications between France and the United States in the French diplomatic archives, there is a manuscript copy of the May 15 Resolution in English. It is part of a memorandum that Deane prepared for his first meeting with the French foreign minister, the Comte de Vergennes. The transcription of the resolution begins with "American United Colonies"— the heading from the *New-England Chronicle*.[74] Thus, because of a British ship captain's decision to bring a Boston newspaper home to England, Deane learned about the May 15 Resolution from the British newspapers. It was the first but not the last time that Deane would learn about important developments in the colonies through the British press instead of directly from the Continental Congress.

There is a line of text crossed out at the top of the manuscript copy of the May 15 Resolution in the French diplomatic archives. The downstroke of a "p," the upstroke of a few "d"s, and a handful of accent marks are still visible—clues that the May 15 Resolution was initially labeled, in French, as a declaration of independence from Great Britain, until the error was discovered and the evidence was erased.[75] This copy of the resolution is prefaced by a note explaining that "Mr Deane has received the following Intelligence which may be relied on as being Authentic," covering up the fact that Deane's source was actually a British newspaper. The manuscript was initially dated "mai 15," but that too was crossed out and replaced with "18 juillet," the date the text was copied out in preparation for the first meeting at Versailles between Deane and the Comte de Vergennes.

Through the Comte de Vergennes's English-speaking secretary, Silas Deane gave assurances that, in the months since he had left Philadelphia, the Continental Congress must have declared independence. The May 15 Resolution was his clue. Deane wanted to know from Vergennes how a formal declaration of independence would be received "by the powers in Europe, particularly by France."[76] But Vergennes did not want to have that conversation yet. Independence was "an event in the womb of time," he argued, and it would be "highly improper for him to say anything on that subject until it had actually taken place."[77] In the meantime, Vergennes warned Deane "not to associate with Englishmen." Although the Committee of Secret Correspondence had hoped that Deane could keep cover as a tourist or a merchant, the British ambassador to France knew that Deane was in Paris. Many spies would be watching the Congress's agent while he waited for the news of independence.

The edict printed in Lisbon, the newspaper printed in Bristol, and the manuscript written in Paris all treated May 15 as a turning point for the Continental Congress. These documents are also evidence of just how little control the Congress had over the ways that their words would be received, especially on the other side of the Atlantic. Virginia delegate Carter Braxton sent a letter to his uncle Landon Carter suggesting that, if the preamble of the May 15 Resolution fell a "little short of Independence," it still would be interpreted as such "by those out of doors on both sides the question."[78] Braxton had no idea just how right he would prove to be, or how far beyond the doors of the Pennsylvania State House the May 15 Resolution would resonate. But in Virginia, Landon Carter had more immediate concerns. On May 15 in Philadelphia, the Continental Congress had taken a step toward formal independence, but in Williamsburg that same day the Virginia Convention had taken a leap. They had issued their own resolution, which Carter thought was "really very well penned," except that it hurried toward a declaration of independence.[79] "God help us all," Carter wrote.

2

Postponed

The Continental Congress Debates
Independence

"United, we stand—Divided, we fall."[1] That was the new message at the top of Alexander Purdie's *Virginia Gazette*. The colonial Virginia coat of arms that had adorned Purdie's newspapers for over a decade was gone, replaced by the words "THIRTEEN UNITED COLONIES." The flag of Great Britain was similarly stripped from the top of the Capitol in Williamsburg and replaced with the "UNION FLAG of the American states."[2] The reason for all this change was a resolution that the Virginia Convention passed on May 15, 1776, empowering Virginia's delegates in the Continental Congress "to propose to that respectable body TO DECLARE THE UNITED COLONIES FREE AND INDEPENDENT STATES, absolved from all allegiance to, or dependence upon, the crown or parliament of Great Britain."[3] The convention also supported "whatever measures may be thought proper and necessary by the Congress for forming foreign alliances, and A CONFEDERATION OF THE COLONIES, at such time, and in the manner, as to them shall seem best."

The Virginia Convention's May 15 Resolution was not a declaration of independence. By comparison to the Continental Congress's May 15 Resolution, however, it was closer in form to the Declaration of Independence to come. The preamble listed grievances about King

George III as well as John Murray, the 4th Earl of Dunmore and royal governor of Virginia. Ever since Dunmore had fled to a British ship, he had been "carrying on a piratical and savage war," including "tempting" white Virginians' enslaved laborers to create a Black British regiment.[4] The resolution itself instructed Virginia's delegates in the Continental Congress to propose a three-part strategy for total separation from Great Britain: a declaration of independence, a plan for foreign alliances, and a plan for confederation. Whether the order of these documents mattered was not made clear. What was clear in the Virginia Convention's resolution—and still hazy in the Continental Congress's resolution of the same day—was that these colonies needed to be "FREE AND INDEPENDENT STATES."[5] At the most elemental level, a declaration of independence needed to articulate a transition in political status: from subjected to free, from dependent to independent, and from colonies to states.[6]

Six weeks passed between the May 15 resolutions—the one in Philadelphia and the one in Williamsburg—and the Continental Congress's approval of the Declaration of Independence. It took time for the Virginia Convention's resolution to travel from Williamsburg to Philadelphia, for the Virginia delegation to propose independence from Great Britain, and for the Continental Congress to consider the proposal. Things moved far too quickly for some delegates and too slowly for others. There was no consensus on what a declaration of independence needed to be, or whether it needed to be issued before or after the plans for confederation and foreign treaties. From its context to its contents to the men who voted for and against it, the Declaration of Independence was a product of specific circumstances, including multiple postponements of the debate about whether or not to separate from Great Britain.

⚜ ⚜ ⚜

The day after publishing the May 15 Resolution, the Continental Congress decided to consult with the commander in chief of the Continental Army.[7] John Hancock wrote to George Washington and asked him to travel from New York to Philadelphia as soon as possible. Newlyweds Dorothy and John Hancock had recently taken up an airy new residence at Fourth and Arch Streets, and whether they knew it yet or not, Dorothy was pregnant with their first child.[8] The Hancocks offered George and Martha Washington a comfortable place to stay while they were in Philadelphia, and their hospitality did not waver when they found out that Martha wanted to be inoculated for smallpox while she was in the city. Ultimately, however, the Washingtons would stay in the home of cabinetmaker Benjamin Randolph. Thomas Jefferson, who had returned from Virginia just before May 15, was lodging with Randolph, but he decided to "get lodgings in the skirts of the town" where he would have "the benefit of a freely circulating air."[9] On May 23, the Washingtons settled in and Jefferson moved out, to the second floor of a newly constructed house at Seventh and Market Streets—remembered as the Declaration House because of what he worked on while he stayed there.[10]

When George Washington came to the Pennsylvania State House, the Continental Congress quickly realized that it would be inefficient for all the delegates to meet with him at once. They therefore created a committee consisting of one representative from each colony. The thirteen committee members conferred with the commander in chief over the course of a week before reporting back to the Committee of the Whole.[11]

At this critical moment, the Congress resolved to send 6,000 militiamen to Canada to reinforce the smallpox-ravaged army, and more than double that number to New York to prepare for a British attack.[12] They also authorized the creation of a flying camp—a mobile strategic reserve—of 10,000 men at Perth Amboy, New Jersey. Every colony from New Hampshire to Maryland would have to commit soldiers to this massive effort.[13]

The Continental Congress's focus on New York and Canada left the Massachusetts delegates concerned about the vulnerability of their home colony. On the evening of June 3, they showed up at John Hancock's house, having planned to accompany him to George Washington's lodgings to make one final pitch to protect Boston. But the delegates found Hancock "very ill of a violent fitt of the Gout" and unable to walk.[14] So instead, George Washington came to Hancock's house, and the two men conversed freely about the colonies' military prospects and personnel. Though the Massachusetts delegates did not get the military support that they wanted, they did get to witness a discussion that, in John Adams's words, "would make a Figure in History."[15]

In between critical conversations with members of the Continental Congress, George Washington sat for local artist Charles Willson Peale. John Hancock had made the arrangements for a portrait of Washington that would celebrate the British evacuation of Boston.[16] But Peale instead captured a somber and contemplative Washington. During his time in Philadelphia, Washington was waiting—to see how his wife responded to smallpox inoculation, to hear when and where the British were going to attack, to know how long he would remain at the head of the Continental Army. By the time he prepared to return to New York, it was clear that Martha would survive inoculation. She decided to stay in Philadelphia to recuperate, knowing that soon she would be able to travel wherever her husband went without fear of smallpox.[17] But being in Philadelphia for thirteen days and seeing the Congress up close gave Washington some new concerns. He complained in a letter to his brother that many delegates were "still feeding themselves upon the dainty food of reconciliation" with Great Britain.[18] Having celebrated the Virginia Convention's "noble" May 15 Resolution, he must have hoped that something would come of it sooner rather than later.[19]

During the two weeks that George Washington was in Philadelphia, the delegates from both Virginia and North Carolina laid new instructions before the Continental Congress. A month before the Virginia Convention, on April 12, North Carolina had become the first colony to instruct its delegates to support independence.[20] But two-thirds of North Carolina's delegation had returned home to participate in the provincial congress. Joseph Hewes, the lone delegate remaining in Philadelphia, held onto his new instructions for a month before presenting them on May 27, just before the Virginia delegates presented their own instructions, which had taken about a week and a half to travel by mail from Williamsburg.[21] Hewes might have been too sick from an "intermitting Fever" to share his instructions any earlier, or maybe the wording of North Carolina's instructions held him back.[22] The North Carolina delegates were empowered to "concur with the delegates of their other Colonies in declaring Independency."[23] The Virginia delegates were empowered to propose independence themselves.

The Virginia delegates waited to make a formal proposal until after George Washington returned to New York.[24] Perhaps they were too preoccupied to take this step any sooner.[25] Benjamin Harrison and Richard Henry Lee were particularly busy on the committee assigned to meet with Washington, but George Wythe, Thomas Jefferson, and Francis Lightfoot Lee were also serving on multiple committees. The front page of the *Pennsylvania Evening Post* on June 6 provides a clue that the time for the Virginia delegates to propose independence had come. The newspaper featured the Virginia Declaration of Rights—not the final version but the committee draft, printed by Alexander Purdie "for the perusal of the members" of the Virginia Convention, not for the public.[26] Someone shared the draft with *Evening Post* printer Benjamin Towne, probably one of the Virginia delegates. On Thursday, Towne's readers got a sneak peek at the first bill of rights on the continent. And on Friday, the Virginia delegates finally made their proposal.

On behalf of the Virginia delegation, Richard Henry Lee read the following resolutions in the Continental Congress on June 7, 1776:

> That these United Colonies are, and of right ought to be, free and independent States, that they are absolved from all allegiance to the British Crown, and that all political connection between them and the State of Great Britain is, and ought to be, totally dissolved.
>
> That it is expedient forthwith to take the most effectual measures for forming foreign alliances.
>
> That a plan of confederation be prepared and transmitted to the respective Colonies for their consideration and approbation.[27]

There are a few key differences between these Resolutions and the instructions from the Virginia Convention, dated May 15. Instead of proposing a change in political status, the Lee Resolutions asserted that the colonies "are, and of right ought to be" states, and that their political connection with Great Britain "is, and ought to be, totally dissolved." This language articulated what Lee, John Adams, and a minority of delegates had been saying for months: that the thirteen colonies already were independent in all but name. The Virginia Convention had suggested that the free and independent states would be "absolved from all allegiance to, or dependence upon, the crown or parliament of Great Britain." However, Lee and his colleagues focused solely on the crown. They added time pressure—"it is expedient forthwith"—to establish foreign alliances. But to the plan of confederation, they added the consent of the governed. Transmitting the plan "to the respective Colonies for their consideration and approbation" would take considerable time, but it was necessary for an independent nation founded on popular sovereignty.

The Continental Congress prepared to debate these resolutions the next day, Saturday, June 8, and encouraged delegates to "attend punctually at 10 o'Clock" in the morning.[28] At ten o'clock on Saturday night, South Carolina delegate Edward Rutledge sat down to write to a friend, New York delegate John Jay. The twenty-six-year-old Rutledge was one of the youngest men in the Congress. That night, he was exhausted. He had been in the Pennsylvania State House for nine straight hours, and almost all that time had been spent debating the resolutions for independence, confederation, and foreign treaties. Rutledge and the "Sensible part" of the Congress "had no Objection to forming a Scheme of a Treaty" of alliance "which they would send to France by proper Persons."[29] They were happy to unite the colonies in a confederacy. But "they saw no Wisdom in a Declaration of Independence." Rutledge believed that the Congress's top priority should be a plan of confederation. The colonies would look "ridiculous in the Eyes of foreign Powers" if the Congress tried "to bring them into an Union with us before we had united with each other." By the end of the letter, Rutledge was too tired to hold his pen. But he let Jay know that on Monday he was going to ask his colleagues to postpone the debate on independence for three or four weeks. Rutledge did not think that his motion would pass. He was wrong.

On Monday, June 10, the Continental Congress resolved that the debate on independence should be "postponed to this day, three weeks"—Monday, July 1.[30] Though Edward Rutledge succeeded in convincing enough delegates to delay the vote, surely they disagreed on the reason why. Some delegates hoped that their home colonies could send new instructions empowering them to support independence. Others, like Rutledge, hoped that the extra time would allow the delegates to confirm that their constituents still did not support independence. Whatever their reasons, the delegates' agreement on a three-week postponement was unusual and specific. Debates in the Congress were routinely postponed, but typically only from one day to the next—if too few delegates were present, or if debate ran too late in the day, or if too many other items on the day's agenda took priority, for example. In his letter to John Jay, Rutledge did not explain what he thought could be accomplished in three weeks. On the one hand, three weeks after June 10 was July 1—a nice number for a national birthday, assuming the Congress could come to a decision quickly. On the other hand, within those three weeks the British fleet could reach New York, obliterate the Continental Army with help from German reinforcements, and force the colonies to reconcile with the king.

Whatever the delegates in Philadelphia might have hoped to accomplish during the postponement, three weeks was not enough time to communicate with all thirteen colonies. The delegates from the northernmost colony, New Hampshire, knew that it took about eleven days for the post riders to bring mail from Philadelphia to Exeter. But Josiah Bartlett and William Whipple were proactive. On May 28, the day after the Congress learned about the new instructions for the North Carolina and Virginia delegations, the New Hampshire delegation wrote a letter home. Having seen the instructions from the southern colonies, Bartlett and Whipple wanted to know the "sentiment" of their colony "on the important subject of a total seperation from Great Britain."[31] Regardless of their own opinions on the matter, they felt "duty bound" to represent their constituents. On June 11, after the Congress postponed the vote on independence, Bartlett and Whipple wrote another letter explaining that, by July 1, "it is expected that all the Delegates who have not already been instructed will receive ample Powers" to support independence.[32] Meanwhile, based on their previous letter, the New Hampshire Assembly agreed to draft new instructions empowering their delegates to vote for independence. On June 15, the assembly approved these instructions, which recognized that the delegates in Philadelphia needed to be informed "without loss of time."[33] New Hampshire's new instructions reached Philadelphia on Saturday, June 29—just in time.[34] Bartlett and Whipple only knew which way to vote when the debate resumed on July 1 because they had written home on May 28. If they had waited until the Congress decided to postpone the debate, not even the fastest post riders could have brought new instructions to Philadelphia before the debate resumed.

The mid-Atlantic colonies were best situated to send new instructions within the three-week postponement. But the political situation in these colonies was challenging. In New Jersey, the royal governor was Benjamin Franklin's son, William.[35] On June 11, a new provincial congress gathered in Burlington, and they determined that Governor Franklin had violated the Continental Congress's May 15 Resolution by scheduling a meeting of the old New Jersey General Assembly in Perth Amboy for later that month.[36] The provincial congress voted to take the governor into custody and cut off his income. The Continental Congress gave the Provincial Congress permission to send Franklin to Connecticut, where a growing number of loyalists were being imprisoned and kept under surveillance.[37] With the royal governor out of the way, the New Jersey Provincial Congress turned its attention to the colony's representation in the Continental Congress. On June 22, they decided to replace New Jersey's entire delegation with five new representatives who would support independence, confederation, and foreign alliances "with the whole force of this Province."[38] Though the distance to Philadelphia was short, only one of the new delegates, Francis Hopkinson, was actually able to join the Congress before the end of June.

The same day that the Continental Congress agreed to imprison Governor William Franklin in Connecticut, they also redefined treason in the united colonies.[39] The Congress resolved that any person who was "adherent to the king of Great Britain, or others the enemies of the said colonies," was guilty of treason.[40] Loyalty to the king—the status quo of British colonial life—had become treacherous. In a letter to George Washington, John Hancock wrote that this resolution was "calculated to suppress Insurrections, and to promote good Order and Obedience to Laws in the United Colonies."[41] Though Hancock believed that the measure was "full and explicit," in reality it was only a half-measure. Any recommendations about laws in the "United Colonies" would be outdated in a week if the Congress decided to declare independence. However, there was another important and timely piece to this resolution on treason. In addition to laws that would punish anyone who committed treason against the colonies, the Continental Congress recommended that each colony should pass laws to punish anyone who counterfeited continental bills or aided in their circulation.

In the last week of June 1776, fears of loyalism, treason, and counterfeiting turned out to be tightly linked. Thomas Hickey was one of George Washington's "life guards," soldiers who kept the commander in chief safe and well attended.[42] Washington held them to strict standards of appearance and behavior.[43] But in mid-June, two of Washington's life guards were jailed for attempting to pass counterfeit bills. One of the men, Thomas Hickey, struck up a conversation with another prisoner, who later testified that Hickey had tried to recruit him into a scheme to "turn against the American Army when the King's Troops should arrive."[44] The news of this "most barbarous and infernal plot" reached the Continental Congress around June 23, just before they passed the resolution on treason.[45]

The Hickey Plot, as it became known, was a conspiracy meant to help the British by cutting off access to New York City, blowing up the powder magazines, and assassinating George Washington and his officers. After the plot was detected, Continental Army soldiers surrounded the Flatbush home of David Mathews, the mayor of New York City, "dragged him from his bed," and arrested him on charges of "dangerous Designs and treasonable Conspiracies."[46] But Mathews claimed that the real mastermind was the royal governor of New York, William Tryon, who was living on HMS *Duchess of Gordon* in New York Harbor. It turned out that Tryon kept a covert intelligence network with his allies on land, including Mathews. One of Tryon's couriers was an enslaved shoemaker named David King.[47] After Mathews's arrest, the New York Provincial Congress offered a $500 reward to detain King. He was "forced to fly," first to Rhode Island and then to England. King would later petition the Loyalist Claims Commission for the £30 worth of leather and shoemaking supplies that he had left behind in New York.[48]

From enslaved shoemakers to disaffected Continental Army soldiers to New York elites, the fallout from the Hickey Plot was extensive. But, as the prevailing name suggests, Thomas Hickey himself suffered the most severe punishment. Hickey was court-martialed on charges of "sedition and mutiny, and also of holding a treacherous correspondence with the enemy, for the most horrid and detestable purposes."[49] He admitted that, at first, he was only interested in "cheating the Tories" and making some money.[50] But when he realized what would happen if he remained at George Washington's side and the king's forces defeated the Continental Army, he committed to the plot so that he might later find safety among the British and avoid the charge of treason against the crown. Instead, the Continental Army court-martial sentenced him to death.

The story of Thomas Hickey's escalating activity—from passing counterfeit money to conspiring against the man whose life he was supposed to protect—terrified the Continental Congress. The June 24 resolution about treason was undoubtedly influenced by the Hickey Plot. Almost every private letter written by a delegate in Philadelphia in the last week of June 1776 mentioned two things: the plot in New York, and the debate scheduled to resume in Philadelphia. On Friday, June 28, a crowd of 20,000 soldiers and civilians gathered in Manhattan to see Thomas Hickey hanged.[51] That same day in Philadelphia, the delegates to the Continental Congress got their first look at the Declaration of Independence.

On June 10, when the Continental Congress agreed to postpone the debate on the first Lee Resolution, the delegates also called for a committee to "prepare a declaration to the effect of the said first resolution."[52] If the Congress resumed the debate on July 1 and agreed to declare independence, they would need a published statement explaining their decision. On June 11, the Congress assigned delegates to not one but three committees to prepare the documents proposed by Richard Henry Lee and the Virginia delegates.[53] A committee with thirteen members—one from each delegation—created a plan of confederation among the colonies. A committee of five delegates worked on a model for treaties with foreign powers. The Declaration of Independence was the work of another small committee, actually remembered as the Committee of Five—John Adams, Benjamin Franklin, Thomas Jefferson, Robert R. Livingston, and Roger Sherman. There was overlap among these committees. Sherman and Livingston were on the declaration committee but also represented Connecticut and New York, respectively, on the confederation committee. Adams was on both the declaration and treaty committees, as was Franklin, who was recovering from gout after a diplomatic trip to Canada. John Dickinson was assigned to the confederation and treaty committees, but not the declaration committee.[54] Meanwhile, Richard Henry Lee was not assigned to any of these committees. He had made plans to return home to Virginia.[55]

The creation of the Declaration of Independence seems such a monumental task and praiseworthy achievement in the collective memory of the United States that generations of Americans have overlooked how quickly it happened. When the Continental Congress postponed the vote on independence by three weeks, they did not expect that a declaration of independence would take three solid weeks to write. Rather, they expected that the drafting committee would meet, discuss, and edit a declaration in spare moments while fulfilling their other assignments. The committee members neither could nor did spend too much time on the document. They worked on the draft for a few days total between June 11 and June 27 before delivering a clean manuscript draft to the

Congress on June 28, the Friday before the debate on independence was set to resume.[56]

Both John Adams's and Thomas Jefferson's accounts of the process, though belated and biased, agree that Jefferson wrote the first draft of the Declaration of Independence. Jefferson recalled that the rest of the committee "desired" him to prepare a draft, and "it was accordingly done and being approved by them," he "reported it" to the Continental Congress on June 28.[57] Adams's autobiography offers more detail, but also more opinion. Adams felt obliged to explain how Jefferson—a young man who rarely spoke in the Congress—had been appointed to a committee of "such importance."[58] It was Jefferson's "Reputation of a masterly Pen" that made up for what he lacked in oratorical skills. According to Adams, the Committee of Five had several meetings about what a declaration of independence should include before they appointed Adams and Jefferson as a "Sub Committee" to pull their ideas together and "cloth them in a proper Dress." Adams remembered that Jefferson had asked him to write the first draft, but he had refused, worrying that he had been "so obnoxious" in promoting independence early on that a draft from his pen "would undergo a more severe Scrutiny and Criticism in Congress" than any draft from Jefferson.

Some of John Adams's account may be true, but Thomas Jefferson had plenty to complain about in 1823 when he heard Adams's version of events. After a Fourth of July orator drew on Adams's memories, Jefferson sent a haughty letter to his friend and presidential successor James Madison.[59] Jefferson remembered "no such thing as a subcommittee" and insisted that the Committee of Five had "pressed" on Jefferson "alone" to draft the Declaration.[60] Jefferson was not surprised that the eighty-eight-year-old Adams had misremembered the events of June 1776. He admitted that, at age eighty himself, he might not have the best memory either, "were it not supported by written notes, taken by myself at the moment and on the spot." But Jefferson did not actually record every detail of the drafting process "on the spot." He wrote his notes later, perhaps as early as August 1776 or as late as 1783. The drafts and letters written by Jefferson and Adams in June and July 1776, though incomplete glimpses at a complex picture, reveal more of the reality of the drafting process than either man's autobiographical reflections or assertions.[61]

The first identifiable draft of the Declaration of Independence is only a scrap of paper. The page is filled with snippets written in different directions and probably at different moments in June and July 1776.[62] Many more pieces of paper like this must have been part of Jefferson's drafting process. He had fewer committee obligations than his colleagues on the Committee of Five, but he was no less preoccupied. Jefferson's heart was at his Monticello plantation with his wife Martha, who suffered a miscarriage sometime that summer, while his head was in Williamsburg at the Virginia Convention, thinking about the colony's new constitution.[63] This scrap paper shows that—regardless of whatever meetings the Committee of Five had and whatever "Sub Committee" John Adams remembered—the Declaration emerged from what Jefferson was already putting on paper before the Continental Congress assigned him to this committee. And the first editor of the Declaration was also Jefferson himself. He crossed out phrases, inserted new words and ideas between the lines of text, and refined the layout.[64]

The draft Declaration had a logical, lawyerly structure: a presentation of generally accepted truths, evidence that those truths had been violated, and a justified conclusion.[65] In Thomas Jefferson's hands, the beginning and end of the text might have looked the same no matter when the Continental Congress decided to declare independence. But the middle—the grievances about King George III—was, like the May 15 Resolution, the product of a specific moment. Jefferson drew inspiration from the newspapers and letters he had read and the reports he had heard during the Congress's daily meetings.[66] The list of grievances escalated from issues that impacted only political leaders to issues that had the potential to affect anyone living in the colonies.[67] The first grievance accused the king of refusing to agree to laws that were necessary for the good of the colonists. The final grievance put the blame for the transatlantic slave trade squarely on "the CHRISTIAN king of Great Britain."[68] No one in the united colonies had experienced every one of these grievances firsthand, but many had been aware of at least one, whether personally, within their local community, or in the columns of their local newspaper.

On the pages Thomas Jefferson labeled as his "original Rough draught," there are edits from John Adams and Benjamin Franklin.[69] Adams replaced "the history of his present majesty" with "the history of the present King of Great Britain." Franklin argued that the colonists had been reduced "under absolute Despotism" and inserted the key word "only" in "our repeated petitions have been answered only by repeated injuries." Both men had limited time with the rough draft, though Adams was able to sit with it for long enough to make a copy of it. It seems that he wanted to share the draft with his wife, Abigail, back home in Massachusetts.[70] On Friday, June 21, Jefferson sent his draft to Franklin, who was suffering from gout. He explained that the "inclosed paper has been read and with some small alterations approved of by the committee"—Adams and perhaps Roger Sherman and Robert R. Livingston as well.[71] But Jefferson wanted Franklin to "peruse it and suggest such alterations as his more enlarged view of the subject will dictate." He hoped that Franklin could work quickly, despite his convalescence, so that Jefferson could share his feedback with the rest of the committee the next morning. On June 21, Franklin also responded to a letter from George Washington. Since he had been too sick to go to the Pennsylvania State House, he could not tell Washington much about what the Congress was working on, but he could assure him that "a Declaration of Independence is preparing."[72]

By the following Friday, June 28, a neatly prepared manuscript copy of the draft Declaration of Independence had been approved by the Committee of Five and was ready for the Committee of the Whole.[73] Josiah Bartlett, who had been working on the Articles of Confederation, thought that the committee draft of the Declaration was "a pretty good one," and hoped it would not be "spoiled" by the Congress.[74] Thomas Jefferson thought the draft was pretty good, too. Around this time, Jefferson learned that he had been reappointed as a delegate to the Continental Congress, but he had received much less support than he had expected. What Jefferson did not realize is that he received fewer votes to stay on as a delegate because he had written so insistently about Martha's poor health and his desire to return to Virginia as soon as possible, and his friends in Williamsburg thought they were being helpful in withholding their votes.[75] Jefferson wrote a letter complaining about the "painful situation" of being 300 miles from Virginia and "thereby open to secret assassination" of his character "without a possibility of self-defence."[76] "If any doubt has arisen as to me," Jefferson remarked, "my country will have my political creed in the form of a 'Declaration &c.' which I was lately directed to draw."[77] The post for Williamsburg was scheduled to leave Philadelphia on Tuesday morning, July 2. Jefferson waited to mail his letter, hopeful that he could add a postscript celebrating the news of independence.

Meanwhile, Edward Rutledge sent a desperate letter to John Jay with "the express Purpose of requesting that if possible you will give your Attendance in Congress on Monday," July 1.[78] Rutledge thought that the rest of the New York delegation was worthless in a debate this important. If the Congress was going to discuss the Declaration of Independence and the plans for confederation and foreign treaties—though those were still in the drafting process—then Rutledge needed Jay's help to "oppose the first, and infuse Wisdom into the others." Jay did not write back until July 6. "Your friendly letter found me so engaged by plots, conspiracies, and chimeras dire," he explained to Rutledge, "that though I thanked you for it in my head I had no time to tell you either in person or by letter."[79] He was simultaneously managing the fallout from the Hickey Plot, preparing for a British attack, and planning for the convention that would create a new constitution for New York. "We have a government, you know, to form," he reminded Rutledge. "God only knows what it will resemble." Jay could not be in two places at once.

✖✖✖

The seemingly arbitrary three-week postponement of the debate on independence proved consequential. If the Continental Congress had decided on a two-week postponement, they would not have known about the Hickey Plot, and none of the colonies would have been able to send new instructions or delegates to participate in the debate. If they had decided on a four-week postponement, the vote might have been swayed by the arrival of the British fleet and the King's Commissioners for Restoring Peace in New York. As John Hancock wrote in a stirring letter to some of the colonies at the end of June, "in the Conduct of Political Affairs, every Moment is precious. A Week—a Day—even an Hour has often proved decisive."[80]

On the morning of July 1, just before the Continental Congress took up the question of whether or not to declare independence from Great Britain, a courier walked into the Pennsylvania State House with new instructions from the Maryland Convention, encouraging Maryland's delegates to support independence. It was a thrilling start to a day that would otherwise prove "an idle Mispence of Time," in John Adams's words.[81] He was frustrated that, in the meeting of the Committee of the Whole, "nothing was Said, but what had been repeated and hackneyed in that Room before an hundred Times for Six Months past."

For John Dickinson, by contrast, it was not time misspent, but rather time for one last argument against independence, in a room where fewer and fewer delegates agreed with him.[82] Dickinson arrived at the Pennsylvania State House on the morning of July 1 having spent the past three weeks drafting a plan of confederation and thinking about the time it would take for the colonies to ratify it, as well as the time it would take to secure a foreign alliance. At least ten weeks of roundtrip ocean travel separated the Continental Congress from their most hoped-for European ally, France. As Dickinson jotted down notes for the speech he planned to give when the debate on independence resumed, his thoughts turned to Silas Deane, who Dickinson expected would reach the coast of France any day if he had not already.[83] Dickinson worried that the French government would be offended if they found out that the Congress had declared independence without Deane's knowledge. From Dickinson's perspective, nothing could be gained domestically or internationally by pushing the first Lee

Resolution before the others. He prepared rebuttals for every argument in favor of declaring independence at that time.

As summer rain poured down outside the Pennsylvania State House on July 1 and the debate on independence resumed, John Dickinson asked his colleagues to imagine a bleak winter scene.[84] A man destroys his house without having anywhere else to live with his family. He calls on his neighbor for help, but the neighbor is caught unprepared. The fate of this man's family is easy to envision: embarrassment, poverty, sickness, perhaps even separation from one another—all because the man did not think through the order and timing of his actions. Dickinson saw a similar fate for the dysfunctional family of colonies represented in the Continental Congress. Declaring independence before agreeing on a plan for confederation and securing a European ally meant tearing down a house that—for all its faults—still provided some sort of cohesion and protection. John Adams later remembered that Dickinson had spoken "not only with great Ingenuity and Eloquence, but with equal Politeness and Candour; and was answered in the same Spirit."[85] That answer came from Adams himself, although he had hoped that "some one less obnoxious" would rise to the occasion.[86]

Over the course of the day on July 1, the Continental Congress heard both sides of the debate. Their numbers increased, too, as three new delegates from New Jersey arrived to support independence.[87] Most—but not all—of the delegations agreed that the time had come to separate from Great Britain. They also believed they were representing the popular sentiments of their colonies. The divisive vote for the preamble of the May 15 Resolution had shown the Congress that, for a decision this important, unanimity was essential. The large Pennsylvania delegation was still divided. Delaware was also split: one delegate for independence, one against, and one absent. Edward Rutledge and the South Carolina delegation pushed the vote to the next day, and this final postponement gave Caesar Rodney "time enough" to ride to Philadelphia through "thunder and Rain" and break the tie in the Delaware delegation in favor of independence.[88] Meanwhile, the New York delegation decided that, because they did not have instructions to support independence, they would need to abstain from the vote. Early on the morning of July 2, they wrote to the New York Provincial Congress with worries about what might happen next. "What Part are we to act after this Event takes Place," they questioned, if "every Act we join in may then be considered as in some Measure acceding to the Vote of Independency."[89]

On the morning of July 2, the Continental Congress voted to declare independence from Great Britain.[90] Twenty-four days after Richard Henry Lee proposed the resolution, the delegates agreed "that these United Colonies are, and, of right, ought to be, Free and Independent States; and that they are absolved from all allegiance to the British crown, and that all political connexion between them, and the state of Great Britian, is, and ought to be, totally dissolved."[91] John Dickinson, having said his piece, decided to skip the vote.[92] Pennsylvania joined the other colonies in supporting independence. The vote took place early enough in the day that Benjamin Towne could include the news in the July 2 issue of his *Pennsylvania Evening Post*. Meanwhile, the New York delegates abstained from the vote and wrote a hasty note to accompany the letter that they had prepared earlier that morning, explaining that "the question of independance has Been put in Congress, and carried in the affirmative without one dissenting vote."[93] Only New York's abstention prevented complete unanimity.

The word began to spread that the Continental Congress was working on a declaration to formally announce their decision. From the afternoon of July 2 through the morning of July 4, the Committee of the Whole debated the Declaration of Independence. They kept the structure of the draft but refined and simplified the language—for example, cutting the second half of the sentence that set up the list of grievances, which initially read: "to prove this let facts be submitted to a candid world, for the truth of which we pledge a faith yet unsullied by falsehood."[94] But most of the discussion focused on the list of grievances itself. The Committee of the Whole cut and combined different grievances, changing some of Thomas Jefferson's original intent.[95] Most notably, the delegates excised the final (and by far the longest) grievance, about the transatlantic slave trade.[96]

The one area of the draft that the Committee of the Whole decided to enlarge rather than condense was the final paragraph. They recognized that, in that moment, the conclusion was the most important part of the Declaration of Independence, for both the inhabitants of the United States and the rest of the world. To make the transition from colonies to states more explicit, the Committee of the Whole made sure that the first Lee Resolution, the one they had voted for on July 2, was incorporated into the final paragraph.[97] They also infused this paragraph with an appeal to "the Supreme Judge of the World for the Rectitude of our Intentions" and "a firm Reliance on the Protection of divine Providence."[98] They changed "assert and declare" to "solemnly publish and declare." Overall, the delegates evidently recognized that the Declaration, more than any of their previous petitions and resolutions, was a communication tool. It needed to reach a wide audience.

On the morning of July 4, 1776, the Continental Congress agreed to the Declaration of Independence—though the New York delegates once again abstained from the vote.[99] The Congress turned to other business, and at the end of the day they assigned John Adams, Benjamin Franklin, and Thomas Jefferson to another committee. These three men were asked to design a seal for the United States.[100] A new national symbol was needed to take the place of the ubiquitous British crown, lion, and unicorn, one that would also serve a ceremonial purpose. Adams expected that a formal copy of the Declaration of Independence would be signed by all the delegates "as soon as an American Seal" was prepared.[101] And the Congress's agent in France, Silas Deane, also anticipated that, when the Congress declared independence, they would send him a formal copy authenticated by a seal. The use of seals on state documents was "a very ancient custom," Deane wrote, and something that the courts of Europe expected to see.[102] But the seal of the United States would in fact take years to design. Adams, Franklin, and Jefferson, who had worked so effectively on the draft Declaration of Independence, turned out to have three distinct designs in mind for a seal and could not reach a consensus. So, when people enthusiastically took down the symbols of the king as the news of independence spread through the United States, there would be nothing to fill the blank spaces that were left.

The Continental Congress voted for the Declaration of Independence before the Articles of Confederation or the Model Treaty were fully drafted. These three, intertwined documents—called for by the Virginia Convention on May 15 and proposed in the Congress by Richard Henry Lee on June 7—rolled out separately and lost their connection to one another. The Congress had not fully realized how much time it would take for plans of confederation and foreign treaties to be debated, approved, and put into action. Nor did they know how much time, manpower, arms, or international support would be required to secure the independence that they articulated in the Declaration.

In John Dickinson's final speech against independence on July 1, 1776, he told the Continental Congress that they were preparing to "Brave the Storm in a Skiff made of Paper." A skiff was a small, lightweight boat, already ill-suited for an Atlantic storm. And a boat made of paper would collapse in on itself and the linen fibers would pull apart from one another. Dickinson was right: the Congress was relying on words on pieces of paper to assert the existence of a new, independent, sovereign nation before they knew how that nation would be governed or who its friends would be. The Declaration of Independence was a "Skiff made of Paper" that the Congress was sending out into the storm, hopeful but unsure about what might happen to it.

3

Publish and Declare

The People Learn the News

In printing offices all over Philadelphia, compositors picked out a capital I from their typecase. They flipped the thin piece of metal on its head, slid it into place in their composing stick, and held it with the tip of their thumb as they reached for the next letter. For most, that next letter was an N; for the German printers in town, it was an M. The compositors worked until the metal type formed a small block of words that they could carefully slide out of their sticks and lock into the form before moving on to the text that would follow the title: In Congress, July 4, 1776. A Declaration by the Representatives of the United States of America, in General Congress assembled. Or, in German: Im Congreß, den 4ten July, 1776. Eine Erklärung durch die Repräsentanten der Vereinigten Staaten von America, im General-Congreß versammlet.

Many people in the United States—beginning in Philadelphia—learned about the Declaration of Independence through public readings and printed broadsides and newspapers. After John Dunlap produced the first broadsides of the text, he and his fellow printers published the Declaration in their respective newspapers. One Philadelphia bookseller even added the Declaration as an appendix to a pseudonymous pamphlet already on the printing press.[1] German printers in Philadelphia produced the first translations of the Declaration within days of July 4. The Pennsylvania Committee of Safety scheduled the first public readings of the Declaration for an election day, when the men who were eligible to vote would decide who would craft a new constitution for the common-wealth. By the time the constitutional convention began on July 15 in Philadelphia, the Declaration was no longer news in the city. It moved on to other places, the columns of other newspapers, and readings in other public squares.

From July through mid-August 1776, the Declaration of Independence was printed and proclaimed across the United States. Many public readings followed a formula that was familiar from years of civic celebrations for King George III and his predecessors, but with a few decidedly different elements. In town after town, civilians and soldiers assembled outside of a courthouse or another central location. A local official, oftentimes the sheriff, read the Declaration aloud, and when he reached the end of the text the people responded with cheers and the soldiers fired off a salute. The celebration often stretched into the evening, lit by bonfires fueled by the wooden coats of arms and signs and symbols of the British crown that were taken down from the buildings around town. People also read the Declaration in private, in their local newspaper or broadsides that some printers made available to purchase.

The Declaration promoted a new national identity and sense of purpose. The process of publishing the news of independence drew people together but also ostracized people who did not want to openly support independence. And, in their haste to spread the news, printers made mistakes—some innocuous but some surprising for a text as important in hindsight as the founding document of the United States.

❈❈❈

The first printer of the Declaration of Independence was John Dunlap. When he was young, Dunlap immigrated from County Tyrone in Northern Ireland to Philadelphia. He learned the printing trade from his uncle, and by 1776 he had been running his own business for a decade. Dunlap had printed many resolutions for the Continental Congress, but the resolution that the Congress asked him to print on July 4 was different.

In his office at the southeast corner of Second and Market Streets, Dunlap set to work on a large broadside of the Declaration. He relied on a clean, handwritten copy of the Declaration as approved by the Congress, and he may have been supervised by one or more members of the drafting committee.[2] Dunlap did not work alone, and he did not work perfectly. A peculiar fragment of one of his broadsides has strange marks (' ') around certain phrases in the first two paragraphs.[3] Perhaps these marks had been inadvertently left on the manuscript that Dunlap was copying, and whoever set the type had initially thought that they were part of the text but then removed them from the typesetting.

John Dunlap designed a broadside of the Declaration of Independence that communicated its importance.[4] Compared to other resolutions of the Continental Congress that Dunlap had printed, the Declaration was large and impressive. Dunlap put "In CONGRESS, July 4, 1776" before the title that had stuck with the text since Thomas Jefferson's rough draft: "A Declaration by the Representatives of the UNITED STATES OF AMERICA, In General Congress assembled."[5] For the first word of the Declaration, "WHEN," Dunlap used a large initial W, the height of six lines of text. On Dunlap's press, the grievances were arranged in separate, indented lines, as they had been in Jefferson's drafts.[6] Small capitals were used to emphasize the first word of each grievance. The final paragraph of the Dunlap broadside contains many more capitalized words than the preceding paragraphs, including, as in the title, "UNITED STATES OF AMERICA."[7] The single, wide column of text would have been easy to read, whether from a platform in front of a clamoring crowd or in a shadowy printing office while trying to find the right letters in the typecase to copy from Dunlap's printing for another broadside or newspaper.

After the type was set correctly, John Dunlap and his workers would have fallen into the repetitive motions of printing. They would have lightly inked the surface of the type, set a sheet of slightly damp Dutch-made paper in the frame, laid the paper against the type form, added pressure to transfer the ink to the page, and hung the freshly printed sheet to dry.[8] There is no record of how many copies of the broadside Dunlap's printing office churned out on the night of July 4 and the morning of July 5, but they surely numbered in the hundreds.[9] As the hours ticked by, the form holding all the pieces of type in place evidently loosened slightly and a word fell out, since one extant Dunlap broadside is missing the word "our" in the phrase "the Ties of our common Kindred" in the penultimate paragraph.[10] Either the printer immediately noticed and corrected the error, or he missed it and this broadside is the lone survivor of a bad batch. During the printing process, the very last line of type—the imprint reading "Philadelphia: Printed by John Dunlap"—shifted slightly to the left.[11] At some point, Dunlap changed the name of the city within the imprint: one surviving broadside reads "Baltimore: Printed by John Dunlap."[12] Perhaps Dunlap hoped to profit from the Continental Congress's order by selling some of these broadsides at his Baltimore printing office.

The most important thing about the Dunlap broadsides is not where they were produced but where they went. Out of the hundreds of Dunlap broadsides that must have been printed on July 4 and 5, only twenty-five with the Philadelphia imprint are known to survive. Each has had a unique history since 1776. None of these copies look as pristine as they did coming off Dunlap's press, with the dark ink shining on bright imported paper. Many were folded before the ink was completely dry, evidence of the haste with which they were disseminated.[13] Some were kept folded up for too long, and the fold lines have made the paper brittle and left lacunae or gaps that make this familiar text hard to read. Charles Thomson, secretary of the Continental Congress, folded up one Dunlap broadside and used red wafer seals to stick it to a page of his handwritten journals. In order to preserve this copy, conservators at the National Archives had to remove it from the journal, wash it with purified water, remove the old adhesive, fill in holes with paper pulp, and use Japanese paper to support the back of the sheet.[14] This copy became the Congress's official record of what the Declaration of Independence would look like as it was sent out across the country. It was the one Dunlap broadside that stayed in place, in the secretary's records, as the rest started to circulate. And it still wore out over time.

On July 5, the President of the Continental Congress, John Hancock, and his private secretary, Jacob Rush, began to send out copies of the

Declaration.[15] Hancock and Rush enclosed Dunlap broadsides in letters to Continental Army generals with instructions to proclaim independence to the soldiers who were actively fighting for it.[16] They also sent Dunlap broadsides to governors, conventions, assemblies, and committees of safety in the different states. Six weeks after the May 15 Resolution, the United States were still figuring their governments out, and the Congress recognized this reality. Hancock directed each of these authorities to share the Declaration of Independence with their "Colony"—a slip of outdated language—"in such Way & Manner as you shall Judge best."[17] As Hancock told these leaders of the United States, "important Consequences" would flow from the Declaration of Independence, and it was essential "that the People may be universally informed of it."

Outside of his official responsibility to share the news of independence, John Hancock also enclosed Dunlap broadsides in his personal correspondence. In a letter to William Cooper, the town clerk of Boston, Hancock wrote that he had been laboring day and night so that the colonists may be "a free and happy people, totally unfetter'd, and Releas'd from the Bonds of Slavery."[18] He recognized that the Declaration did not guarantee this freedom, but he assured Cooper and the rest of his friends in Massachusetts that "Congress have done, and will still do, more" to promote independence. Every letter Hancock sent out on July 5 and 6 enclosing the Declaration of Independence—whether public or private—bore the signature made famous by the parchment copy of the Declaration he would sign a month later.

The mail leaving Philadelphia on July 5 and 6 included letters from other delegates in the Continental Congress, sharing the Declaration with their correspondents. John Adams and Elbridge Gerry both sent broadsides to friends in Massachusetts.[19] One of the newly appointed New Jersey delegates, Abraham Clark, shared a Dunlap broadside with one of the former delegates, William Livingston, then serving as a brigadier general in the state militia. Clark explained that the Declaration needed to be "Published in all the Colonies, And Armies," and hoped that Livingston would share the news with his brigade in Elizabethtown.[20] North Carolina delegate Joseph Hewes kept a Dunlap broadside in his

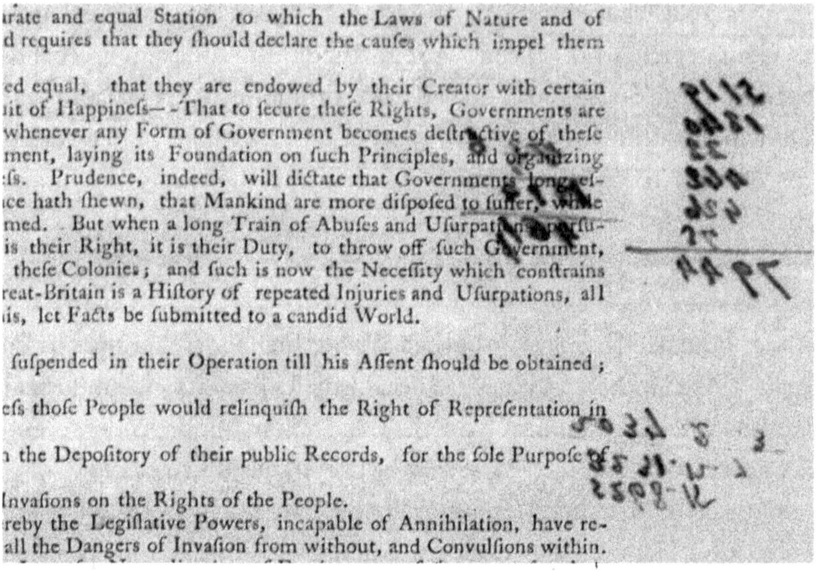
irate and equal Station to which the Laws of Nature and of
d requires that they ſhould declare the cauſes which impel them

ed equal, that they are endowed by their Creator with certain
iit of Happineſs—-That to ſecure theſe Rights, Governments are
whenever any Form of Government becomes deſtructive of theſe
ment, laying its Foundation on ſuch Principles, and organizing
ſs. Prudence, indeed, will dictate that Governments long eſ-
ce hath ſhewn, that Mankind are more diſpoſed to ſuffer, while
med. But when a long Train of Abuſes and Uſurpations, purſu-
is their Right, it is their Duty, to throw off ſuch Government,
theſe Colonies; and ſuch is now the Neceſſity which conſtrains
reat-Britain is a Hiſtory of repeated Injuries and Uſurpations, all
is, let Facts be ſubmitted to a candid World.

ſuſpended in their Operation till his Aſſent ſhould be obtained;

eſs thoſe People would relinquiſh the Right of Repreſentation in

the Depoſitory of their public Records, for the ſole Purpoſe of

Invaſions on the Rights of the People.
reby the Legiſlative Powers, incapable of Annihilation, have re-
all the Dangers of Invaſion from without, and Convulſions within.

Figure 3.1 Detail from John Dunlap broadside, originally owned by Joseph Hewes. Chapin Library, Williams College, Williamstown, Massachusetts.

personal papers.[21] He folded this large sheet of paper into a small square and marked it "Declaration of Independence." But he also used the folded-up broadside as scrap paper. The ink from a few of his arithmetical calculations bled through the right margin of the page, obscuring the second paragraph of the Declaration. Hewes's Dunlap broadside was not unique. A number of copies of the Declaration are covered in math.[22]

In these early days, the Declaration of Independence was treated as the product of the Continental Congress. Unlike *Common Sense* and other pseudonymous essays, there was no public speculation about who had authored the Declaration. Only John Dunlap's Baltimore newspaper reported that the Declaration was "the production of an eminent Gentleman of Virginia."[23] But Thomas Jefferson wanted his friends to see the Declaration as he had intended it, and he put his own publication plan in motion. He created clean handwritten copies of the draft that the Committee of Five had presented to the Congress,[24] Jefferson sent these manuscripts from Philadelphia to Virginia—to Richard Henry Lee and George Wythe, who had taken leave of the Congress to work on Virginia's new constitution, but also to Edmund Pendleton, John Page, and Filippo Mazzei, Jefferson's Albemarle County neighbor. Jefferson asked his friends to "judge" whether the final Declaration was "better or worse for the Critics."[25] Although Lee had not witnessed the editing sessions in the Committee of the Whole firsthand, he could see that the Congress had "mangled" the committee draft.[26] Pendleton concurred with Lee's assessment, and told Jefferson that the Congress had "altered it much for the worse."[27] "However," Lee assured Jefferson, "the Thing is in its nature so good, that no Cookery can spoil the Dish for the palates of Freemen."[28] The Congress had declared independence, and that was what mattered most.

As the Declaration of Independence started to spread throughout the United States, only a handful of people knew how the Committee of the Whole had changed what the drafting committee had proposed. Thirty years later, when Thomas Jefferson was President of the United States, a new generation of newspaper readers would see the draft Declaration for the first time. In 1806, George Wythe was poisoned to death by his grand-nephew, and his papers—including the copy of the draft Declaration that Jefferson had sent to Wythe—ended up in the hands of the editor of the Richmond *Enquirer*, who was eager to print it.[29] In 1776, the vast majority of the people who read the Declaration had no idea that the text had been drafted and revised by Jefferson, edited by John Adams, Benjamin Franklin, and perhaps Roger Sherman and Robert R. Livingston, and then refined and amended by all the delegates in Philadelphia.

The Pennsylvania Committee of Safety was quick to follow John Hancock's instructions to share the news of independence. On Saturday, July 6, in Philadelphia, the committee read Hancock's letter and resolved that the Declaration of Independence should be "publish'd on Monday next," July 8, "at the places where the Election for Delegates are to be held."[30] The purpose of this election was to send representatives to a constitutional convention for Pennsylvania. The eight men who received the most votes in each county would come to Philadelphia the following week to work on a new plan of government. Pennsylvanians had been called to vote in a series of elections in the spring and summer of 1776, and they had experienced a jarring change in the political scene. Two weeks after an election in which the majority of Pennsylvania voters favored reconciliation over independence, the Continental Congress passed the May 15 Resolution.[31] The conservative Pennsylvania Assembly agreed to allow a conference to decide how to conform to the resolution. This conference concluded that "the present government of this province is not competent to the exigencies of our affairs," quoting the Congress's resolution, and the members joined in the call for a constitutional convention.[32]

The Committee of Safety planned for Pennsylvania electors to hear the Declaration of Independence, vote in the election, return home, and share the news with the rest of their community. The committee decided that, in Philadelphia, the sheriff would read—or "Cause to be Read"—the Declaration outside the Pennsylvania State House at noon on Monday, July 8. The committee paid a rider £11 to take Dunlap broadsides to Bucks, Chester, and Lancaster counties, as well as to Pottsgrove at the western edge of Philadelphia County.[33] Other riders must have brought the Dunlap broadsides to Berks and Northampton counties, so that the counties closest to Philadelphia could all hold public readings on July 8. The counties further west were not mentioned in the Committee of Safety's plans, perhaps because there was not enough time to get Dunlap broadsides to them before election day.

On Monday morning, John Dunlap printed a notice in his *Pennsylvania Packet*: "THIS DAY at Twelve o'clock, the DECLARATION of INDEPENDENCE, will be PROCLAIMED at the STATE-HOUSE."[34] At noon, a crowd of electors as well as people from across the city and county gathered in the warm sunshine on the south side of the Pennsylvania State House.[35] The sheriff of Philadelphia, William Dewees, stood by as John Nixon, colonel of a battalion of Pennsylvania Associators, read the Declaration of Independence aloud from a Dunlap broadside.[36] John Adams looked on as Nixon stood on "that awfull Stage, in the State house Yard," surrounded by the Committee of Safety, the Committee of Inspection, and "a great Crowd of People."[37] Adams had predicted that "Pomp and Parade" would be part of the celebration of independence, but he was bothered by all the noise.[38] The crowd cheered and applauded as Nixon finished his reading. The Pennsylvania battalions fired a *feu de joie*—"notwithstanding the Scarcity of Powder," Adams noted—and bells and chimes rang out through the day. Adams was grateful that, amid "all this Lurry," the election was carried out "with the Utmost Decency, and order."[39] The day ended with a fiery finale: the king's arms were taken down from the walls of the Pennsylvania State House and "burned amidst the acclamations of a croud of spectators."[40]

Hundreds, perhaps thousands, of people participated in and observed the day's activities, including nine-year-old James Forten. The words of the Declaration of Independence would stick with him for the rest of his life as he became one of Philadelphia's most prominent and influential Black citizens.[41] There were surely other free Black and enslaved people in the crowd. Some delegates to the Continental Congress had brought enslaved laborers to Philadelphia, including William Whipple. Late at night on July 8, after the bonfires had burned out, Whipple wrote a letter to his brother-in-law, enclosing a copy of the Declaration and noting that "it was this day publishd in form at the State House in this City."[42] He felt "Lighter." Whipple wrote that "we are now free from those Cursed Shackles" that had "embaresed" the Continental Congress "ever since the Commencement of the war." An enslaved servant named Prince had accompanied Whipple from New Hampshire to Philadelphia. Whipple did not record whether Prince listened to the reading of the Declaration, and he did not see the irony in talking about "Cursed Shackles" in this moment. But the words of the Declaration became a source of hope for Prince, whether he heard them read aloud in July 1776 or not. Three years later, he would be one of twenty "natives of Africa" who petitioned for freedom, arguing that the "God of nature gave them life and freedom, upon terms of the most perfect equality with other men." Eventually he would be manumitted by Whipple.[43]

The words of the Declaration of Independence rang out across eastern Pennsylvania on July 8, from the large assembly outside the

Pennsylvania State House to smaller but still substantial readings at other polling places. In Reading, Sheriff Henry Vanderslice rang the bell in the tower of the Berks County courthouse and then stood on the courthouse steps to read the Declaration to the gathering crowd. In Easton, a battalion of soldiers paraded in front of the Northampton County courthouse, and the sounds of their drums and fifes excited "a great number of spectators."[44] Robert Levers, the county clerk, read the Declaration, and the crowd "gave their hearty assent with three loud huzzas, and cried out, 'MAY GOD LONG PRESERVE and UNITE the FREE and INDEPENDENT STATES of AMERICA.'"[45]

There was also a reading of the Declaration of Independence on July 8 on the other side of the Delaware River, where the people already had a new constitution. Shortly after the New Jersey Provincial Congress called for Governor William Franklin's arrest, they adopted a new constitution. In Trenton, outside the Hunterdon County courthouse, both the New Jersey Constitution, dated July 2, and the Declaration of Independence, dated July 4, were read aloud and "received with loud acclamations" by a crowd of soldiers and civilians.[46]

The New Jersey Constitution was a document caught between progress and regress. The fourth article granted suffrage to "all Inhabitants"—including women and free Black people—who were of age and had property.[47] But the constitution was a plan of government for a colony, not a state. The final paragraph indicated that, "if a Reconciliation between Great Britain & these Colonies should take Place, and the latter be again taken under the Protection & Government of the Crown of Great Britain, this Charter shall be null and void." John Adams was "Somewhat alarmed" by this provision.[48] In a letter to Jonathan Dickinson Sergeant, one of the former New Jersey delegates to the Continental Congress, who had helped to draft the constitution, Adams wrote that it was "a pity that the Idea, of returning under the Yoke" of Great Britain was part of an otherwise promising plan of government. There must have been an obvious, anxious dissonance in Trenton as the crowd learned about both the Declaration of Independence and a state constitution that could be nullified if independence proved to be short-lived.

In the weeks that followed July 8, there were dozens of public readings of the Declaration. Sheriffs were the officials most often asked to read the text aloud, and courthouses were the most popular locations. Many of these readings were described in newspapers, and the accounts were reprinted across the United States.[49] In his *Pennsylvania Packet,* John Dunlap described public readings of the Declaration in New Jersey, New York, New Hampshire, Massachusetts, Maryland, and South Carolina.[50] These accounts reassured the Continental Congress that the Declaration of Independence was being well received.[51] The same sorts of descriptions of its reception recur in many different settings. The celebrations at the college in Princeton, New Jersey, the state house in Newport, Rhode Island, and the courthouse in Richmond, Virginia, were all "conducted" with great "decorum."[52] The reading of the Declaration in Newburyport, Massachusetts, was a "joyful occasion," and the soldiers at Fort Ticonderoga, New York, "manifested their joy with three cheers."[53] Learning about these readings and seeing similarities between celebrations in different places reinforced a sense of community and common purpose for the United States.[54]

The readings of the Declaration of Independence in the first few weeks of July were confined to the northern and mid-Atlantic states because it took more time for the post to travel by land to the southern states. Ordinarily, it would have been easier for a ship to carry the news of independence from Pennsylvania to the Carolinas and Georgia, but there were British ships all along the coastline, and the key port of Charleston had narrowly escaped British occupation. The southern division of the Continental Army, led by Major General Charles Lee and Colonel William Moultrie, had repelled a British attack on Sullivan's Island on June 28.[55] The British forces had sustained significant casualties and the loss of HMS *Actaeon,* one of several warships piloted by enslaved men who the British navy had impressed into service.[56]

It took a month for the Declaration of Independence to reach Charleston by land, but when it did it prompted a day-long celebration on August 5. At noon, Charles Lee joined the president of South Carolina, John Rutledge, and other political and military leaders at the statehouse to hear it read aloud.[57] The group processed to the exchange building on the waterfront, an important site of commerce for Charleston, for another reading, which was celebrated with cheers and cannon fire. Lee ordered all the soldiers in town who were not on duty to assemble at three o'clock at the liberty tree, where the Declaration was read aloud for the third time in as many hours. The following day, there was yet another reading on Sullivan's Island.

Officials in Savannah, Georgia, similarly planned a day full of public readings of the Declaration on August 10. First, the provincial council met in their chamber and read John Hancock's letter and the Dunlap broadside enclosed with it.[58] Next, they processed to Johnson Square, one of the town's oldest public squares, where "a great concourse of people" listened to the Declaration, and the grenadier and light-infantry companies fired a celebratory volley. The crowd moved to the nearby liberty pole, which the Sons of Liberty had raised a year earlier, for another reading. The procession continued east to the Trustees' Garden, where the Declaration was read for the fourth time that day, and the council celebrated with a dinner under the cedar trees.

As night fell, there was another procession through town—a mock funeral cortege for George III. The local militia marched with muffled drums and somber fifes, followed by "a greater number of people than ever appeared on any occasion before" in Georgia. They buried their loyalty to the king with a solemn prayer "that he will never obtain a resurrection to rule again over these United States of America." When George III was "interred" in front of the courthouse in Savannah, the people needed a substitute for the king's body. For decades, colonists had taken out their frustrations on effigies of the king's men, including enforcers of the Stamp Act, royal governors, and printers. But in the summer of 1776, the newly independent people of the United States created effigies of the king himself. These effigies reinforced the message of the Declaration, that the king had driven his colonists to independence. In Huntington County, Long Island, where the reading of the Declaration of Independence on July 22 was "approved and applauded by the animated shouts of the people," an effigy of George III, "hastily fabricated out of base materials," was wrapped in a flag that used to wave on a liberty pole.[59] The flag-draped king was covered with gunpowder, hung from a gallows, blown up, and burnt to ash. The *New-York Journal* reported a few more symbolic details. The face of this effigy was "black, like *Dunmore*'s Virginia regiment" of enslaved men.[60] On its head was a wooden crown as well as feathers. This effigy was a physical manifestation of the final grievance in the Declaration of Independence, which blamed the king for encouraging enslaved people and Native Americans to fight alongside the British against the colonists.

Amid all the celebration and seeming unanimity at these public readings, people who did not support independence felt suddenly exposed. Robert Christie, the sheriff of Baltimore County, was supposed to "proclaim Independency" at the courthouse on Monday, July 29.[61] But having promised to read the Declaration, he instead fled town. At noon on July 29, with Christie nowhere to be found, a member of the Committee of Observation took on the task.[62] After the reading, Baltimoreans continued the celebration by carting an effigy of George III through town, and hundreds of people cheered as the effigy went up in flames.[63] Though Christie remained the county sheriff, he thereafter worried for his safety. Four months later, he received a written warning: "Your conduct has been such in this State during our struggle for liberty, that we are at this present moment determined that unless you leave the town instantly, and the State within six days, your life shall be sacrificed by an injured people." The note was simply and ominously signed, "LEGION."[64] Christie went into hiding and eventually fled Maryland. When he later petitioned the Loyalist Claims Commission for financial compensation, he could truthfully say that he "never in any respect conformed to the Measures of the Rebels."[65]

On Saturday, July 6, as the Pennsylvania Committee of Safety made plans for public readings of the Declaration of Independence, Benjamin Towne published the first newspaper copy of the Declaration.[66] Towne's strategy of publishing the *Pennsylvania Evening Post* three times a week—on Tuesdays, Thursdays, and Saturdays—really paid off in the first week of July 1776. He printed the news of the Continental Congress's

July 2 vote that same day.[67] Towne did not mention the Declaration in his paper on Thursday, July 4. Instead, the news that the Congress had approved the Declaration of Independence first appeared in German, in Henry Miller's *Pennsylvanischer Staatsbote*, on Friday, July 5. The Declaration was said to be "jetzt in der Presse"—now in the press—in English, since Miller knew that printing was in progress at John Dunlap's press, and perhaps knew the same was true at Towne's shop as well.[68]

There were generations of German-speaking people living in and around Philadelphia in 1776. From the descendants of the first thirteen families of Germantown to more recent immigrants from Europe, Pennsylvania Germans were politically engaged, and they needed the same access to the Declaration of Independence as their Anglophone neighbors. The local printers anticipated that there would be an audience for the complete text both in German broadsides and in the pages of the *Pennsylvanischer Staatsbote*. The printers worked quickly to translate the text and then to set the type, and within days of July 4 the public was provided with two German printings of the Declaration: in Henry Miller's *Pennsylvanischer Staatsbote* on July 9, and as a broadside printed by Melchior Steiner and Charles Cist perhaps as early as July 6.[69] In the final paragraph, these printers used larger type to highlight "freye und Unabhängige Staaten" (free and independent states), as well as "Vereinigten Staaten von America" (United States of America). The Fraktur typeface makes these copies of the Declaration visually distinct from any other copies printed in the United States.

The Philadelphia translations from English to German are remarkable not only for their speed but also for their grasp of the complexity of the Declaration's argument.[70] These printers had a vocabulary for the revolutionary moment, especially by comparison to the translations of the Declaration in German-language newspapers in Europe later that summer. The semantic translation by Melchior Steiner, Charles Cist, and Henry Miller successfully maintained the writing style of Thomas Jefferson and the Continental Congress for their German-reading audi-

Indem wir, derohalben, die Repräsentanten der Vereinigten Staaten von America, im General-Congreß versammlet, uns wegen der Redlichkeit unserer Gesinnungen auf den allerhöchsten Richter der Welt berufen, so Verkündigen wir hiemit feyerlich, und Erklären, im Namen und aus Macht der guten Leute dieser Colonien, Daß diese Vereinigten Colonien Freye und Unabhängige Staaten sind, und von Rechtswegen seyn sollen; daß sie von aller Pflicht und Treu-ergebenheit gegen die Brittische Krone frey- und losgesprochen sind, und daß alle Politische Verbindung zwischen ihnen und dem Staat von Großbrittannien hiemit gänzlich aufgehoben ist, und aufgehoben seyn soll; und daß als Freye und Unabhängige Staaten sie volle Macht und Gewalt haben, Krieg zu führen, Frieden zu machen, Allianzen zu schliessen, Handlung zu errichten, und alles und jedes andere zu thun, was Unabhängigen Staaten von Rechtswegen zukömmt. Und zur Behauptung und Unterstützung dieser Erklärung verpfänden wir, mit vestem Vertrauen auf den Schutz der Göttlichen Vorsehung, uns unter einander unser Leben, unser Vermögen und unser geheiligtes Ehrenwort.

Unterzeichnet auf Befehl und im Namen des Congresses,

John Hancock, Präsident.

Bescheiniget,
Carl Thomson, Secretär.

Figure 3.2 Broadside printed by Melchior Steiner and Charles Cist. Pammi Sheaffer, Photographer. Special Collections and College Archives, Musselman Library, Gettysburg College, Gettysburg, Pennsylvania.

ence. By contrast, the quick turnover of news in Europe, where printers were less invested in the project of independence than the printers in Philadelphia, called for a more literal translation of the Declaration. The printer of the *Reichspostreuter* in Altona, near Hamburg, translated the word "usurpations" as "Usurpationen."[71] But Steiner and Cist thought that "Eingriffen" more usefully expressed the repeated violations of the colonists' rights. The word "facts"—in the phrase, "let Facts be submitted to a candid World"—reads as "Vorfälle" or "Begebenheiten" in European newspapers, words that imply events or incidents. But in Philadelphia, "facts" was translated as "Facta," as in the Latin, legal understanding of the word. When the German translators in Europe saw the list of grievances, they understood it as a list of episodes. But the Philadelphia translators understood that the Declaration of Independence built up evidence against King George III to support the logical conclusion that the king could no longer be the ruler of the colonists.

The Declaration of Independence appeared on the front page of almost every Philadelphia newspaper, beginning with Benjamin Towne's

Evening Post, John Dunlap's *Packet*, and Henry Miller's *Staatsbote*, even though, in eighteenth-century newspapers, the most important news of the week did not necessarily show up on the front page. The first and fourth, or front and back pages of a newspaper, were printed at the same time, on one side of a large sheet of paper. Printers would work on these pages in advance, especially if their newspaper was only issued once a week, and would fill the last page with advertisements and the first page with longer essays or the news from London. The middle pages of the newspaper were set and printed on the other side of the sheet of paper, and they often contained news in roughly geographical order, from the furthest away to the closest to home, so the most local news could usually be found on the third page. In Philadelphia, newspaper readers almost always had to open their papers and look at the interior for the latest resolutions from the Continental Congress. But on this occasion, many printers in Philadelphia and across the United States resisted both convention and convenience and put the Declaration on the front page.

In the weeks following July 4, the Declaration of Independence was printed in every active newspaper in the United States.[72] Most printers formatted the Declaration in the regular columns of their newspaper like any other piece of news. But two printers—John Holt in New York City and Benjamin Dearborn in Portsmouth, New Hampshire—decided to set it off from the rest of the week's news.[73] Holt explained that he placed the Declaration on its own page *"to oblige a number of our Customers, who intend to separate it from the rest of the paper, and fix it up, in open view, in their Houses, as a mark of their approbation of the INDEPENDENT SPIRIT of their Representatives."*[74] Holt used the same typesetting to create a broadside of the Declaration, with an important update. The New York delegates in the Continental Congress had felt compelled to abstain from the votes on July 2 and 4 because they did not know if their colony supported independence. But when the New York Convention reached a quorum on July 9, they swiftly resolved to support the Declaration, and Holt published their decision.[75]

Taking the opposite approach from John Holt, the printers in New Haven, Connecticut, published a broadside of the Declaration of

Independence and reused the typesetting for their weekly newspaper. An advertisement in Thomas and Samuel Green's *Connecticut Journal* on July 10 told readers that "The Resolves of the Congress, declaring the United Colonies, FREE and INDEPENDENT STATES" would be "ready for sale" the next day.[76] This was a bold business decision, because the Greens had been suffering from paper shortages for weeks. While they waited for a paper mill to be constructed in New Haven, they printed their newspaper as a single sheet.[77] Despite the limited quantities of paper, the Greens printed copies of the Declaration of Independence for people to purchase. To create their broadsides, they formatted the Declaration in two columns separated by a line of ornamental type.[78] In the next issue of their *Journal* on July 17, the Greens squeezed the same two columns of type onto the back page and used a border of ornamental type to separate the Declaration from other pieces of news and advertisements. They also corrected an error in the typesetting—an upside-down letter "u" that made the word "Country" read as "Conntry." Since the *Connecticut Journal* was typically organized in three skinny columns, and the two columns of the Declaration did not quite fill the page, the Greens added a perpendicular row of advertisements along the right side of the page to avoid wasted space—an awkward arrangement that nevertheless reflected the printers' efficiency at this critical moment.

As different printing offices across the United States set to work publishing the Declaration, they changed the text. They infused their own style through their capitalization and punctuation decisions.[79] As a comparison, apart from the first word of each sentence, there are a limited number of capitalized words in the Declaration as published in the *Maryland Gazette*—including "God," "Great Britain," "English," "British," "Indian," and "United States of America"—while more than 300 words were capitalized in the *Providence Gazette*.[80] When copying the text, compositors also added and omitted words and used alternative or incorrect spellings. Some even misspelled Hancock as "Hacock" and Thomson as "Thompson."[81] In Mary Katharine Goddard's *Maryland Journal*, the type size decreased near the end of the list of grievances to fit all the text on the front page. In the process, Goddard's compositor inadvertently skipped a line in the penultimate paragraph.[82] Goddard also prefaced the Declaration in her newspaper with a bold announcement that "THE THIRTEEN United STATES OF AMERICA, Have declared INDEPENDENCY."[83] This was correct, though Goddard had no way of knowing it, since she printed her newspaper on July 10, the day after the thirteenth state—New York—agreed to independence and before word of the vote had reached Maryland. These errors were unintentional and innocuous, but they still surely affected the reader's experience, whether the reader noticed or not.

Some of the changes to the printed Declaration can be traced back to a common source, giving a sense of how printers operated at this time. Three newspapers printed in New Hampshire and northern Massachusetts omitted the same four words.[84] Two of the missing words are in a single sentence: the first "our" and "would" in "we have conjured them by the Ties of our common Kindred to disavow these Usurpations, which, would inevitably interrupt our Connections and Correspondence." Apart from the tense, the absence of these words does not affect the meaning of the sentence, but it does show a connection between these printings. In one of these newspapers, the *New Hampshire Gazette*, two erroneous homophones appear in one sentence: "Mankind are more disposed to suffer, while Evils are sufferable, then to right themselves by abolishing the Forms two which they are accustomed"—perhaps because someone was reading the text aloud as the compositor picked out the letters from the typecase for this extraordinary issue of the *Gazette*.[85]

The *Massachusetts Spy* is a good—or rather, bad—example of how much the Declaration of Independence could change in the printing process. In June 1776, Isaiah Thomas, the printer of the fiery *Spy*, handed over his Worcester business to William Stearns and Daniel Bigelow and moved to Boston. Thomas had to make several journeys between Worcester and Boston to collect payments from his former subscribers, and he happened to be in Worcester on July 14 when the news of independence arrived.[86] Thomas climbed the steps of the town meeting house and spontaneously read the Declaration aloud. But although Thomas was one of the printers who had pushed for independence, he did not get to print the Declaration himself. That task was performed by his successors, even though, according to Thomas, they had "no experience in editing, much less in printing a newspaper."[87] As printed in the *Massachusetts Spy*, there are 1,319 words in the Declaration, one fewer than the number of words in the Dunlap broadside—but that number accounts for five deleted words, three added words, and one un-hyphenated word.[88] A number of other words were misspelled, including "goverment," "desolved," "declareing," "seperation," and most notably, in the last paragraph, "SATES" rather than "STATES."[89] Perhaps the most glaring mistake appeared in the second sentence: "We hold these truths to us self-evident...." But though Stearns and Bigelow were poor successors to Thomas, their error-riddled version represented the first and perhaps only access that some readers in central Massachusetts had to the Declaration.

The *Massachusetts Spy* shows how, if the timing of the Declaration of Independence had been different, the people involved in publishing the news would have been different, too. Some printers had kept the same newspaper going for decades. Others had just launched their paper weeks earlier.[90] In New York, printers were preparing to evacuate the city if the British attacked. In South Carolina, printers needed to reassemble their presses to publish the news of independence after the Battle of Sullivan's Island. The cohort of printers who produced broadside and newspaper copies of the Declaration of Independence in the United States in the summer of 1776 reflects the instability of their profession during the war.[91]

When the Declaration of Independence was news, it was fleeting. Public readings—even the all-day series of readings in Charleston and Savannah—were momentary. They offered people an opportunity to come together, listen to one voice for about ten minutes, and perhaps participate in toasts and cheers before going back to their everyday activities. The newspaper columns that contained the Declaration of Independence in one issue contained completely different news in the next issue, arranged from the same pieces of metal type. Nevertheless, the common experience of the news of independence would have a lasting impact.

4

Melted Majesty

Statues Fall and Tensions Rise in New York

The white and red of St. George's Cross gleamed at the fore-topmast of HMS *Eagle* as Vice Admiral Richard Howe sailed into New York Harbor on July 12, 1776.[1] The late-day sun illuminated a picturesque scene, which Howe's secretary, Ambrose Serle, described in his journal. "Nothing could exceed the Joy, that appeared throughout the Fleet and Army" upon Howe's arrival, Serle wrote.[2] The *Eagle* was "saluted by all the Ships of War in the Harbour, by the Cheers of the Sailors all along the Ships, and by those of the Soldiers on the Shore." But when the *Eagle* anchored at Staten Island, Serle's mood quickly darkened as he learned the news of the Declaration of Independence.

"The Congress have at length thought it convenient to throw off the Mask," Serle complained.[3] The Declaration of Independence proved that the Continental Congress had never truly wanted to reconcile with Great Britain. Independence had been "their Object from the Beginning." Serle had never seen "a more impudent, false and atrocious Proclamation" than the Declaration. As he vented in his journal, Serle noted that, in their previous petitions, the Congress had "thrown all the Blame and Insult upon the Parliament and ministry," but in the Declaration they had "the Audacity to calumniate the King and People of Great Britain." Even worse, they dared to invoke divine protection. "'Tis impossible to read this Paper," Serle wrote, "without Horror at the Hypocrisy of these Men, who call GOD to witness the uprightness of their Proceedings."[4]

New York Harbor in the summer of 1776 was one of the most fluid spaces in the entirety of the war.[5] People were constantly moving in and out, families separating and reuniting, thousands of soldiers and militiamen converging, and two armies preparing to face off. It was a place where authority and loyalty were being worked out in real time. The first British ships arrived just three days after General George Washington's life guard Thomas Hickey had gone to the gallows for plotting to sabotage the Continental Army the moment that British forces reached the harbor. Soon after, the long-anticipated King's Commissioners for Restoring Peace collided with the news of the Declaration of Independence. In the time between when one commissioner, General William Howe, sailed into New York Harbor and the other commissioner, his brother Vice Admiral Richard Howe, joined him, the united colonies became the United States. The Continental Army and the British army would spend weeks in a state of tension between potential peace and potential war, reacting—and purposefully striving not to react—to the news of independence.

⊗⊗⊗

As soon as George Washington found out that King George III was going to appoint Commissioners for Restoring Peace, he worried that he himself would be "under much embarrassment respecting the manner of receiving them."[6] Washington did not know how many commissioners there would be or whether they should be treated as ambassadors. He wondered if they should be given passports and allowed to travel through the colonies, or if they should instead be restrained. On July 1, as he watched British ships sail into New York Harbor, Washington made "every preparation" to receive the commissioners as representatives of the British government who could negotiate peace between the colonies and the Crown.[7] But he also expected that these British ships would "make an attack as soon as possible." The king and his ministers made overtures about peace and reconciliation. By targeting New York instead of Philadelphia, they showed that they wanted to subdue the colonies through military victory. The pressure was on the Continental Army—

rather than the Continental Congress—to deal with the king's commissioners, if a deal could be made.

The timing of the king's commissioners' arrival is remarkable. Vice Admiral Richard Howe's departure from England had been delayed by a debate over which powers should be granted to the commissioners. The secretary of state for North America, Lord George Germain, threatened to resign rather than allow the commissioners to do anything more than grant pardons to colonists who swore oaths of allegiance to George III.[8] When Howe was finally able to set sail, he planned to rendezvous with his brother and co-commissioner near Halifax and proceed to New York together. But the younger Howe started sailing south before his brother reached the Canadian coast. On June 25, on board HMS *Greyhound*, General William Howe reached Sandy Hook, a beachy spit that juts out of northeast New Jersey marking the entrance to New York Harbor. As the news of General Howe's arrival spread, loyalists began to flock to the British ships, eager for protection from political persecution.

On July 2, George Washington issued orders that read like a rallying cry in the face of a growing number of British ships in the harbor. He reminded his men that "the fate of unborn Millions will now depend, under God, on the Courage and Conduct of this army."[9] Washington knew that there was supposed to have been a vote on independence in Philadelphia on July 1. If the Continental Congress agreed on and asserted a political independence from Great Britain that the Continental Army could not defend, it would make the defeat all the more devastating. Washington admitted that, "if we now shamefully fail, we shall become infamous to the whole world." He called on his officers to remain cool and his soldiers to be attentive and obedient. Washington was acutely aware that the actions or inactions of even one man, regardless of his rank, could destroy any potential for peace in this tenuous moment.

Washington's orders captivated Hezekiah Hayden, a soldier from Windsor, Connecticut. He wrote a letter to his parents on July 4 and copied out the general's orders almost word for word.[10] Hayden wished that he could write more—perhaps words of his own, in addition to his commander's—but the drumbeat called him to action. Two months later, Hayden would die of starvation as a prisoner of war.

As General Washington called his soldiers to action, General William Howe's ship anchored at Staten Island and the British forces quickly transformed the island. Howe settled into the home of Adriaan Bancker on the road that ran along the Kill van Kull, the strait separating the northern shore of the island from New Jersey. Bancker had been pre-scient enough to send his wife, Anna, and their children to New Jersey for their safety, before he was detained on a British man-of-war.[11] Howe's troops set up camp around the Watering Place, the natural spring in the northeastern part of the island, which supplied the occupying force with plenty of fresh drinking water.[12] Washington and the New York Provincial Congress had tried to remove livestock and horses from the farm-rich island before the British arrived, a measure of "Self Preservation" for the Continental Army "tho' painful & disagreeable" to residents of Staten Island.[13] But the local Committee of Safety delayed the order, and some residents hid their animals.[14] The British forces gathering at Staten Island had potable water, room to spread out, trees for firewood, residents more willing to hand their livestock over to the British army than to the Continental Army, and a clear view across the water to Manhattan. It was the perfect spot for Howe to wait for his brother.[15]

Within a few days, an estimated 10,000 British soldiers had set up camp on Staten Island, to the delight of William Tryon.[16] After living on HMS *Duchess of Gordon* in New York Harbor for nine months, Tryon was pleased to see the inhabitants of Staten Island "welcome the arrival of their Deliverers" and share "every Supply & Accommodation in their Power."[17] The former—and, if the Continental Army failed, future— royal governor of New York hoped that this sentiment would spread through the entire province.

Not everyone on Staten Island welcomed the British, however. Two brothers, John and Joshua Mercereau, ran a stagecoach between Philadelphia and Staten Island, so they knew transportation to and from the mainland better than almost anyone. Still, they barely made it off the island before the British learned of their movements. Some soldiers quickly took advantage of the casks of wine in the cellar of the Mercereau family's tavern, the Blazing Star.[18] The Mercereaus' sister and brother-in-law stayed on Staten Island, in their home obscured by the woods. Two weeks after he made his escape, John Mercereau returned to his sister's home in secret to gather intelligence on the British occupation—the first act of a spy ring that would include multiple members of the family.[19]

The soldiers in the Continental Army and those in the British army were eager to confront each other. In their letters and journals from this time, peace was not the topic of conversation. Samuel Blachley Webb, one of George Washington's newest aides-de-camp, immediately recognized that the soldiers landing at Staten Island were "the fleet which we forced to evacuate Boston."[20] Webb's sister, Sarah, and her husband had lived in occupied Boston. As soon as the British left town, Webb had taken leave from the Continental Army and had flown "on the wings of Impatience" to find his sister.[21] But Sarah and her husband had evacuated, and their Boston mansion "look'd more like a covering for the Dead than a habitation for the liveing." In New York, Webb observed a sadistic glee spreading through the Continental Army. He had never seen "Men more chearfull."[22] His fellow soldiers relished the opportunity for a rematch with the British troops that had done so much damage in Boston. Meanwhile, on Staten Island, one British officer wrote to his brother that the island was "a very pretty One," almost like "the fine parts of Holland without the Cannals."[23] But he also thought that what he could see of New York City looked "very pretty." He hoped to address his next letter home from there.

George Washington anticipated an immediate British attack, but by July 4 he realized that General William Howe would hold off until Vice Admiral Richard Howe arrived.[24] During this calm before the storm, Washington's officers sent reassuring letters to their wives. Adjutant General Joseph Reed expected that his pregnant wife, Esther, had heard "many Reports" of General Howe's troops "penetrating into the Jersey."[25] He assured her that Howe meant "only to take Possession" of Staten Island and wait there "for the foreign Troops who they say they hourly expect." Reed was confident that his "dear Hetty" and their children would be safe in Burlington, New Jersey. On July 4, Henry Knox wrote two letters to his wife, Lucy, and—unsure of where she was—he sent one to Fairfield, Connecticut, and the other to Stamford. On the morning of July 1, when the Knoxes had looked out the second-story window of their lodgings on Broadway and seen British ship masts, Henry had panicked. He hurriedly packed trunks for his wife and newborn daughter, and put the two of them on the road to Connecticut.[26] But Lucy refused to travel more than a few hours' ride from her husband. "I left my Harry in a state of mind, that prevented me an opportunity of saying a word to him of the tender kind—of which I had many in my heart," she wrote.[27] She hoped to have the opportunity for "a more affectionate parting." On July 4, Henry apologized for the pain and anxiety he had caused Lucy in their last moment together, with "your Harry scolding the enemy approaching, all in Confusion."[28] Henry told Lucy that the British ships they had seen were "received with a hearty welcome" by the "rascally tory Inhabitants" of Staten Island. In his second, shorter letter of the day, Henry assured Lucy that there had been no battle yet—but "we think we can beat them with the blessing of heaven."[29]

⁂

Late in the evening on July 4, the news of July 2 reached Manhattan from Philadelphia. The next morning, the postmaster of New York City, Ebenezer Hazard, wrote a hurried letter to Major General Horatio Gates at Fort Ticonderoga. Hazard shared the good news that he had heard at the coffeehouse the night before: the Continental Congress had voted to declare independence. Although the delegates from New York had abstained, Hazard was confident that, as soon as the New York Convention met, they would "doubtless concur with the other Colonies."[30] Word spread quickly through the streets of New York. Lieutenant Isaac Bangs, from Massachusetts, recorded the news in his journal, along with his hope that the United States would "be able to Support themselves free & Independent and never again be brought under the Yoke of Bondage by Cunning & designing Men."[31] In the afternoon on Saturday, July 6, Bangs joined a group of Continental

Army officers at a tavern to toast the "happy news of Independence." Even in the privacy of his journal, he was embarrassed to admitted that, after a few too many bowls of wine, he had inadvertently become the subject of one of the toasts.

The news was also printed in the *Constitutional Gazette* on July 6, and one of the people who found out from this New York newspaper that the Continental Congress had declared independence was General William Howe.[32] On July 7, Howe wrote a letter to the British secretary of state, Lord George Germain, describing his arrival at Staten Island and explaining his decision to wait for his brother before attacking the Continental Army. Howe had "great reason to expect" that "a numerous body of the inhabitants" of the colonies were eager to join the British side of the war.[33] Sixty men from Shrewsbury had come to Staten Island, "all desirous to serve"—the vanguard of hundreds more in that area of New Jersey alone. Howe believed that the time was right for the king's commissioners to negotiate a reconciliation. But he also believed that peace could not be restored until the "Rebel Army" was defeated, and he would take all the help he could get. On July 8, Howe wrote another letter to Germain. More men had come to Staten Island since he finished his letter the previous day, bringing with them "a newspaper of the 6th," the *Constitutional Gazette*.[34] At the end of his letter, without any comment, Howe told the secretary of state "that the Continental Congress, on the Tuesday preceding, had declared the United Colonies free and independent States."

As Continental Army officers toasted independence and British army officers waited for reinforcements, a postrider 100 miles to the southwest began his journey from Philadelphia to Manhattan, carrying a letter from John Hancock to George Washington. "The Congress, for some Time past, have had their Attention occupied by one of the most Interesting and important Subjects," Hancock explained.[35] Benjamin Franklin had hinted to Washington that a Declaration was in the works.[36] However, in the month of near-daily correspondence since Washington and Hancock had last spoken in person in Philadelphia, Hancock had not mentioned independence at all.[37] With the conviction "that our

Affairs may take a more favourable Turn," Hancock wrote, the Congress "judged it necessary to dissolve the Connection between Great Britain and the American Colonies."[38] Hancock did not say anything about the abstention of the delegates from New York, the state where Washington and his troops were preparing for a British attack.

The Continental Congress empowered George Washington to have the Declaration of Independence proclaimed at the head of the Continental Army.[39] One of the most fragmentary surviving Dunlap broadsides—missing the entire bottom third of the sheet—remains in Washington's wartime papers at the Library of Congress.[40] But John Hancock must have sent Washington a stack of Dunlap broadsides, which ended up on Adjutant General Joseph Reed's desk.[41] The broadsides needed to be distributed to the brigades in New York and forwarded on to other divisions of the army.[42] Washington understood that the Declaration did not simply assert political independence from Great Britain, but also "asserted the claims of the American Colonies to the rights of Humanity."[43] It gave him a clear sense of what the Continental Army was defending.

On Tuesday, July 9, at six o'clock in the evening, the Continental Army in Manhattan assembled in parade formation. Officers with Dunlap broadsides in hand stepped up and read the Declaration of Independence aloud.[44] The army of the free and independent United States responded with three huzzahs, so loud that they reverberated off the trees that surrounded the clearing where the soldiers had gathered.[45] Washington hoped that hearing the Declaration would provide a "fresh incentive to every officer, and soldier, to act with Fidelity and Courage, as knowing that now the peace and safety of his country depends (under God) solely on the success of our arms."[46] He wrote to let John Hancock and the Continental Congress know that he had shared the Declaration with the army and that "the measure seemed to have their most hearty assent—the expressions and behaviour, both of Officers and men, testifying their warmest approbation of it."[47] July 9 had particular importance for Washington. It was the anniversary of the 1755 retreat remembered as Braddock's Defeat, when a much younger, less-experienced Colonel

George Washington saw firsthand what could happen when generals failed to plan and soldiers failed to act with courage.[48]

A few hours after the first reading of the Declaration of Independence to the Continental Army in New York, George III lay "prostrate in the dirt, the just desert of an *ungrateful Tyrant!*"[49] The gilded statue of the king on horseback had been constructed on the Bowling Green at the southern tip of Manhattan in 1770. Everything about this statue—the subject, the timing of its construction, the proportions of the king "about 1/3 larger than a Natural Man," the gold leaf, the fifteen-foot-high marble pedestal holding it aloft—felt out of place in this moment when the Continental Army was celebrating independence while the British army was staring them down from across the harbor.[50] The question of who "tumbled down and beheaded" the king's statue was answered with a flurry of speculation.[51] Massachusetts soldier Isaac Bangs said it was "the Populace."[52] Newspaper printer John Holt credited the "Sons of Freedom."[53] George Washington's aide-de-camp Samuel Blachley Webb suggested that his fellow soldiers "long had an inclination" to tear it down, and "tho't this time of publishing a Declaration of Independence, to be a favorable opportunity."[54] The next morning, Washington felt the need to address the statue's destruction in his general orders. Washington understood that whoever had "pulled down and Mutilated the Statue" of George III had been "actuated by Zeal in the public cause," but this reaction to the news of independence gave "the appearance of riot and want of order."[55] Such things needed to be "avoided by the Soldiery, and left to be executed by the proper authority." Washington did not disagree with the statue coming down, but he recognized that the eyes of his newly independent country—and the world—were on New York. The Continental Army needed to meet the moment.

Unlike the wooden coats of arms that were ripped from public spaces and burned in bonfires after readings of the Declaration of Independence, this leaden symbol of the monarchy would be put to good use. The broken pieces of the statue of the king were carted off to Connecticut to be melted down. John Holt reported in his newspaper that the "lead where-with this monument was made, is to be run into bullets, to assimilate

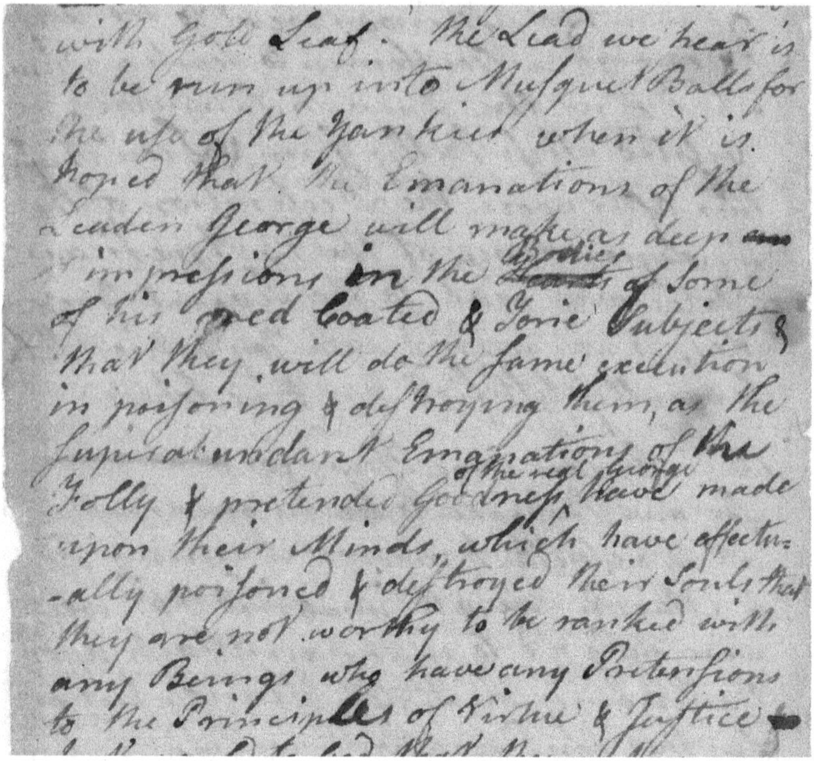
with Gold Leaf. The Lead we hear is
to be run up into Musquet Balls for
the use of the Yankees when it is
hoped that the Emanations of the
Leaden George will make as deep
impressions in the Bodies of some
of his red Coated & Torie Subjects &
that they will do the same execution
in poisoning & destroying them, as the
superabundant Emanations of the
Folly & pretended Goodness of the real George have made
upon their Minds, which have effectu-
-ally poisoned & destroyed their Souls that
they are not worthy to be ranked with
any Beings who have any Pretensions
to the Principles of Virtue & Justice

Figure 4.1 Isaac Bangs Diary. Collection of the Massachusetts Historical Society.

with the brain of our infatuated adversaries."[56] It was a powerful metaphor which Isaac Bangs struggled to articulate in his journal.[57] He recognized that bullets made from the "Leaden George" could poison the body in the same way that the "Folly & pretended Goodness of the real George" had poisoned the minds of British soldiers and loyalists. Postmaster Ebenezer Hazard put it more simply in another letter to Horatio Gates, enclosing a copy of the Declaration of Independence. The king's troops were going to have "melted Majesty fired at them."[58]

On July 12, the Continental Army spotted HMS *Eagle*, the flagship of Vice Admiral Richard Howe, at Sandy Hook. George Washington spent the morning debating a strategy to attack Staten Island.[59] But his advisors agreed that they had run out of time. Meanwhile, the British saw an opportunity. They decided to send two men-of-war and three tenders up the Hudson River. A brisk breeze and rising midday tide quickly carried HMS *Phoenix* and HMS *Rose* past Bedloe's Island, the future site of the Statue of Liberty, and all the way to the Tappan Zee, where the Hudson River widens. The Continental Army batteries on the New York and New Jersey sides of the river fired on the king's ships. But a number of soldiers, instead of listening to the drummers' alarm and manning their posts, simply stood on the banks of the Hudson "gazing at the Ships."[60] No one was killed by British fire, only a cow. But six of Henry Knox's artillerymen died and many others were wounded by accident as they hastened to return fire.[61] "How much I thank Heaven you were not here," he wrote to Lucy.[62]

The physical and psychological damage caused by the fast-paced British incursion on July 12 dimmed a week's worth of joy at the news of independence. As the sun began to set, things only got worse for the Continental Army as the *Eagle* sailed through The Narrows, the strait separating Staten Island and Brooklyn. From Manhattan, George Washington could see Vice Admiral Richard Howe's flagship. He could hear the salutes of the hundreds of British ships that had assembled near Staten Island by that time. Washington dispatched an express rider to Philadelphia with a letter that condensed the Continental Army's embarrassment over the British incursion that afternoon into a single paragraph. For the first time in their history, the Continental Congress met on a Sunday, July 14, to discuss what additional support they could send to the Continental Army at this critical moment.[63] It was a gloomy day of drenching rain in Philadelphia, and the scene was not much better in New York Harbor, where a British lieutenant sailed through the bad weather to bring a message to George Washington.

Vice Admiral Howe wanted to meet with Washington. On June 20, somewhere off the coast of Nova Scotia, Howe had drafted a declaration. He wrote that the king was "desirous to deliver all his subjects from the Calamities of War" and restore the colonies "to His Protection and Peace."[64] He described how George III had appointed Howe and his brother as Commissioners for Restoring Peace. He promised pardons "to all those, who, in the Tumult and Disorder of the Times may have deviated from their just Allegiance" to the king. Howe decided that the best way to share his declaration with the colonists would be to send it to the royal governors. But seven governors had taken refuge on British warships, and New Jersey Governor William Franklin was on his way to prison for violating the May 15 Resolution.[65] Only the governors of Connecticut and Rhode Island stayed in office as the united colonies transitioned to the United States.[66] Oblivious to this, Howe dispatched three lieutenants from HMS *Eagle*. One went south with copies of his declaration for the governors of the mid-Atlantic and southern colonies, one went north with copies for the New England governors, and one crossed the harbor with a copy for George Washington.[67]

Vice Admiral Howe hoped that a conversation with Washington might "prevent the further Effusion of Blood, and become productive of Peace and lasting Union between Great Britain and America."[68] Howe wanted to sail the *Eagle* as close to New York City as possible and invite Washington on board, with assurances that he would be perfectly safe and free to return to shore. Joseph Reed, Henry Knox, and Samuel Blachley Webb took a barge out into the harbor in the pouring rain to receive Howe's message from British Lieutenant Philip Brown. Peace should have been appealing to the three Continental Army officers, each of whom had in-laws whose loyalties lay with the British. In a letter to Lucy, Henry Knox described the encounter with Lieutenant Brown. After greeting each other with bows and pleasantries, Brown took the invitation from Howe out of his pocket and presented it to Reed, Knox, and Webb. Knox showed his wife how the letter was addressed:

> George Washington Esqr
> New York
>
> Howe[69]

Reed told Brown that there was no "George Washington Esquire" in the Continental Army, and Washington's three men therefore refused to touch the letter.[70]

The commander in chief could not accept a letter from the British commander that was addressed to him as a private citizen. And he certainly could not accept a letter that was, according to Lieutenant Philip Brown, "rather of a civil than Military nature."[71] Although the seats of civil power were shifting in every state, Washington's officers knew that the Continental Congress held the ultimate civil power in the United States at this moment. "George Washington Esquire" could not negotiate peace with Great Britain. Brown asked Joseph Reed how Washington would prefer to be addressed, but Reed noticed how he fumbled over the question, saying "General" before correcting to "Mr. Washington."[72] Reed reminded Brown that Washington's station was well known, and "certainly they could be at no loss how to direct him." As Brown prepared to return to the *Eagle,* he mentioned how much Vice Admiral Howe had wanted to be here "a little sooner."[73] Reed, Knox, and Webb all understood what Brown meant—that Howe thought that he could have prevented the Declaration of Independence. The four men exchanged bows—but not Howe's letter—and parted ways.

George Washington supported his officers' decision. He told John Hancock, "I deemed It a duty to my Country and my appointment to insist upon that respect which in any other than a public view I would willingly have waived."[74] If the message was urgent, and if the king's commissioners really had the power to prevent further bloodshed, then the Howes would have to figure out a way to address him properly. But, in case they needed a hint, Washington sent his own brief message to General William Howe on July 15, signed "Comr in Chief of the Continental Forces."[75] Nevertheless, when General Howe responded the next day, he fell into the same quagmire as his brother, addressing his message to "George Washington Esqr. &c. &ca."[76] The etceteras "implied everything & they also implied any thing."[77] Howe's officers tried to trick Washington's officers into accepting this letter by wrapping it in a blank sheet of paper. Joseph Reed "could not help smiling" at the ploy.[78] Washington again insisted that he could not correspond with the king's commissioners if they could not outright recognize his military rank.

Though the Howe brothers could not get their message across, their repeated attempts to talk with Washington created an opportunity for more personal communication. The Continental Army officers shared letters from British prisoners of war. The king's commissioners requested safe passage from Manhattan to Staten Island for Margaret Moncrieffe, the teenaged daughter of a British officer.[79] When Lucy Knox found out that her husband was communicating with the British, she asked Henry to gather intelligence on her sister, Hannah, who had gone to Halifax with her husband when the British evacuated Boston.[80] If Lucy Knox had married a loyalist gentleman rather than a rebel bookseller, she knew that she herself might have done the same. Samuel Blachley Webb likewise tried to use British channels to reconnect with his sister, Sarah. He wrote her a letter, but admitted to her that it was a "delicate Situation."[81] Webb could not entrust British communication networks with too many details or too much emotion.

Another letter that crossed from one side of New York Harbor to the other during this impasse was from Esther Reed's brother, Dennis DeBerdt, in London. Esther and Dennis, the children of a colonial agent, had taken to opposite sides of the Atlantic and opposite sides of the conflict, and they had not seen each other in six years.[82] DeBerdt had arranged a meeting with Vice Admiral Richard Howe before he sailed for North America and had made sure that Howe knew Joseph Reed's name. DeBerdt hoped that his brother-in-law would see that "Lord Howe goes to America as a Mediator, & not as a Destroyer," adding "I firmly believe it upon my Honor."[83] DeBerdt thought that if he could influence Reed—whether through kinship or common sense—then Reed could influence George Washington, and together Howe and Washington could end the war. "The very Thought my dear Friend of being instrumental in bringing about a Peaceful Accommodation is better felt, than express'd," DeBerdt wrote. Reed shared DeBerdt's letter with Washington and sent a copy to his wife in Burlington. He confided to Esther that no one could "wish more for Peace or would promote it more heartily" than him.[84] But the Declaration of Independence and Howe's declaration of pardons had complicated things. Reed expected that the combination of the commissioners' limited powers and the promise of political independence would unite the people against reconciliation with Great Britain. "From the printed Declarations you will see what little Prospect there is of Negotiation," he told Esther.[85]

Joseph Reed also sent a copy of Dennis DeBerdt's letter to Philadelphia, where the Continental Congress had just intercepted Vice Admiral Richard Howe's declaration.[86] Thomas Jefferson, Robert Treat Paine, and Charles Carroll of Carrollton—on his first day as one of Maryland's newly appointed delegates—formed a committee to read and respond to Howe's declaration and the circular letter that he had tried to send to the royal governors.[87] The next day, July 19, on the committee's recommendation, the Congress resolved to publish Howe's declaration in the newspapers, so "that the good people of these United States may be informed of what nature are the commissioners, and what the terms, with the expectation of which, the insidious court of Britain has endeavoured to amuse and disarm them."[88] The delegates hoped that Howe's declaration would convince "the few, who still remain suspended by a hope founded either in the justice or moderation of their late King" that reconciliation was impossible. Carroll felt confident that Howe's "silly declaration" would "soon unite all parties, & make all Americans Independents."[89] But Howe's declaration was not the only text that the Congress wanted to see in the newspapers.

The delegates in Philadelphia learned that, as the news of independence was traveling south, the news of the Battle of Sullivan's Island was working its way north.[90] On July 19, they ordered printers to publish an extract of a letter that Major General Charles Lee had sent to the Continental Congress describing the Continental Army's scrappy victory in South Carolina. Lee understood that this news would give "no small credit to the American arms."[91] Even those men who had lost limbs had not lost "their spirits; for they enthusiastically encouraged their comrades never to abandon the standard of liberty and their country." What happened in Charleston Harbor on June 28 arguably was just as important for public morale as what happened in Philadelphia on July 4. The news of Sullivan's Island was an antidote to the anxiety in New York

Harbor, where the Continental Army had been embarrassed by the British ships moving up the Hudson River and George Washington was locked in a communication stalemate with the king's commissioners. Lee's letter seemed to be timely proof that the Continental Army could, in fact, defend independence.

On July 19, the Continental Congress also resolved that the Declaration of Independence should be inscribed in a large, clear hand on parchment, "with the title and stile of 'The unanimous declaration of the thirteen United States of America.'"[92] When the parchment was ready, it would be "signed by every member of Congress." These decisions—to sign a parchment copy of the "unanimous" Declaration and to ensure that both Vice Admiral Richard Howe's declaration and Major General Charles Lee's account of the Battle of Sullivan's Island were printed in every newspaper in the United States—were inextricably connected. If the Congress had been waiting for New York to support independence, they could have ordered a parchment copy on July 15, when the news from the New York Convention reached Philadelphia.[93] Instead, the delegates simultaneously decided to sign their Declaration and disseminate Howe's declaration.

In their correspondence, the delegates to the Continental Congress made no mention of the parchment that they would be expected to sign, but they had plenty to say about Vice Admiral Howe's declaration, as well as the victory at Sullivan's Island. John Adams believed that Howe's declaration had "let the Cat out of the Bag."[94] New Hampshire delegate William Whipple thought that things would go "much better" for the Continental Congress "since we have got rid of that fantom reconciliation."[95] There had been widespread speculation that one of the reasons why the Howe brothers had targeted New York instead of Philadelphia was so that they could cut off the more rebellious New England colonies from the more moderate mid-Atlantic and southern colonies. But the victory in South Carolina proved that all thirteen of the United States were fighting back. Charles Carroll did not know that Howe had sent copies of his declaration separately to the New England governors, and so, he assumed the worst. He wrote to his father that it was "remarkable that even these harsh terms of Submission & pardon" in Howe's declaration "have not been offered to the N. England Govts. They, I suppose, must expect no mercy."[96]

On July 20, Vice Admiral Howe's month-old declaration first appeared in Philadelphia newspapers. Howe had hoped that his words would reach an understanding audience. But his declaration was printed by order of the Continental Congress, alongside his circular letter to ousted royal governors and Charles Lee's letter about the British defeat at Sullivan's Island, as well as reports that George Washington kept rejecting attempts by the Howe brothers to communicate with him on unequal terms.[97] This combination of news items made the King's Commissioners for Restoring Peace seem out of touch with reality. The date of June 20 on the declaration showed that Howe had promised pardons before the Congress had declared independence. But Howe's decision to send out his declaration and circular letter to the royal governors proved that the Declaration of Independence had not changed anything for the commissioners. This, along with the "George Washington Esqr" and "&c. &ca." incidents, showed that the commissioners did not think—or were not allowed to think—that they could secure peace with the independent and sovereign United States. Instead they saw that peace could only be achieved through reconciliation and subjugation.

The image of molten lead transforming from a symbol of the king's sovereignty into musket balls that could be fired at his troops captures what it was like in New York in July 1776. Emotions, loyalty, authority—everything was in a state of transition. Everyone was living through an unprecedented moment, waiting to see what would happen next. In the days between the arrivals of General William Howe and Vice Admiral Richard Howe, the terms of the conflict changed. It was no longer a colonial rebellion, but rather a war between Great Britain and the independent United States.[98] However, the King's Commissioners for Restoring Peace were not able to acknowledge such a change. They had to hope that "melted Majesty" could be re-formed. The Howes continued to call the United States "the Colonies in Rebellion." They treated George Washington as "the Commander in Chief of the Rebel Armies."[99] Ultimately, Vice Admiral Howe's declaration had the opposite impact of what he had intended. Howe thought that the Declaration of Independence could be ignored or reversed. Instead, his declaration prompted the Continental Congress to create a parchment copy of their Declaration to be signed and preserved. Howe's declaration made the Declaration of Independence indelible.

5

The Reigning Subject

Inoculation and Independence in Massachusetts

"The secret is out," John Adams wrote to Abigail.[1] Sometime in June, before the Continental Congress declared independence, John had copied out the draft Declaration and sent it to his wife in Massachusetts.[2] But John was talking about a different secret, one that Abigail had tried to keep from him: she and their four children had been inoculated for smallpox. When he found out, John went into a spiral of grief and guilt, desperate for news of his family. "Nothing, but the critical State of our Affairs should prevent me from flying to Boston, to your Assistance," John assured Abigail.[3] Of course, she knew that he could not leave Philadelphia and abandon his responsibilities in the Congress. That was why she wanted to keep her plans to herself. Though Abigail Adams had consistently written to her husband while he was in Philadelphia, in June and July 1776 she let weeks go by without a single letter to him—at first because of painful eye inflammation, and then to keep John from worrying.[4]

Abigail and the Adams children were inoculated in Boston on July 12, 1776, two days before the only daughter, also named Abigail, turned eleven years old, and a day after John Quincy turned nine. The younger boys, Charles and Thomas, were aged six and three.[5] On July 13, after weeks of silence, Abigail picked up her pen and wrote to her husband

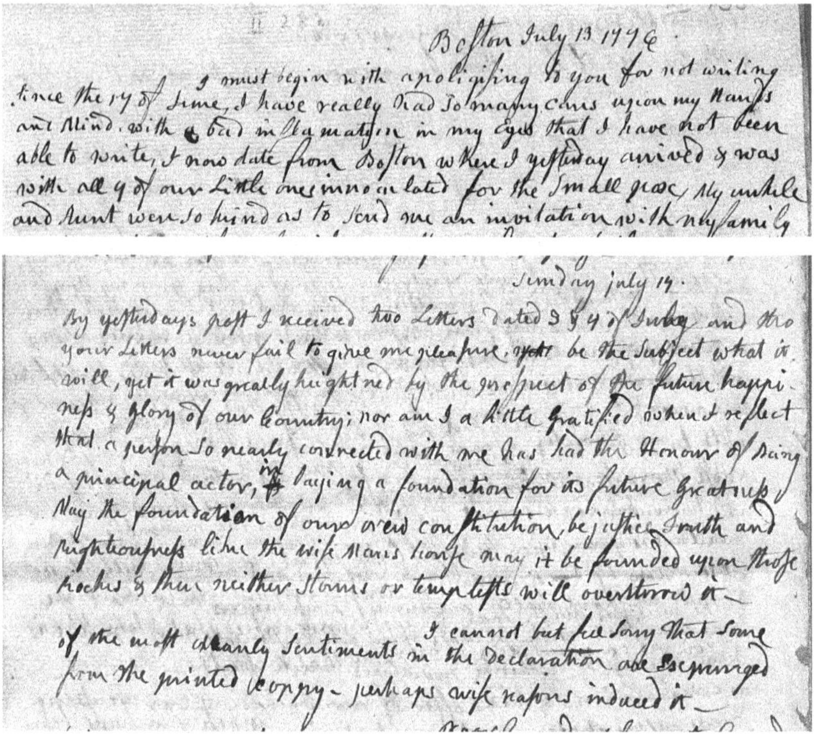

Figure 5.1 Letter, Abigail Adams to John Adams, July 13–14, 1776. Collection of the Massachusetts Historical Society.

that "our Little ones stood the operation Manfully."[6] After she finished detailing one of the most important updates in her young family's lives, she received two letters from her husband detailing the most important update in their civic lives.[7] On Sunday, July 14, she picked up her pen again to add to her letter.

Abigail Adams was always glad to hear from her husband, but the letters she received on July 13 were "greatly heightened by the prospect of the future happiness and glory of our Country."[8] As she read through the Declaration of Independence, she felt proud to be "so nearly connected" to someone who had "the Honour of being a principal actor" in the founding of the United States. Straining her still-inflamed eyes, Abigail compared the draft in John's handwriting to the final, printed version.[9] She could not help but feel "sorry that some of the most Manly Sentiments" in the Declaration had been "Expunged from the printed coppy." Abigail Adams was among the few outside the Pennsylvania State House who knew that the draft Declaration had included a grievance about the transatlantic slave trade. She mused that perhaps there were "wise reasons" for this revision. Adams was a politically savvy woman, and she knew the concessions that her husband had been obliged to make in his push for independence. Nevertheless, the published Declaration of Independence was a balm to her as she waited for pustules to erupt on her skin.

Smallpox profoundly impacted the news and reception of the Declaration of Independence in Boston. Only four months had passed between mid-March, when the British occupation of Boston ended, and mid-July, when the news of independence arrived. Amid the chaos of people leaving and returning to town, a smallpox outbreak was hard to avoid, especially because inoculation was illegal. The number of smallpox patients increased so quickly that, for a short window of time in July 1776, the Massachusetts General Court allowed for legal inoculation in Boston. The opportunity for inoculation brought people into Boston who would not have been there otherwise when the first copies of the Declaration reached the city. Smallpox kept soldiers in Boston who would have gone to New York, where they were desperately needed, if they were healthy. The "Spirit of innoculation," in Abigail Adams's words, overtook Boston at the same rate as the spirit of independence.[10] But it was hard to anticipate the outcome of either independence or inoculation. Only time would tell if either would take full effect.

❈❈❈

The *variola* virus, the cause of smallpox, had impacted the course of history in North America for a long time before the American Revolution. European settlers had brought the disease with them, and it had devastated Native communities. Massachusetts had been the site of a number of smallpox epidemics since the seventeenth century. The virus typically incubated in the body for ten to fourteen days before symptoms would start to appear, most notably skin eruptions. If patients survived, they would have lifelong scars, or pockmarks, but they would also gain life-long immunity. Variolation, or inoculation, offered another path to immunity from smallpox. The procedure involved intentional exposure to *variola* taken from the skin of an infected person. The ideal outcome of inoculation was a mild case of smallpox, just enough to provoke an immune response but without the unpredictable and often fatal symptoms from a natural infection.

The earliest experiments with inoculation in British North America had taken place in Boston during a terrible epidemic in 1721. Fifty-five years later, the procedure was still controversial. Public officials could not shake the worry that, if inoculated patients did not properly isolate, they could infect other people. Inoculation was thus illegal in Massachusetts and most of the colonies, though it was allowed in Philadelphia, the meeting place of the Continental Congress. Many delegates chose to be inoculated as soon as they arrived, but Rhode Island delegate Samuel Ward had refused, and he was subsequently infected naturally. His quick demise is recorded in a letter between the New Hampshire delegates. William Whipple initially wrote that Ward's case was "not dangerous," but at ten o'clock that same evening he added a postscript to his letter saying that Ward was "extream Ill, the Chance much against him."[11] Two days later, Ward was gone. John Adams wrote to Abigail about his frustration that Ward's stubbornness had cost the Congress "a very valuable Friend of the Colonies."[12] "Numbers, who have been inoculated, have gone through the Distemper, without any Danger," Adams explained. But no such arguments had convinced Ward.

The Continental Congress and the Continental Army were faced with two enemies: the British and the *variola* virus. For his part, John Adams described smallpox as "an Enemy more terrible in my Imagination, than all others" and "ten times more terrible" than the British.[13] After General William Howe evacuated the British forces and loyal civilians from Boston, General George Washington tried to limit communication between civilians and soldiers, fearing that "the Small Pox will be communicated to both."[14] Still, he would not allow soldiers to be inoculated.

Meanwhile, smallpox "Crept in among the Troops" in Canada.[15] After the death of Major General Richard Montgomery at Quebec, the Continental Congress sent Major General John Thomas to command the northern division of the army. Unfortunately, Thomas had never had smallpox, and he had not been inoculated. As he led the army in retreat, he became infected and died. John Adams wrote to Abigail about Thomas's death. "Cruel small Pox!" he lamented, "worse than the sword!"[16] But the news that smallpox had killed Thomas steadied Abigail Adams's resolve. "Every day some circumstance arises and shews me the importance of having that distemper in youth," she wrote to her husband.[17]

Abigail Adams had spent twelve years watching her husband work and travel with the liberty of immunity from smallpox.[18] During an epidemic in Boston in 1764, when she was nineteen years old, her parents had kept her from being inoculated alongside her then-fiancé and their friends. After the worst of John's symptoms had passed, he had written to Abigail that "Parents must be lost in Avarice or Blindness, who restrain their Children."[19] A decade later, in the fall of 1775, dysentery had ravaged the Adams household. While John had been home during a break from the Continental Congress, a laborer on the Adamses' farm had fallen ill. Shortly after John had left for Philadelphia, Abigail had started experiencing the same symptoms. She had made the difficult decision to let her husband return to the Congress, rather than sending for him to come back and risk getting sick as well.

Dysentery had spread quickly through the Adams family members, servants, and neighbors. In one letter—so melancholic that Abigail had told her husband to destroy it after reading—she had written that "the small pox in the natural way was never more mortal than this Distemper has proved."[20] Every day had brought another funeral for someone who had died from dysentery. Abigail's mother, Elizabeth, had come to help care for her daughter and grandchildren, but she, too, had become ill. Abigail's heart had burst open on the page when she had written to tell John that her mother had died.[21] Soon after he had received this dreadful letter, John had asked Abigail to come to Philadelphia to be inoculated for smallpox.[22] But Abigail had stayed in

Braintree, tending to her household by day, mourning her mother by night.[23] There was no way for the Adamses to know if or when dysentery would come back, and there were no effective means of preventing it. But smallpox was different.

In the spring of 1776, while her husband was in Philadelphia, Abigail Adams committed to protecting herself and her children from smallpox. She hoped that the rising rate of infections in Boston would convince local officials to legalize inoculation.[24] Abigail's aunt and uncle, Elizabeth and Isaac Smith, stayed in Salem during the British occupation, and when Isaac returned to Boston for the first time in early April, he saw that the town was primed for an outbreak. Isaac invited Abigail and her children to come to his Boston house "Iff there should be liberty to Innoculate."[25] Abigail promised her husband that she and the children would be among the first to be inoculated and that they would convalesce at her aunt and uncle's house.[26]

On July 3, the Massachusetts General Court made smallpox inoculation legal in Boston, but only until July 15. News of the court's order spread quickly, mostly by word of mouth. Isaac Smith met Abigail Adams and her children in Roxbury and accompanied them to Boston.[27] The Smiths' house quickly filled up with the people who wanted to be inoculated and those who would take care of them: Abigail, her four children, John Quincy's tutor, Abigail's sisters and their families, several cousins, and a number of white and Black servants, including Abigail's former nurse.[28] The Smiths' hospitality soon had competition from John Hancock. When he learned that Abigail and her children had been inoculated, he offered the use of his mansion and gardens. Doctors believed that fresh air, exercise, and a good diet were essential to successful inoculation, and Hancock knew that his property on Beacon Hill was "Bless'd with a free Air."[29] Adams and the children stayed with her family. But since the British had cut down the Smiths' fruit trees and currant bushes, she gladly accepted Hancock's offer of fresh fruit from his gardens.[30]

Smallpox brought civilians to Boston, but it also kept soldiers in and around Boston. Major General Artemas Ward, the commander of the troops in Massachusetts, was worried about bringing infected soldiers to New York to face an imminent British attack. On July 4, Ward wrote to General George Washington and explained that so many soldiers had smallpox that "the remainder of them must soon be inoculated."[31] Washington thought that it was "extremely unlucky that smallpox should prevail in the Army at this time."[32] He wanted Ward to quarantine the sick soldiers in Boston, conscious of the "Calamities that would flow" from smallpox spreading to the rest of the army. But Washington did not say anything about inoculation. Ward could not wait for Washington's permission anyway. He decided that, since "so many of the Troops in Town had taken the disorder," it was prudent to allow soldiers to be inoculated.[33] Soon after he made this decision, Ward received a letter from Washington enclosing the Declaration of Independence.[34] Washington wanted all the Continental battalions around Boston to hear the news of independence—which they would, on July 17—and then march to New York. But Ward decided to wait until the risk of spreading smallpox to the rest of the Continental Army abated.

Nearly 5,000 people were inoculated in Boston in the first two weeks of July 1776, and a quarter of them were from outside of the city. This included James and Mercy Otis Warren, who came from Plymouth "into the Croud of Patients" in Boston as the window for legal inoculation closed.[35] "The rage for Inoculation prevailing here has whirled me into its vortex," James Warren wrote to John Adams, reporting that a "Collection of Good, Bad, and Indifferent of all Orders, Sexes, Ages and Conditions" were gathered in the city. Warren was quick to assure Adams that Abigail and their children were among the good sort. The prevailing hope for all these people—the reason why the Massachusetts General Court allowed for inoculation in the first place—was that a few weeks of discomfort and isolation from the rest of the world could restore the town's health and security for the long term.

Smallpox was the "reigning subject of Conversation" in Boston until it was dethroned, briefly, by the news that arrived from Philadelphia on

July 13.[36] "The Decleration came on Saturday, and diffused A general Joy," James Warren wrote.[37] Inoculation patients congratulated each other in the streets as "freemen," and every person in Boston felt "more Important than ever." Warren appreciated how the news of independence "really raised our Spirits to A Tone Beneficial to mitigate the Malignancy of the small pox" and inspired "every one to support, and defend the Independency he feels." Samuel Cooper, minister of the Brattle Street Church, which the Adams family attended whenever they were in Boston, congratulated John Adams on the Declaration, which "is admir'd, diffuses Joy, and will have great Effect." Cooper checked in on Abigail and the children at the Smiths' house and promised John that he would "continue to visit them, and contribute all in my Powers to amuse, and make their Stay here agreable." For a moment, Boston was filled with hope for the future.

The city prepared for a public reading of the Declaration of Independence on July 18. It was an important day in the typical timeline of smallpox inoculation. Anyone who had been inoculated on July 4— the day after the court order made it legal—expected to be erupting in pustules fourteen days later.[38] Perhaps local officials planned the public reading around this two-week timetable, which was what John Adams and those who had been inoculated in Boston in 1764 had experienced. No one knew yet that many people would need to be inoculated multiple times before they became symptomatic, and some people would ultimately be infected naturally, incurring a much greater risk.[39]

Abigail Adams took part in the celebration on July 18, six days postinoculation and still in good health. She started her day at church and then processed "with the Multitude," joined by her brother-in-law Richard Cranch and perhaps other members of her family as well.[40] It was a large crowd, to be sure, but Adams knew that smallpox had "prevented many thousand from the Country" from being there.

The crowd gathered on the regrettably named King Street, the same site that had witnessed the Boston "Massacre" six years earlier. At midday, Colonel Thomas Crafts stepped onto the balcony of the State House, overlooking the large audience. A decorative painter who had been swept up in political protest, Crafts had been a member of the Loyal Nine and the Sons of Liberty, had destroyed tea in December 1773, and had fought the British during the occupation of Boston. On this day, he had the opportunity to read the Declaration of Independence. The responsibility should have fallen to the sheriff of Suffolk County, William Greenleaf, but, as Greenleaf's son later wrote, his father's voice was too weak to carry across the crowd, so he needed Crafts's help.[41] As Crafts read out the final words of the Declaration, the political leaders of Massachusetts who had joined him on the balcony shouted, "God save our American States," and the people below responded with three huzzahs.[42] As cheers, bells, and cannon fire rang out, Abigail Adams noticed that "every face appeared Joyfull." "Thus ends royall Authority in this State," she wrote to her husband, "and all the people shall say Amen." When evening fell, the royal coats of arms were taken down all over Boston to fuel a bonfire on King Street.[43]

When it came to printing the Declaration of Independence in Boston, the after-effects of the British occupation were keenly felt.[44] In 1775, Benjamin Edes had fled from Boston to Watertown, and he had printed the *Boston Gazette* there throughout the British occupation.[45] His printing partner of twenty years, John Gill, had stayed behind in Boston, and in May 1776 he had started his own newspaper, the *Continental Journal*. Shortly after Samuel Hall printed the issue of the *New-England Chronicle* with the May 15 Resolution—the source for all the British newspaper reprintings—Hall turned over control of that paper to Edward Eveleth Powars and Nathaniel Willis. All this transition meant that the only active newspaper printers in Boston in July 1776 were John Gill and the firm of Powars and Willis. The two printing houses published their newspapers on the same day of the week, Thursdays.

On Thursday, July 18—the same day as the public reading in Boston— the Declaration of Independence was on the front page of both Gill's *Continental Journal* and Powars and Willis's *New-England Chronicle*. Harbottle Dorr, a Boston merchant, added the *Continental Journal* to his collection of newspapers from the last decade, which he meticulously annotated and made searchable through a detailed index. The front page of Dorr's July 18 issue contains almost as many handwritten annotations as printed words. He covered up the masthead with a scrap of paper filled with notes, linking each grievance in the Declaration of Independence to different articles in earlier newspapers. He did this work "at considerable expence, and Very GREAT Trouble, in hopes that in future, they may be of some service, towards forming a Political History of this Country."[46] John Gill, Edward Eveleth Powars, and Nathaniel Willis also teamed up to produce a broadside of the Declaration that they could sell in Boston. The neighboring printing offices saw an opportunity for collaboration at this moment, when supplies were low but the city was full of potential customers.[47] There are two surviving versions of this broadside: one without the printers' names, and the other with a bold imprint "AMERICA: Boston, Printed by JOHN GILL, and POWARS and WILLIS, in Queen-Street."[48]

Daniel Gould purchased one of the Boston broadsides of the Declaration of Independence and signed his name just below John Hancock and Charles Thomson's printed names. A twenty-two-year-old soldier from Topsfield, Massachusetts, Gould had marched as a minuteman to Lexington and Concord in April 1775 and then joined the Continental Army. During the British occupation of Boston, he was recruited to be a life guard, first for Major General Charles Lee and then for Major General Artemas Ward.[49] Gould might have heard the Declaration of Independence read aloud to the Continental Army

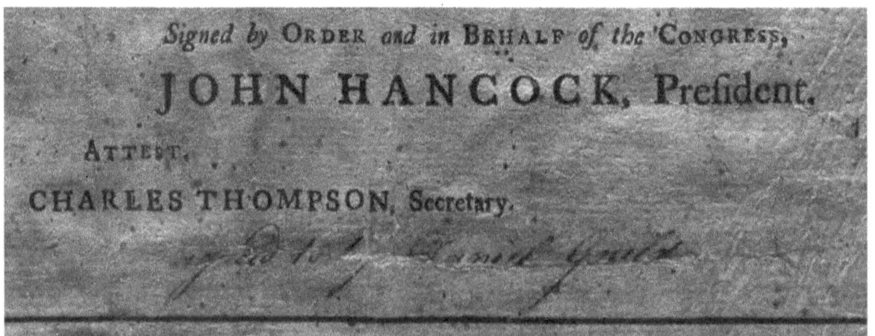

Figure 5.2 Broadside printed by Gill, Powars, and Willis, originally owned by Daniel Gould. Courtesy of the John Carter Brown Library.

regiments around Boston on July 17, or he might have heard the reading from the balcony of the State House on July 18. But his broadside reveals that Gould carefully read the text himself. Next to each grievance, he added a number, a strategy for reading through the list of complaints against George III. He lost track of his numbering near the end of the list and wrote "27" next to the twenty-sixth grievance before correcting his mistake.[50] Gould treasured this broadside. He added a note on the back so that other people would understand its significance when he was no longer around to tell the story: "I bought this when the Declaration of independence was first celebrated in Boston in the year 1776 and when I was a soldier in the American Army." A few weeks after he purchased this broadside, Gould would sail for New York, accompanying two large iron mortars that the British had left behind in Boston.[51] Gould's signature and annotations are a vivid reminder of the clarity that the Declaration provided to the soldiers in the Continental Army about their fight for independence.

These three printings—two newspapers and one collaborative broadside—were the only printings of the Declaration of Independence created in Boston in 1776. When the Massachusetts Council commissioned broadsides of the Declaration to send out to every town in the state, they turned to Ezekiel Russell, a printer in Salem. Perhaps the council did not think the printers in Boston or Watertown, where the council was meeting, could manage such a large order. It would take hundreds of broadsides to reach all the towns in Massachusetts. Or maybe the council was worried about smallpox. Some people believed that the disease could spread from person to person through paper, including currency and letters.[52] Abigail Adams knew that, back in Braintree, everyone who came to town had to be "smoaked there upon their return with all their money and papers," since sulfur smoke was thought to stop the spread of illness.[53] The town officials in Salem were similarly vigilant about smallpox.[54] It may have seemed like a safer space for this important work than Boston at this time.

The Massachusetts Council wanted to send broadsides of the Declaration of Independence "to the Ministers of each Parish, of every

Denomination, within this State."[55] At the conclusion of services on the first Sunday after these ministers received their broadsides, they were "*required* to read" the Declaration to their congregations.[56] Afterward, they were expected to hand the broadside off to the clerk in their town, who was "required to record" the Declaration in the town books, "to remain a *perpetual* Memorial thereof." The council approved this plan on July 17, the day before the public reading in Boston. But it took time and effort to execute. Ezekiel Russell shared his Salem printing office with John Rogers, who had recently launched a weekly newspaper. The *American Gazette* was only active for seven issues, but those weeks happened to coincide with the news of independence. Rogers printed the Declaration in his newspaper on July 16, and he used the same skinny columns of type to produce a broadside of the text as well.[57] The next issue of Rogers's newspaper included an apology. He could only give his readers a half sheet of news because "some Work of Importance to the State, was doing in the Office."[58] This is a clue that Ezekiel Russell had started working on the Massachusetts Council's order of a larger, more formal broadside of the Declaration. By August 5, the Russell broadsides were ready.[59] John Avery, the secretary of the Massachusetts Council, instructed Sheriff William Greenleaf to "take proper care that they be distributed through this State as soon as may be, that every town may have them publicly read in each religious assembly."[60]

For these broadsides, Ezekiel Russell used more capitalization and italics than any other printer of the Declaration of Independence in 1776, and this would have helped the ministers tasked with reading the text. Russell emphasized the "*manly* Firmness" of the provincial governments, the "*foreign* mercenaries" and "*merciless* Indian Savages," and George III's status as a tyrant who was "unfit to be the Ruler of a FREE PEOPLE!"[61] Small capitals highlighted the first word of each grievance, though the compositor forgot to use a small capital in the "He" at the beginning of the ninth grievance. It seems that Reverend Nathan Stone got tripped up at the same spot in the text when he read the Declaration to his congregation in Southborough. Starting with the ninth grievance, he added a small stroke of ink over the first word of each of the king's offenses to avoid repeating himself or skipping over any of them.[62]

Each of Ezekiel Russell's broadsides was marked on the back with a minister's name and a town: Mr. Frisbie in Ipswich.[63] Mr. Gay in Hingham.[64] Mr. Curtis in Charlton.[65] Mr. Holyoke in Boxford.[66] Mr. Everett in Dorchester.[67] In the North End of Boston, Samuel Mather was among the first ministers to read from a Russell broadside, on Sunday, August 11. Surely there were people in the pews who were recovering from smallpox inoculation. On the back of his broadside, Mather wrote that, "after the Conclusion of Divine Service, I read this Declaration, conformable to the Order of the Council of State; and spake in Favour of a Compliance with the Continental Declaration."[68] The following Sunday, August 18, Ezra Stiles read the Declaration to his congregation in Dighton. Stiles traveled back and forth between Dighton and Newport, Rhode Island, where he had first read the Declaration privately on July 13.[69] On the back of the Russell broadside that was sent to him, Stiles wrote that it was "Read in the public Congregation of the South Society in Dighton, By Ezra Stiles."[70] It took a month for a Russell broadside to reach Gideon Hawley, who had been a missionary on Cape Cod for almost twenty years. On September 8, he read the Declaration of Independence to a meeting of more than 100 Mashpee Wampanoag people.[71] Hawley did not leave a record of whether he read the Declaration in English or translated the text for his audience.

The Massachusetts Council's order was not clear about what exactly should happen after the ministers in each parish read the Declaration.[72] Parishes and towns did not overlap neatly, and while some towns only had one church, others had many churches of different denominations. Certain ministers handed their broadsides over to the town clerks as requested, while others held onto their copies.[73] Clerks made their own decisions about whether it was best to insert the printed broadside into the town record book or hand-copy the Declaration onto the pages of the book. Some clerks made a mess of the text. In Cambridge, the title of the Declaration alone filled half the page, in large and legible capital letters, though the town clerk missed the "R" in "CONGRESS" and the

"M" in "ASSEMBLED."[74] The clerk in Natick used massive, thickly inked capital letters for "A DECLARATI" before running out of room and consigning "ON" to the next line.[75] These handwritten copies of the Declaration are a challenge to read, especially by comparison to the Russell broadside.

When a minister read from one of Ezekiel Russell's broadsides on a Sunday afternoon in August or September 1776, the Declaration of Independence would not have been news to many of the people in the congregation. This publication process was performative, almost ritual. Churches had been important sites of local governance in Massachusetts for a long time. The Massachusetts Council could not control how many people would turn out to a reading of the Declaration in a public square, especially when many people were worried about smallpox spreading from town to town. But there was a social expectation that people would attend church regularly and that what they heard from the pulpit would influence their worldview.

When Samuel Cooper read the Declaration to his congregation at the Brattle Street Church in Boston on Sunday, August 11, he had a unique perspective on the text. When Cooper had visited Abigail Adams and her children after they were inoculated, he had seen the draft of the Declaration. He wrote to John Adams, "I could wish, however, that some great Strokes I saw in a Manuscript Draught had not been omitted."[76] Cooper would have been glad to read aloud the condemnation of the transatlantic slave trade. Nevertheless, he thought the published Declaration was "Masterly" and that it would have a "deserved Weight upon the Minds of the People."

Abigail Adams was at the Brattle Street Church when Samuel Cooper read the Declaration of Independence.[77] She was two weeks "free from paine," with only one pustule to show for her suffering.[78] Her son John Quincy had gone through inoculation "exactly as one would wish, enough to be well satisfied and yet not be troublesome." But the other Adams children had to be inoculated multiple times. As she sat in a pew on August 11, Adams knew that inoculation was working for three of her children; all except Charles. John Quincy and Thomas were

"quite Recoverd," and young Abigail was finally symptomatic and deal-
ing with hundreds of pustules.[79] Her body was so sore and swollen that
she could not find comfort standing, sitting, or laying down. This uneven
experience of inoculation was not uncommon. The Adamses' friend
James Warren was "cleverly spatterd" in pustules, but inoculation weak-
ened his wife, Mercy, to "a State little better than nonexistence."[80]
Smallpox inoculation proved to be far more unpredictable than anyone
who had come to the city in early July could have anticipated.

After a month in Boston, Abigail Adams was frustrated that "the
Town instead of being clear of this distemper are now in the height of it,
hundreds having it in the natural way through the deceitfulness of innoculation."[81] In the days that followed the reading of the Declaration at
the Brattle Street Church and other churches around town, the Adamses'
extended family members returned to their homes. Mercy Otis Warren
recovered her health, and the Warrens prepared to travel back to
Plymouth. But Abigail and her children had to stay in Boston. Young
Abigail was still covered in a thousand pustules—"enough for all the
family beside"—and six-year-old Charles needed to be inoculated a third
time.[82] "I have had a Seige of it," Abigail wrote to John.[83] "I long for the
compaign to be over."

The war on *variola* continued for the Adams family long after Boston's
planned isolation period ended and the joy over the news of independence had faded. Repeated inoculations did not work for Charles, who
eventually became infected naturally. The quick onset of intense symptoms made his mother anxious and his father inconsolable when he
found out a week and a half later.[84] Abigail Adams seriously considered
sending horses to Philadelphia to bring John home, especially after
Charles deliriously offered her a dollar to "get a Horse for Pappa."[85] The
news of Charles's condition "fixed an arrow" in John Adams's heart,
"which will not be drawn out untill the next Post arrives," and he worried that, "then, perhaps, instead of being withdrawn, it will be driven
deeper" if he received bad news.[86] Mercifully, the next batch of mail from
Boston brought him a more positive update: Charles would survive
smallpox. Relieved, Adams sent love to his "little Speckeled Beauty,

Nabby," and admitted to Abigail that he "did not know what fast Hold that little Pratler Charles" had on him until the boy's life was in question.[87] After all, Adams had been preoccupied by revolutionary politics for much of his six-year-old son's life. By September 2, Charles was well enough that the Adams family could finally leave Boston. "This is a Beautifull Morning," Abigail wrote.[88] "I see it with joy, and I hope thankfulness." She had come to Boston with her "treasure of children," and they had "passd thro one of the most terrible Diseases to which humane Nature is subject, and not one of us is wanting." Finally, twelve years after her husband, Abigail Adams was free from the worry of smallpox.

The main story in Boston in July 1776 was smallpox. It impacted the lives of everyone in the city—including people like the Adamses, who ended up staying for much longer than they had planned. The news of independence offered a long-expected but ultimately temporary moment of joy amid the fear and uncertainty of inoculation. Over the course of her family's journey through inoculation, Abigail Adams experienced the Declaration of Independence in different ways. She first read the draft in her husband's handwriting while she was preparing to move her family to Boston. Then she read the final, printed version the day after she and her children were inoculated. Later that week, she joined the crowd below the balcony of the State House to cheer a reading of the Declaration. After she made it through inoculation successfully, she heard it read again by the minister of her family's church in Boston. Adams wrote to her husband about each of these interactions with the Declaration, and these paragraphs in their correspondence are remarkable. But Abigail wrote many, many more paragraphs to John about her family's experience with smallpox inoculation. The Adams family would bear the scars of July 1776 for the rest of their lives.

6

Words and Wampum

Native Americans Acknowledge
Independence

Ambrose Bear looked at the silver gorget with disgust. The crescent-shaped metal collar was engraved with the royal coat of arms and busts of the king and queen. But he did not want anything to do with the British monarchy anymore. The Wolastoqey chief handed the gorget over to James Bowdoin, the president of the Massachusetts Council, and demanded a new one, decorated with the bust of a different George—General George Washington—and symbols that represented the united colonies. A few days later, Ambrose Bear and the other representatives from Wabanaki nations who had traveled to Massachusetts learned that the united colonies had become the United States. An interpreter translated the copy of the Declaration of Independence that arrived in the middle of their treaty negotiations. Ambrose Bear responded, "We like it well."[1]

During conferences in the summer of 1776, representatives of Indigenous nations learned about the Declaration through translations and presentations of wampum. According to the minutes of the conference in Watertown, Massachusetts, in July 1776, the interpreter "fully explained" the Declaration of Independence in French to the Mi'kmaq and Wolastoqey representatives who understood that language.[2] But a full explanation would have required the interpreter to translate all the grievances about George III, including the last one on the list, which claimed that the king had "endeavoured to bring on the inhabitants of our Frontiers, the merciless Indian Savages, whose known Rule of Warfare, is an undistinguished Destruction, of all Ages, Sexes, and Conditions."

At the founding of the United States, the delegates in the Continental Congress had two conflicting images of Native Americans.[3] There were friendly Indigenous peoples who fought alongside the Continental Army or, at the very least, stayed neutral and peaceful. But there were also "merciless Indian Savages." Only one of these visions made it into the Declaration of Independence.

All through the spring and summer, the delegates in Philadelphia met with Native representatives. A Haudenosaunee delegation from the Six Nations even gave John Hancock a new name—Karanduawn, the "Great Tree of Liberty."[4] The Congress encouraged their Commissioners for Indian Affairs to draw up treaties of alliance and friendship with these nations.[5] But, at the same time, the Declaration reflected deep-seated fears about British officials encouraging Indigenous men to terrorize communities at the edges of the Congress's authority.[6] The Declaration of Independence asserted the sovereignty of the United States, yet it failed to represent the sovereignty of Indigenous nations, and instead painted those people as "Savages" wreaking havoc on the "Frontiers."

The Wolastoqiyik and Mi'kmaq sent representatives from the Wabanaki homeland to Massachusetts in July 1776 to meet with George Washington. The previous winter, during the British occupation of Boston, Washington had forged a connection with a leader of the Wolastoqiyik, or St. John River tribe, who told him that "the English people are mad & very cross & want us to fight against the New England people."[7] But the Wolastoqiyik wanted to fight alongside George Washington. On July 10, three Wolastoqey chiefs and seven Mi'kmaq chiefs arrived in Watertown, Massachusetts, with a letter from Washington encouraging them to support the united colonies. They did not know that the war had since taken the commander in chief to New York. They were greeted instead by the Massachusetts Council, led by James Bowdoin, and asked where they lived and which tribes they represented. The men answered in turn, naming themselves and their villages in Nova Scotia and New Brunswick. The council hurriedly prepared for a formal treaty conference.

On Friday, July 12, the Massachusetts Council invited the Wolastoqey and Mi'kmaq representatives into their meeting room on the second story of a private home in Watertown, which had become the center of government during the British occupation of Boston and remained so during the subsequent smallpox outbreak. The council's secretary, John Avery, agreed to take minutes, and the council asked John Prince, a student at Harvard College, to translate the conference proceedings into French. Some of the Indigenous men knew that language and could translate further for the rest of their cohort.[8] Avery and Prince were sworn into their important roles, and—according to Avery's minutes—Wolastoqey Chief Ambrose Bear acknowledged them by saying, "We like it well." This phrase of acknowledgment would be repeated throughout the conference.

Ambrose Bear formally presented James Bowdoin with the letter he had from George Washington, along with a treaty from 1760. This treaty of peace and friendship between the Wolastoqey and Passamaquoddy nations and Great Britain recognized the sovereignty of King George II and his successors. Ambrose Bear showed the Massachusetts Council the gorget with the royal coat of arms, as well as a sword and pistol he had recently received from a man he believed to be a British agent, who had tried to bribe the Wolastoqiyik to fight for the British, encouraging them to go to Halifax instead of Boston. But the men could not be bought off. As Ambrose Bear explained, the Wabanaki nations were "all one people, and of one tongue and one heart."[9] They wanted "nothing to do with Old England."

Bowdoin appreciated the chief's candor. Putting the conflict in terms that he expected the Indigenous representatives to understand, Bowdoin explained in detail why "the English people beyond the great water have taken up the hatchet, and made war against the United Colonies in America."[10] He said that Great Britain had been "unbrotherly and unkind." Bowdoin recounted the Battles of Lexington, Concord, and Charlestown, and how the "great warrior" General Washington had driven the British army out of Boston. In this conflict, he said, "we ought to be, and it is our interest to be mutual friends" with Native peoples. On behalf of the colony of Massachusetts and the united colonies in North America, he and the council received the Wolastoqiyik and Mi'qmaq in friendship and brotherhood. He offered them the "free choice" to join with the united colonies in the war or to remain neutral. Ambrose Bear responded that they would need some time to consider their decision. Bowdoin asked John Prince to give the British gorget back, but, "with great vehemence and displeasure," Ambrose Bear refused to take it. The council sent out an order for a new gorget, a present that they hoped would be ready by the end of the conference.

The conference resumed the next afternoon, and Chief Ambrose Bear pledged that the Wolastoqiyik and Mi'kmaw would join the war on the side of the colonies. Three of the Mi'kmaq chiefs—Joseph Denaquara, Sabbatis Netobcobwit, and Peter André—were so eager to join George Washington in the fight against the British that they jumped from their seats and offered to go to New York immediately.[11] James Bowdoin wanted to calculate how many Mi'kmaq and Wolastoqey men the united colonies could count on. He turned to each chief and asked how many men from his village would be willing to go to war. Though some of the Mi'kmaq chiefs hesitated to pledge too many men, since their villages in Nova Scotia needed protection, Bowdoin and the council calculated that the Mi'kmaq villages could provide about 120 men.[12] Even so, it would take months for these men and anyone else that could be recruited from other Mi'kmaq villages to join the war. But the Wolastoqiyik lived further south, closer to Massachusetts, and Bowdoin expected that thirty of their men could be in New York that fall. Each Indigenous fighter would receive a rifle shirt, a blanket, and either buckled shoes or moccasins, and they would be paid monthly for the length of their service. As for weapons, Ambrose Bear explained that the men who had guns would need to leave them at home "for our children to hunt with in our absence." But Bowdoin insisted: every man who had a gun had to bring it with him. As night fell, Bowdoin offered a toast to the Mi'kmaw and Wolastoqey nations and "wished that the friendship now established might continue as long as the sun and moon shall endure."

The Declaration of Independence reached Watertown in the middle of this conference between the Massachusetts Council and representatives of the two nations. When Ambrose Bear and the other chiefs returned to the council's meeting house on Tuesday, July 16, James Bowdoin explained that, on July 4, the "great Council at Philadelphia"—the Continental Congress—had declared independence from Great Britain.[13] The united colonies had become the United States, forming a "long and strong chain" that was "made longer and stronger by our brothers of the St. John's and MicMack Tribes joining with us." The council brought out a printed copy of the Declaration, and John Prince translated it into French. Ambrose Bear responded simply, "We like it well."[14]

Four words from Wolastoqey Chief Ambrose Bear—"We like it well"—mark the first formal acknowledgment of the independent and sovereign United States of America by another nation. "This is the Declaration of the United States," Bowdoin explained.[15] "You and we, therefore, have nothing to do with Great Britain." The Indigenous men agreed. Bowdoin presented a treaty, which the Massachusetts Council had crafted after the Declaration arrived. At this point, Bowdoin had to leave for Boston—perhaps to prepare for the public reading of the Declaration there on July 18—so he shook hands with each of the chiefs and left the rest of the council to go over the treaty with them.

The first paragraph of the treaty of alliance and friendship quoted the last paragraph of the Declaration of Independence. The Massachusetts Council felt empowered by this paragraph to "contract Alliances." Since the Council did not have the authority to effect an alliance between the United States and a foreign power, this document, which would become known as the Treaty of Watertown, represented an alliance between the Mi'kmaw and Wolastoqey nations and the state of Massachusetts only.

The Treaty of Watertown called for the Wolastoqey and Mi'kmaw nations and the United States to "be at peace with each other and be considered as friends and brothers united and allied together for their mutual defense, safety and happiness."[16] The ten articles of the treaty laid out the Massachusetts Council's expectations for their Indigenous neighbors. The Wolastoqiyik and Mi'kmaq would give the people of Massachusetts and the other United States, "during their present war with the King of Great Britain, all the aid and assistance in their power." This included sending 600 men, "or as many as may be," to New York. The council expected that the chiefs who signed this treaty would return home and "use their utmost influence" with the other Wabanaki nations, including the Passamaquoddy, to convince them to send additional men to fight for the United States. Since three of the Mi'kmaq chiefs had "manfully and generously offered to enter immediately into the war," they prepared go to New York right away. If any misunderstanding or conflict came up between the United States, the Wolastoqiyik, and the Mi'kmaq the treaty stated, "no private revenge shall be taken, but a peaceable application shall be made for redress." Each of these provisions was meant to ensure that Indigenous men would fight for—not against—the former colonists.

The final article of the Treaty of Watertown nullified all former treaties that these or any other Wolastoqey or Mi'kmaq representatives had made "with any other power, State or person."[17] This included the 1760 treaty with Great Britain that Ambrose Bear had presented on the first day of the conference. The independence of the United States made the history of colonial British North America "void." All that mattered was this new connection, this new chain of friendship that stretched from Nova Scotia down the coast to Georgia. On July 17, the representatives of the state of Massachusetts added their names to the bottom of the treaty, alongside the pictographic marks of the ten Mi'kmaq and Wolastoqey chiefs. The next day, the council secretary, John Avery, read the Declaration of Independence aloud from one of the second-story windows of the house where the treaty conference had taken place.

As three of the Mi'kmaq chiefs prepared to join the Continental Army in New York, the Massachusetts Council learned that their conference had been very well-timed. On July 8, the Continental Congress had

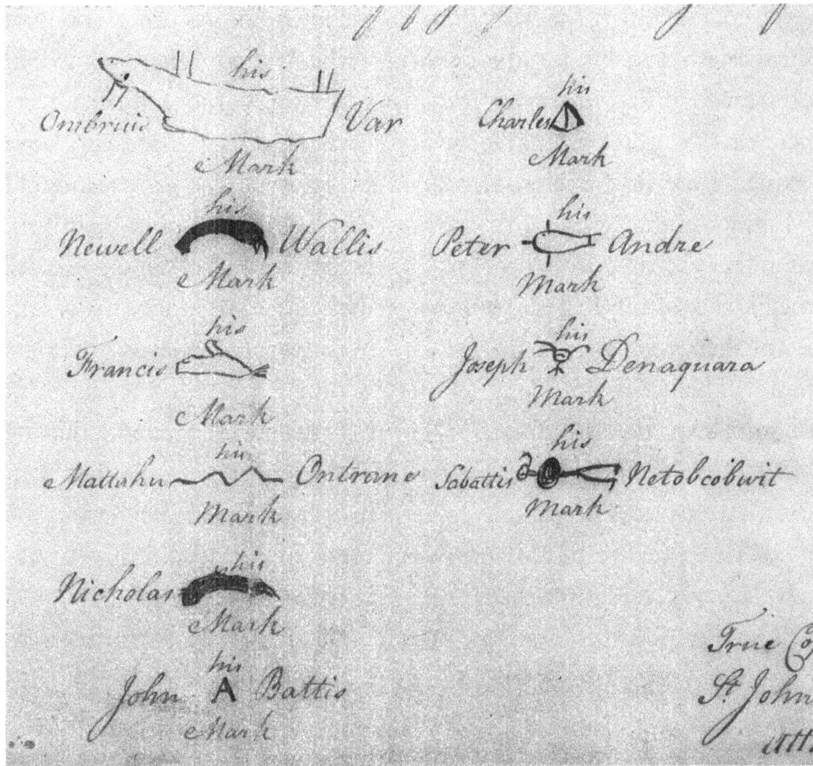

Figure 6.1 Treaty of Watertown. Massachusetts Archives, Boston.

granted George Washington the authority to "call forth and engage in the service of the United States, so many Indians of the St. Johns, Nova Scotia and Penobscot tribes, as he shall judge necessary."[18] On July 11, Washington—unaware of the delegation that had just arrived in Watertown—wrote a letter to the leaders of the Massachusetts government. With the words of the final grievance in the Declaration of Independence fresh in his mind, Washington expressed his frustration that the British had employed "foreign mercenaries" and "excited Slaves and Savages to arms against us."[19] He asked for help recruiting "Five or Six hundred Men" from the Wabanaki nations and marching them "with all possible expedition to Join the Army here."

James Bowdoin excitedly shared the news of the Watertown conference with George Washington. "At the time your Excellency's Letter was received, requesting the Aid of this Government in procuring a body of the Eastern Indians for the Service of the United States," Bowdoin explained, "it happened very fortunately, that a Number of them were here, as Delegates from the St John's & Mickmac Tribes in Nova Scotia."[20] Bowdoin enclosed a copy of the Treaty of Watertown and told Washington that some of the signatories would join him in New York soon. It was his hope that these Mi'kmaq chiefs would "not only secure the Fidelity of the Tribes to which they belonged, but induce many others of them to engage in the Service." Washington expressed his "most hearty Thanks" to the Massachusetts Council for "their readiness in undertakeing the late Treaty."[21] He was particularly grateful that he would have the assistance of a few Mi'kmaq men sooner rather than later. After weeks of waiting for the British to attack New York, the moment seemed to be at hand. Washington told Bowdoin that "a very few days will Determine the fate of this City."

Though Bowdoin sent a copy of the Treaty of Watertown to Washington, he did not send one to the Continental Congress.[22] This oversight reflected the priorities of the conference. Both the Massachusetts Council and the Mi'kmaq and Wolastoqey representatives were most concerned with helping Washington and the Continental Army, not communicating with the Congress. John Hancock asked Washington if he could share Washington's copy of the treaty, but Washington was not sure where it was. Soon after receiving Bowdoin's letter, he had decided to box up all the state papers that he had, "Lest by any Accident" they might fall into British hands.[23] Washington thought the treaty might be in this box, which he had sent to Philadelphia in the trusted hands of Bowes Reed, Adjutant General Joseph Reed's brother. "If Congress are desirous of Seeing It—they will be pleased to have the Box opened," Washington wrote.[24]

❧❦❧❦❧❦

A few days after the Continental Congress received the box of George Washington's papers, they learned about another conference. In mid-June, Major General Philip Schuyler had invited the Six Nations to a meeting in German Flatts, on the Mohawk River west of Albany, New York.[25] As one of the Congress's Commissioners for Indian Affairs for the northern department, Schuyler was concerned that some of the Six Nations were changing their neutral position.[26] Samuel Kirkland, a Presbyterian missionary among the Oneida, warned Schuyler about the influence of Colonel John Butler, the acting British superintendent for the Six Nations, based at Fort Niagara. Kirkland told Schuyler that the Oneida and Tuscarora "expressed great concern on account of Colonel Butler's growing strength and influence."[27] Butler, "by threats and proffers," had convinced "the greater part of the Senecas, Cayugas, and Onondagas" to join with some of the Mohawk to "renounce the cause of the Colonies, and engage on the King's side." A group of thirteen Oneida men met with Schuyler in Albany and confirmed that "Indians are daily successfully urged to take up arms for the King."[28] Kirkland convinced Schuyler that it was "impracticable" for Native Americans "to continue much longer in a state of neutrality."[29] The Commissioners for Indian Affairs needed to meet with the Six Nations and "demand who are friends and who are not."

Philip Schuyler arrived at German Flatts on July 16 hoping to find a "very numerous" gathering of men, women, and children from the Six Nations, but instead he found "very few Indians."[30] Still, he heard some positive news from Peter Ryckman, a trader from Albany who had been detained for months at Fort Niagara "on a well-grounded suspicion of his affection to the American cause."[31] Ryckman had escaped the fort and arrived at German Flatts on the same day as Schuyler, in the company of twenty-one Senecas. Ryckman told Schuyler that Guyasuta, a Seneca sachem, had delivered a lengthy, bitter speech against Colonel Butler's attempts to coerce Native nations to join the war.[32] Guyasuta insisted that the "father and son"—Great Britain and the colonies—should settle their differences without Indigenous peoples' interference. Ryckman was hopeful that Guyasuta's speech "opened the eyes of the Indians to their true interest."[33] Schuyler was relieved, because he regarded the Seneca as "the nation who could distress us most" if they joined the war on the British side or targeted white settlers.[34] Still,

Schuyler worried about Butler's influence, especially after he heard a rumor that Butler had sent a spy from Fort Niagara to the meeting at German Flatts.[35]

The day after Philip Schuyler came to German Flatts, he received a letter from George Washington enclosing copies of the Declaration of Independence.[36] Schuyler agreed to send the Declaration along to Major General Horatio Gates at Fort Ticonderoga, who would follow Washington's order to share the Declaration with the Continental Army. Meanwhile, Schuyler had the opportunity to share it with the Six Nations. But he would have to wait a while. It took much longer than Schuyler expected for all the Native Americans who were invited to German Flatts to make the trip. "Their Delays distress me beyond Imagination," Schuyler told Washington.[37] But the extra time allowed Schuyler to consider how he and the other Commissioners for Indian Affairs would organize the conference, and how he would adjust his language in talking about the colonies-turned-states. Schuyler was certain that the reaction to his opening speech would give a sense of the Six Nations' "Temper and Intentions" and would dictate how the rest of the conference would go.[38]

By August 8, more than 1,700 men, women, and children from the Six Nations, as well as the Delaware and Mohegan nations, had gathered at German Flatts, and the conference with the Commissioners for Indian Affairs began.[39] The commissioners presented a string of wampum, small

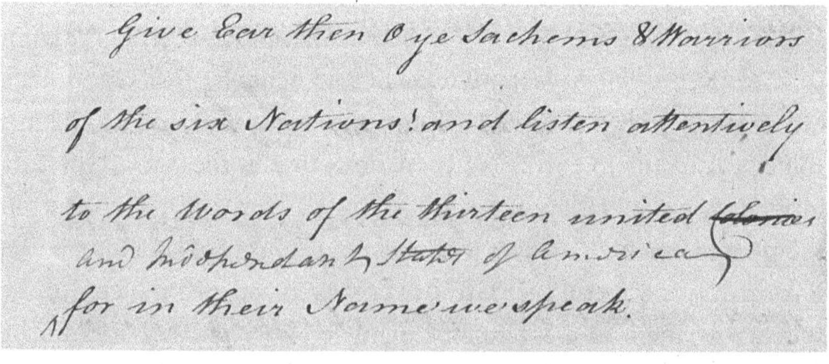
Give Ear then O ye Sachems & Warriors
of the six Nations! and listen attentively
to the Words of the thirteen united ~~Colonies~~
and Independant States of America
for in their Name we speak.

Figure 6.2 Notes in Philip Schuyler's Indian Papers, ca. August 1776. The New York Public Library.

cylindrical beads made from clam shells, and asked the sachems and warriors who were present to let this string "open your ears, that you may plainly hear what the Independent States of America have to say to their brethren of the Six Nations."[40] Then, the commissioners explained that the united colonies had hoped to reconcile with King George III, but that he would not listen to their petitions. The king had "become a cruel and oppressive father" who had raised armies against his colonists and encouraged enslaved laborers to rise up in insurrection. The colonies "accordingly proclaimed to all the world that they will never hereafter acknowledge him, or any of his family, to be their King, but they will always be and remain a free and independent people." The commissioners asserted that they themselves no longer represented colonies or provinces, but "must, for the future, be called the Commissioners of the United and Independent States of America." The commissioners presented a wampum belt to help "remember this great event." They told the Six Nations that the United States intended to "live in friendship, and cultivate a good understanding, and maintain a friendly intercourse with all Indians." But they needed to know the Six Nations' intentions. At the end of their opening speech for the conference, the Commissioners for Indian Affairs presented a larger wampum belt, "which denotes what we hope will take place, that, is, a firm union between the Six Nations and the Thirteen United States of America."[41]

The next day, Abraham, a Mohawk sachem, held up the large wampum belt as he responded to the commissioners' speech.[42] He himself presented another belt, with beads that formed four diagonal bars and a square, as a gift to the commissioners for bringing the Six Nations together for this important meeting. Abraham acknowledged that the colonists had declared independence because the king had failed to redress their grievances. He recognized that this belt represented the determination of the United States to be "forever free and independent."[43] Abraham took the opportunity, on behalf of the Six Nations, to thank Philip Schuyler and the other commissioners for sharing the news of independence "in so publick a manner." Abraham acknowledged the "thirteen independent states" with yet another belt, made of eight rows of white beads. In contrast to Ambrose Bear's entirely verbal response to the Declaration of Independence, the Mohawk sachem responded with wampum as well.

After a few days of listening to Abraham and other sachems express their interest in peace and present different wampum belts, the Commissioners for Indian Affairs responded. They held up all the belts that had been shared, including the one with which the Six Nations "answered the Declaration of the Thirteen United Colonies, that they had become States independent of the King of Great Britain."[44] All these wampum belts together signified a "covenant of peace" among the Six Nations and the United States. The commissioners warned that, "if any of the Six Nations join the enemy and fight against us, the peace will again be broken," a rupture that could not be fixed with "words and wampum only." They thereupon presented yet another belt and proclaimed that "peace and good understanding prevails between the Independent States of America" and the Six Nations.

Philip Schuyler returned to Albany with "great hopes that no depredations will be committed on the frontier inhabitants."[45] He expected that "a few" of the Six Nations "will always join the Enemy in Canada," but otherwise the nations were committed to remaining neutral.[46] As James Bowdoin had done with the Treaty of Watertown, Schuyler decided to send a copy of the conference proceedings to George Washington "for his perusal."[47] But Schuyler also told John Hancock, "I cannot possibly find time to make two copies of the transactions." He had not expected to spend a full month in German Flatts and he had to catch up on his other responsibilities with the Continental Army. So he asked Washington to pass his copy of the proceedings along.[48] Washington responded that he understood that the time spent in German Flatts must have been "sufficiently irksome & disagreeable."[49] "However," he told Schuyler, "if the Good Consequences Which You meant should be produced from it"—if the United States remained at peace with the Six Nations—"You will think It was extremely well spent." Washington sent the conference proceedings along to Hancock and the Continental

Congress on August 23, the day after thousands of British troops disembarked at Long Island to prepare for the long-awaited battle.[50]

The Declaration of Independence was communicated to Native American nations in 1776 through two different binary methods: dark ink on light paper, and dark shell beads strung together with light beads. The formal presentations of a printed copy of the Declaration in Watertown, Massachusetts, and wampum belts in German Flatts, New York, were meant to convey an important change, from colonies to independent states. The two conferences coincided with the news of independence. However, these meetings had two different premises. The Massachusetts Council could only secure a treaty of alliance on behalf of the state of Massachusetts, while Philip Schuyler and the Commissioners for Indian Affairs could negotiate on behalf of the Continental Congress and the United States. The Wolastoqiyik and Mi'kmaq were eager to join the war and fight under George Washington, but the Six Nations decided to pursue neutrality, even in the face of British coercion. Though there was no place for Native neutrality or alliances in the Declaration of Independence—only "merciless Indian Savages"—allies in the Wolastoqey and Mi'kmaq nations and neutrals among the Six Nations were a key part of the Declaration's audience in 1776.

7

Embarrassment

Clergymen Close Churches and Change Prayers

In August 1776, the Declaration of Independence reached Peter De La Roche in Lunenburg, on the southern shore of Nova Scotia. De La Roche did not think that the fire for independence would reach Lunenburg, but he worried that his community would be "either suffocated by the smoke or scorched to death by the heat."[1] The Swiss-born minister had been in Canada for a few years. He had been ordained in the Church of England in 1771 and had sworn an oath of allegiance to the king, the sovereign head of the Anglican church. The church's missionary arm, the Society for the Propagation of the Gospel in Foreign Parts, had sent him to St. John's Church in Lunenberg. When De La Roche read the Declaration of Independence five years later, he was shocked to learn that the Americans had "thrown off all Allegiance to the British Crown." Though he had expected the Continental Congress to declare independence from Great Britain and Parliament, he had still thought "they would retain the king as supreme."

The Declaration of Independence caused a moment of reckoning for many of Peter De La Roche's fellow clergymen in the United States. For months, what was happening inside Anglican churches had not matched the lived experience outside the church doors. The *Book of Common Prayer*, which guided Anglican services, included prayers for the king to defeat his enemies. But as the war raged on, the king's enemies filled the church pews. After independence was declared, ministers who were supported by the Society for the Propagation of the Gospel (SPG) were forced to choose among three uncomfortable paths.[2] They could change the liturgy to eliminate the prayers for King George III and the royal family, and thereby risk betraying their ordination oath and being excommunicated from the Church of England. They could close their churches for the safety of themselves, their families, and their parishioners. Or they could abandon their congregations and perhaps even leave the United States altogether. The ministers who chose to edit the *Book of Common Prayer* faced a further decision: whether prayers for the king should be replaced with prayers for the Continental Congress or the provincial governments, or simply be erased entirely. In their annual reports to the SPG secretary in London, ministers would need to explain their situation and justify the decisions they made after the Declaration of Independence.

At the start of the American Revolution, there were over 300 Anglican ministers in the thirteen colonies.[3] Each of these men, whether they were born in the colonies or in Europe, had to be ordained by a bishop in England, because there were no bishops in North America. In doing so, they had to swear an oath to the king's sovereignty over every earthly power, and promise to adhere strictly to the *Book of Common Prayer*, according to the Act of Uniformity that was passed after the Restoration. The SPG, which was established in 1701, sent Anglican clergymen and educators to establish and sustain churches and schools in the colonies. The rector, or the minister in charge of each church, was supported by the vestry, a group of male parishioners who made decisions about the church's organization and finances. In most of the colonies, the SPG provided stipends for these ministers and expected annual reports on the state of their churches, including the numbers of people who were baptized, married, and buried.

The *Book of Common Prayer* provided a consistent experience for Anglican churchgoers in the colonies. The book detailed the order of scriptures and prayers for daily morning and evening services, as well as holidays and other special circumstances. There were morning and evening prayers for the king and the royal family, in which Anglican ministers asked God to grant "our most gracious sovereign Lord," George III, with "health and wealth long to live," so that "he may vanquish and overcome all his enemies."[4] During holy communion, there were two options for prayers for the king. The first was a prayer that "we and all his subjects" would "faithfully serve, honour, and humbly obey him," and the second focused on the king himself, "that in all his thoughts, words, and works, he may ever seek thy honour and glory." There was also a prayer for Parliament, "that thou wouldest be pleased to direct and prosper all their Consultations to the advancement of thy glory, the good of thy church, the safety, honour, and welfare of our Sovereign and his Kingdoms." There was a special prayer for times of "War and Tumults." And finally, a service of thanksgiving on October 25, the anniversary of the king's ascension to the throne. It was similar to the services for other church holidays except that all the prayers were for George III—for a long life, for victory over his enemies, for his ministers to be righteous, and for peace under his reign.

As the Continental Army fought the king's troops and support for independence increased in the colonies, so too did tensions around the *Book of Common Prayer.*[5] The Maryland Convention decided that prayers for the king no longer made sense. They argued that "the good People" of Maryland and the other colonies had "taken up arms to defend their rights and liberties."[6] The people could not, "with any sincerity or devotion of heart, pray for the success of his Majesty's arms." On May 25, 1776, the convention resolved that every prayer and petition for the king in the *Book of Common Prayer* should be "omitted in all Churches and Chapels in this Province, until our unhappy differences are ended."[7] One minister in Chaptico, Maryland, decided that, rather than omitting the prayers altogether, he would change the subject from the king to the Continental Congress. He crafted new prayers on strips of paper and pasted them into his book.[8]

On July 5, after agreeing to a new constitution and declaration of rights, the Virginia Convention also decided to change the *Book of Common Prayer*. The convention resolved that the prayers for the king should be replaced with prayers for "the magistrates of this common-wealth."[9] They listed out every passage that needed to be edited, clarifying that all the rest of the liturgy should be "retained, without any alteration." A Scottish minister, Alexander Cruden, refused to follow these instructions. The Bishop of London had ordained Cruden in 1749, and the SPG had sent him to South Farnham along the Rappahannock River. Cruden believed that praying for provincial officials instead of the king was "incompatible with his Duty to his Sovereign, and the Oaths which he had taken" more than twenty-five years earlier.[10] Cruden and other Anglican ministers in Virginia received their income from the provincial government in the form of tobacco rather than a stipend from the SPG. Before independence, Cruden had received an annual salary of 16,000 pounds of tobacco, as well as 250 acres of land and nine enslaved laborers.[11] After independence, Cruden lost all this property and abandoned his parish.

As rector of Christ Church in Philadelphia, Jacob Duché was the first minister who was forced to consider what the Declaration of Independence would mean for the Anglican church. Duché did not have the time or opportunity to consult with his "spiritual superiors" in London.[12] On July 4, the Christ Church vestry decided that, since the Continental Congress "resolved to declare the American Colonies to be free and Independant States," and the prayers for the king were "inconsistent with the said Declaration," these prayers should be omitted from the liturgy.[13] The vestrymen slashed long black lines through the *Book of Common Prayer* and replaced one passage with a new prayer for the "Congress of these United States."[14] The Christ Church vestry recommended that other churches should omit these prayers as well, "for the peace & welfare of the congregations."[15] Duché later admitted that the vestry's decision was the "sad alternative" to closing Christ Church altogether. He knew that, if he continued to pray for the king in

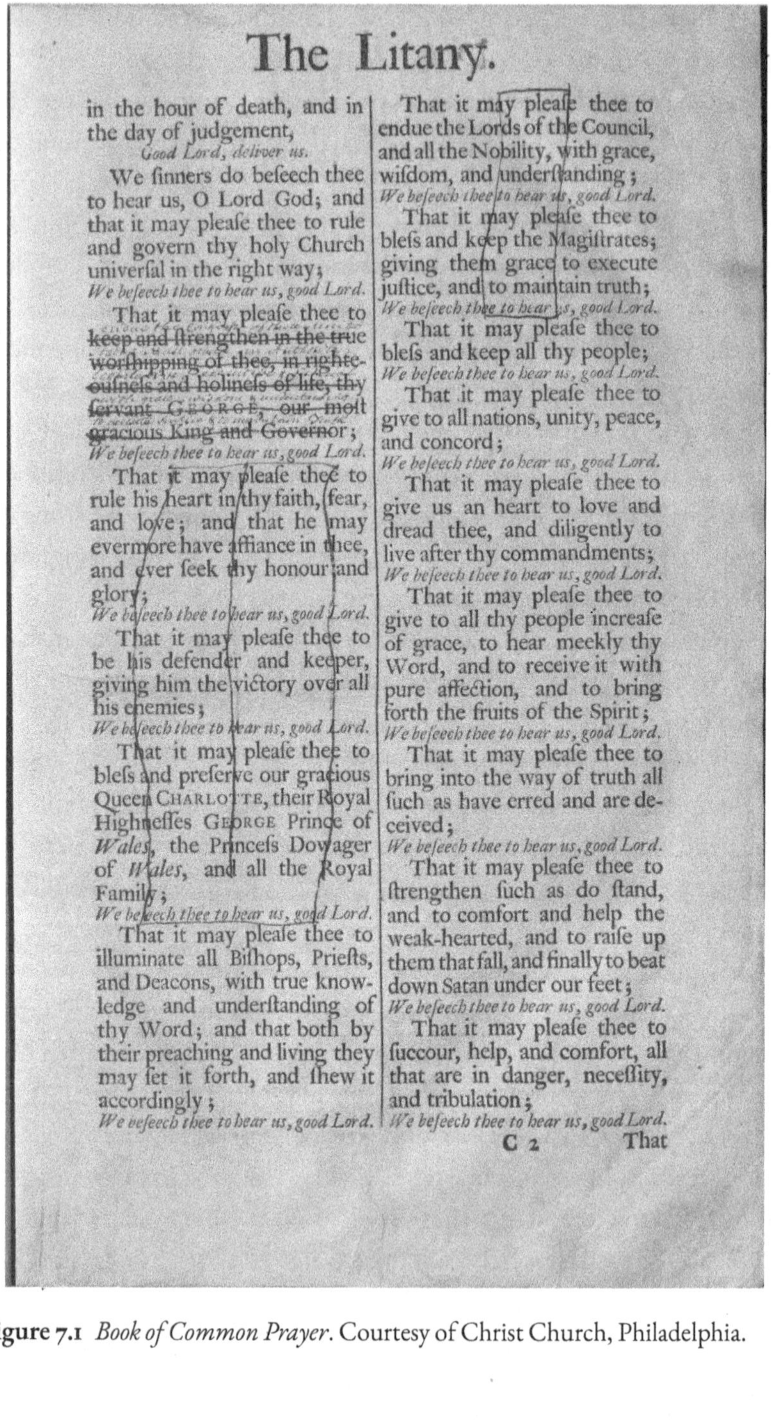

The Litany.

in the hour of death, and in the day of judgement,
Good Lord, deliver us.

We sinners do beseech thee to hear us, O Lord God; and that it may please thee to rule and govern thy holy Church universal in the right way;
We beseech thee to hear us, good Lord.

That it may please thee to ~~keep and strengthen in the true worshipping of thee, in righteousness and holiness of life, thy servant GEORGE, our most gracious King and Governor;~~
We beseech thee to hear us, good Lord.

That it may please thee to rule his heart in thy faith, fear, and love; and that he may evermore have affiance in thee, and ever seek thy honour and glory;
We beseech thee to hear us, good Lord.

That it may please thee to be his defender and keeper, giving him the victory over all his enemies;
We beseech thee to hear us, good Lord.

That it may please thee to bless and preserve our gracious Queen CHARLOTTE, their Royal Highnesses GEORGE Prince of *Wales,* the Princess Dowager of *Wales,* and all the Royal Family;
We beseech thee to hear us, good Lord.

That it may please thee to illuminate all Bishops, Priests, and Deacons, with true knowledge and understanding of thy Word; and that both by their preaching and living they may set it forth, and shew it accordingly;
We beseech thee to hear us, good Lord.

That it may please thee to endue the Lords of the Council, and all the Nobility, with grace, wisdom, and understanding;
We beseech thee to hear us, good Lord.

That it may please thee to bless and keep the Magistrates; giving them grace to execute justice, and to maintain truth;
We beseech thee to hear us, good Lord.

That it may please thee to bless and keep all thy people;
We beseech thee to hear us, good Lord.

That it may please thee to give to all nations, unity, peace, and concord;
We beseech thee to hear us, good Lord.

That it may please thee to give us an heart to love and dread thee, and diligently to live after thy commandments;
We beseech thee to hear us, good Lord.

That it may please thee to give to all thy people increase of grace, to hear meekly thy Word, and to receive it with pure affection, and to bring forth the fruits of the Spirit;
We beseech thee to hear us, good Lord.

That it may please thee to bring into the way of truth all such as have erred and are deceived;
We beseech thee to hear us, good Lord.

That it may please thee to strengthen such as do stand, and to comfort and help the weak-hearted, and to raise up them that fall, and finally to beat down Satan under our feet;
We beseech thee to hear us, good Lord.

That it may please thee to succour, help, and comfort, all that are in danger, necessity, and tribulation;
We beseech thee to hear us, good Lord.

C 2   That

Figure 7.1 *Book of Common Prayer.* Courtesy of Christ Church, Philadelphia.

the de facto capital of the independent United States, the church would be subject to violence. Duché barely had time to process these changes to the *Book of Common Prayer* when he received "greatly alarming" news from John Hancock: the Continental Congress had appointed Duché as their chaplain.[16]

Jacob Duché thought that he had made his sentiments against independence clear. He later testified to the Loyalist Claims Commission that, "when the idea of independence was first broached he publicly expressed his disapprobation of the measure" and "continued to persevere" in this opinion even as those around him conformed.[17] Nevertheless, according to John Hancock, the Continental Congress unanimously chose Duché to be their chaplain because of his "uniform & zealous Attachment to the Rights of America."[18] Duché acquiesced, because he worried what might happen to himself and his church if he refused. By his own account, Duché kept to his specific duties and remained "perfectly ignorant" of the Congress's activities while he was chaplain. However, after two and a half months, he felt compelled to resign. A year later, on the first Sunday after British troops marched into Philadelphia, Duché was able to pray for the king in Christ Church once again. But any comfort or nostalgia that he may have felt in doing so faded when he walked out of the church and was detained by British officials. They were highly suspicious of Duché because he was widely known to have been the chaplain of the Continental Congress. After this experience, Duché begged George Washington to convince the Congress to rescind their "hasty & ill-advised declaration of Independency."[19]

In Providence, Rhode Island, the parishioners of King's Church forced John Graves to stop praying for the king before the Declaration of Independence arrived. The Rhode Island Assembly had renounced all allegiance to King George III on May 4, without calling for any changes to the *Book of Common Prayer*. However, on July 8, forty-four members of Graves's congregation signed a letter to their minister asking him to omit all the prayers for the king and the royal family and instead use the prayer meant for times of "War and Tumults."[20] The *Book of Common Prayer* was "perfect," in the parishioners' opinions, except that they could not "in conscience" pray for the king anymore. Graves had served his congregation well for many years, and they trusted that he would make the right decision. But they warned him that, if he continued to pray for the king, his community would turn on him, his wife, Ann, and their seven children.

On Saturday morning, July 13—the same day that the Declaration of Independence was printed in the newspaper in Providence—John Graves wrote a letter to his congregation.[21] In it he condemned the "variety of Motives, Threats, and Promises" that his parishioners had made against him.[22] He argued that it was not in his power to stop praying for the king, "as a Minister of that Church over which, under God, he is the Head, and in whose Comunion I desire to live and die." Graves claimed that no other clergyman in Rhode Island or all of New England had been "so long and vigorously attacked, by his People."[23] He had planned to write a much longer letter in his defense. But then he learned about the Declaration of Independence. "I shall quietly lay aside my publick Ministry," he explained to his parishioners, "and freely serve your spiritual Interest, while among you, in any other way, not inconsistent with the Laws of the Country." Rather than cease or change his prayers for the king, Graves closed King's Church, though he continued to baptize children, visit the sick, and bury the dead. Because Graves agreed to his congregation's demands, his parishioners provided financial support for his large family in Providence.[24]

On July 20, a week after John Graves made the decision to close his church, the Rhode Island Assembly prohibited all prayers for the king.[25] In the wake of the Declaration of Independence, any person in Rhode Island who acknowledged the king as "rightful Lord and Sovereign," even "under Pretence of preaching or praying," would be guilty of a high misdemeanor. Anyone convicted would face a £100 fine and jail time. Congregationalist minister Ezra Stiles copied this resolution into his diary and described how Anglicans in Newport, Rhode Island, "cried out" when they learned the news.[26] Reverend George Bissett immediately removed the *Book of Common Prayer* from Trinity Church in Newport and locked the doors.

"The Church of England has now no longer an existence in the united Colonies of America," Philip Reading explained to Richard Hind, the secretary of the SPG.[27] For thirty years, Reading had been the minister of St. Anne's Church near the Appoquinimink River in what is now Middletown, Delaware. The king's sovereignty over the Anglican church was "judged incompatible" in the independent United States, he wrote. Reading could only obtain limited reports of how other ministers were responding to the Declaration of Independence, but he knew that some ministers had modified the prayers for the king and the royal family, or adapted the prayer for Parliament into a prayer for the Continental Congress. "As to myself," Reading explained, "I was at no loss in determining what part I should bear in this important Juncture." He regularly reread his ordination vows and the articles of faith that undergirded the Anglican church. He was adamant that ministers could not alter the *Book of Common Prayer* at their own discretion or "leave out parts of it to serve particular purposes" and that anyone who changed the prayers for the king, "whether Clergyman or Layman," would be excommunicated from the Church of England.

Philip Reading's resolve was tested on Sunday, July 21. The first two Sundays after the Declaration of Independence were normal for Reading, but on this third Sunday, one of the vestrymen approached Reading's pew and asked him to skip over the prayers for the king and the royal family. This recommendation was motivated by "pure kindness and friendship," and concern that "the temper of the prevailing party was such that they would no longer bear the reading of those prayers."[28] But Reading told the vestryman that he would rather close the church than change the service. "Being now assured on all hands of the danger with which I was threatened, if I persisted in complying with my oaths, vows, and subscriptions," Reading wrote, he thought it was "high time" to prioritize his family's safety. On the following Sunday morning, July 28, Reading made an emotional announcement to his parishioners. He could no longer read the liturgy "without offending against the new Government and incurring the resentment of the people." Reading decided to close St. Anne's Church for six weeks, in hopes that independence would be only temporary. But two years later, in another letter to the SPG secretary, Reading admitted that his church was still closed, because "the maintenance of Independence still continues tenaciously adhered to, & such laws are Multiplying among us as Militate against the discipline of the Church of England."[29] He prayed that the SPG would understand and respect his decision to keep his church shut. Reading died in 1778 and was buried next to the entrance to St. Anne's. The inscription on his tombstone honors his "Soundness of Judgment" and "Steadiness of Principle."

After July 4, Anglican ministers felt isolated, unsure of whether independence was momentary or permanent. They did not know what decisions other ministers had made, which churches were still open, or how they would be able to provide for themselves and their families. Uzal Ogden, Jr., had been ordained by the Bishop of London only eighteen months before the Battles of Lexington and Concord. He served four congregations and attended services in fifteen different locations in New Jersey. The Declaration of Independence made him question whether he could "use Part of the Liturgy and omit the Rest," so he decided to omit all of it. He would preach but not pray.

The difficulty of transatlantic communication during the war made it almost impossible for ministers in North America to receive guidance from the SPG headquarters in London. This also meant that they could no longer receive their annual stipends. Some congregations provided financial support to their ministers, for a variety of reasons, as evidenced by the quid pro quo at King's Church in Providence. But other ministers faced a bleak future in the independent United States. In North Carolina, Charles E. Taylor thought it was best to leave his parish after the Declaration of Independence. He was forced to give up his property, then his land—and finally his honor, when he was reduced to begging for assistance.[30]

In Massachusetts, some Anglican ministers evacuated with the British in March 1776, but Samuel Parker stayed behind, and that meant he had to reckon with the Declaration of Independence. On Sunday, July 14—the day after the news of independence reached Boston—Samuel Parker was interrupted during prayers in Trinity Church. He received "many Threats & Menaces" warning him not to pray for the king.[31] On July 18, the day of the first public reading of the Declaration in Boston, Parker told the vestry of Trinity Church that he "could not with Safety perform the Service of the Church for the future; as the continental Congress had declared the American Provinces free & independent States." The vestry debated what to do and decided that there were only two options: "to shut up the church & have no public Worship; or to omit that Part of the Liturgy wherein the King is prayed for." Changing the liturgy seemed like a better solution. The vestry asked Parker to omit specific prayers for the king but insisted that "no other Alterations be made, nor any Additions be Substituted," and Parker reluctantly agreed. His flexibility meant that his congregation not only stayed together but grew in numbers. He was "uncertain" of what his superiors in London would think about his decision to change the language in the *Book of Common Prayer*, "but considering the disagreeable Dilemma we were reduced to, we cannot but hope our Conduct will be viewed with Candour, & the Error (if such it is) imputed to the Head & not to the Heart."[32]

When Abigail Adams returned home to Braintree in September after two months in Boston, she was shocked to see that Christ Church was still open and that Edward Winslow was still praying for George III and the royal family.[33] Winslow knew that, after the Declaration of Independence, Trinity Church in Boston was able to remain open only because Samuel Parker had agreed not to pray for the king. But Winslow himself refused to make that change, and he believed that he had the support of his Braintree congregation, even as a "Spirit of Intolerance" against Anglicanism rose up all around them.[34] He wrote to the SPG secretary about the possibility that ministers in Massachusetts, like their colleagues in Rhode Island, would be required to pray "for the present Rulers" rather than the king. If that happened, Winslow was determined to close his church. In the meantime, he believed that it was his "Duty, to risque the Consequences of waiting." The "conscientious parson," as

Abigail Adams described him, kept Christ Church open until April 1777, when he preached a farewell sermon accompanied by "much weeping and wailing" before he closed the doors.[35]

Local Anglican ministers' views on the Declaration of Independence were further complicated because they were obliged to take part in the Massachusetts Council's publication plan. They were expected to read the Declaration aloud from one of Ezekiel Russell's broadsides.[36] The Russell broadside that was intended for Jacob Bailey had taken a long time to reach Pownalborough, up the Kennebeck River in the part of Massachusetts that would later become Maine. When it finally did, Bailey refused to comply with the Massachusetts Council's order, and on Sunday, September 22, he refused to read the Declaration.[37] This action, he claimed, did not stem "from any contempt of authority," but rather "from a dread of offending that God who is infinitely superior to all earthly power."[38] On October 28, the Pownalborough Committee of Correspondence, Inspection, and Safety called Bailey to respond to three charges: refusing to read the Declaration of Independence, praying for the king, and preaching sedition.[39]

These were not Bailey's first offenses. In May 1776, the committee had responded to a complaint that Bailey had been "unfriendly to the Cause of Liberty" and was "Guilty of a criminal Neglect in not reading Proclamations issued by the Continental and Provincial Congresses."[40] The Pownalborough committee had put Bailey under a £40 bond at that time, which would be waived if he behaved. Instead, Bailey had continued to disregard orders that contradicted his principles.

During Jacob Bailey's October hearing, the Pownalborough committee claimed that his refusal to read the Declaration of Independence to his congregation would "undermine the Foundation of the United States of America."[41] His continued prayers for George III, the committee maintained, were tacit endorsement of the king's "Tyrannical Measures, against these States." Bailey was "in Principle and Practice, a most inveterate and dangerous Enemy to the Rights and Liberties of these United States." But Bailey was unmoved. He responded by describing the sacred oath that he and every other Anglican minister had taken at their ordination. Bailey baited the committee with a Cromwellian nightmare: What if he took an oath of allegiance to the Continental Congress, and then the Continental Army rose up against the Congress and proclaimed George Washington to be the king of America? Would he be forced "to publish such a proclamation in a place of public Worship?"[42]

Jacob Bailey assured the Pownalborough committee that he was not an anarchist. He did not hold enough power, influence, or money to undermine the United States. The committee included classmates from Harvard College, men who had known him since they were teenagers. He asked them: "have I taken up Arms in favor of Britain? have I gone into any publick Meetings to defend or establish the Pretensions of either the King or Parliament? have I prevented any one from enlisting into the Service? have I by Word or Writing conveyed any Intelligence to the Enemy?"[43] Bailey's only crime was his unwillingness to compromise his relationship with God and the Church of England for what he believed to be a temporary change in political authority. The chairman of the committee reminded Bailey that George III had broken the oath that he had sworn at his coronation to protect his people. Bailey refused to concede. He was placed under bond again.

Jacob Bailey would get caught up in accusations around other SPG ministers' reactions to the Declaration of Independence as well. His brother-in-law, Joshua Wingate Weeks, was a minister in Marblehead, and, like Bailey, he refused to read the Declaration or stop praying for the king.[44] Weeks complained to the SPG about certain ministers in Massachusetts who had changed the *Book of Common Prayer* and acquiesced to the demands of the rebel leaders. He specifically called out Edward Bass, who had been serving St. Paul's Church in Newburyport for more than twenty years. Bass had, in fact, omitted certain prayers, but only at the insistence of his congregation. In mid-July 1776, the church wardens and vestrymen wrote him a letter explaining that "the representatives of the United Colonies in America having in Congress declared said Colonies free and independent States, and disavowed all allegiance to the King of Great Britain," it was necessary to omit all prayers for the king, the royal family, and the British government.[45] They assured Bass that, "without such omission," St. Paul's would "immediately cease" to exist. Bass replied that, if it was "necessary to the existence of the Church in this place," he would leave out those prayers.

A few weeks later, Edward Bass was required to read the Declaration of Independence aloud, and the question of whether he did so or not would follow him for years. Joshua Wingate Weeks and other SPG ministers insisted that Bass had acquiesced to read the Declaration. Weeks claimed that, according to his brother-in-law, Jacob Bailey, Bass had preached a sermon to raise support for the Continental Army. But Bailey refuted this story and came to Bass's defense. So did William Walter, who had evacuated Boston, leaving Samuel Parker as the new rector of Trinity Church. Walter had heard from a reliable source that after the Russell broadsides of the Declaration were sent out to Massachusetts churches, Bass had "positively refused" to read it, "saying he was no Herald to publish the Proclamations of War."[46] Bass had conceded that "he coud not prevent it" if the sheriff or the clerk of St. Paul's Church wanted to read it, but he "woud have nothing to do wh. it himself." Bass repeatedly told the SPG that he only did what was necessary to keep his church doors open. A decade after independence, still refuting Weeks's charges against him, Bass would write his own account of these events, which was published in London.[47]

The question remains: If Edward Bass did not read the Declaration of Independence at St. Paul's Church, then did anyone there follow the Massachusetts Council's order? It seems reasonable that Tristram Dalton, a prominent merchant and one of the church's vestrymen, might have read the Declaration aloud. When he first heard the news of independence in mid-July 1776, he wrote, "We are no longer to be amused with delusive prospects. The die is cast. All is at stake. The way is made plain. No one can now doubt on which side it is his duty to act."[48] For Dalton, independence was the clear path forward. He had signed the letter asking Bass to stop praying for the king, but he still had empathy for the minister. He even contributed £10 to cover part of Bass's lost salary from the SPG.[49] The decision of which side to support was not as straightforward for Anglican ministers like Bass as it was for an Anglican parishioner like Dalton.

✶✶✶

Across the United States, Anglican ministers held out hope that independence would be overruled and that, after closing the doors of their churches or omitting certain prayers for a short time, they would be able to resume worship services according to the *Book of Common Prayer*. This was very nearly the case for ministers in New York City. On October 31, 1776, Reverend Charles Inglis, the rector of Trinity Church, wrote a lengthy report to the SPG secretary recounting what had happened to him and his church that year.[50] Inglis was not surprised by the Declaration of Independence. In February 1776, Inglis had felt compelled to write a response to Thomas Paine's *Common Sense* because it was "one of the most virulent, artful & pernicious Pamphlets" that he had ever read and had "seduced thousands" to support independence. The first edition of his anonymous treatise, printed in New York, had been "seized by the Sons of Liberty & burnt."

An incident that occurred between the publication of *Common Sense* and that of the Declaration of Independence proved that Charles Inglis could not be intimidated. Soon after George Washington arrived in New York, one of his officers told Inglis that Washington was planning to come to church services and would be "glad" if Inglis omitted the prayers for the king and the royal family.[51] Inglis "paid no regard to this message." One Sunday while Inglis was conducting a service in Trinity Church, a company of Continental Army soldiers marched in "with Drums beating & Fifes playing" and "their Guns loaded & Bayonets fixed, as if going to Battle." Inglis continued the service unfazed, while women in the congregation fainted and the "Rebels stood thus in the Aile for near fifteen Minutes." Then the church sexton asked the soldiers to move into the pews, and they complied.

Inglis claimed that he could fill an entire book with stories like this, of how he and other Anglican clergymen had been threatened, "reviled with the most opprobrious Language," and "treated with brutal Violence."

According to Inglis, the Declaration of Independence "increased the embarrassment of the Clergy."[52] Any clergyman who officiated a service and did not pray for the king and the royal family, he claimed, was going against "their Duty & Oath," as well as the "Dictates of their Conscience," while anyone who continued to pray as if nothing had changed "would have drawn inevitably Destruction on them." In mid-July 1776, Inglis took down the royal coat of arms in Trinity Church—"or else the Mob would do it"—and talked to the vestry members. They decided that it was better to "submit to that temporary Inconvenience" of closing the church than to omit the prayers for the king.

Inglis shared with the SPG secretary everything he knew about other churches and clergymen and how they had responded to the news of independence. He shared a rumor that one minister in Connecticut "officiated as usual after Independence was declared" and insisted that he would "pray for the King till the Rebels cut out his Tongue." Otherwise, it seemed that many clergymen made the same decision as Inglis, and that was "remarkable" to him. They could not "consult each other on this interesting Occasion; yet they all fell upon the same Method in shutting up their Churches."

When the British forces attacked the Continental Army weeks after the Declaration of Independence was issued, Charles Inglis went into hiding on Long Island. By mid-September, New York City was under British control, and Inglis returned to his home to find that it had been "plundered of everything by the rebels."[53] Inglis thought he could safely reopen his church, but then a fire devastated the city and the "venerable edifice" of Trinity Church burned, along with the rector's house and the SPG-sponsored school.[54] Joseph Hildreth, the schoolmaster, returned to the city a few days after Inglis and was grief-stricken by the destruction of "our Antient Beautiful Parish."[55] He found a vacant house and started collecting students. Hildreth had only twenty-five boys and ten girls, as well as a growing number of young Black catechumens. But loyal citizens were seeking refuge in New York City and Hildreth expected the number of students to grow quickly. Meanwhile, Inglis was confident that the king's forces would prevail.

"I have not a doubt but, with the blessing of Providence, his Majesty's arms will be successful, and finally crush this unnatural rebellion," Inglis wrote. He expected that the Anglican church in North America would "indubitably increase." But Inglis's prediction would turn out to be wrong. At the end of the war, the Church of England and the SPG had only half the number of ministers compared to the start of the war. Some had died, some had retired, and some had left the United States, including Inglis. In 1787, Inglis became the first Anglican bishop in North America, for the diocese of Nova Scotia.

On July 11, 1776, when the New York Convention wrote to the Continental Congress to share their support for the Declaration of Independence, they offered a suggestion. They wondered if the Congress might take "some measures for expunging from the *Book of Common Prayer* such parts, and discontinuing in the congregations of all other denominations all such prayers as interfere with the interest of the American cause."[56] The New York Convention was "afraid to meddle" with the *Book of Common Prayer* themselves because there were so many adherents of the Anglican church in their state. The Congress read the New York Convention's letter but never took action. Some colonial and state governments made the decision to alter or omit prayers for the king. But, for many ministers, this choice remained a personal one, made after thoughtful consideration and sometimes under duress. Anglican ministers were torn between the allegiance they had sworn at their ordination and the reality of living in the United States after the Declaration of Independence. Their limited ability to communicate with the SPG during the war meant that they would spend years after independence worried about whether they had made the right decision.

The Declaration of Independence challenged the sovereignty of King George III. It was written to show that the king was undeserving of the supreme political authority that he held over the colonists. This was a problem for Anglican ministers, who believed that the king held not only political authority but also spiritual authority. Modifying the prayers in the *Book of Common Prayer* was not a simple matter of cutting and pasting or scribbling something new. Clergymen had to think carefully about whether they could, in good conscience, stop praying for the king or start praying for the new ruling powers in the United States. They had to consider what it would mean for them to read the Declaration aloud. They had to accept the powerlessness that came with closing the doors of their churches. These ministers' choices were filled with emotions—anger, disappointment, fear, and embarrassment. Jacob Duché described the Declaration of Independence as "fatal," and for many Anglican ministers it was.[57] It killed any hope of keeping the king as the head of their churches, and it threatened the lives and ministries of clergymen across the United States.

8

Intercepted

Broadsides in British Hands

On July 9, 1776, the Declaration of Independence was printed on the front page of the *Pennsylvanischer Staatsbote*. On the back page was an advertisement for Jonas Phillips's shop on Market Street. Phillips offered fine French indigo, the best writing paper, checked and striped fabrics, needles and pins, umbrellas, wines, and other sundries for sale.[1] In the British Colonial Office papers at the National Archives, there is a similar list of products that would "sell to Advantage" in Philadelphia, handwritten by Phillips for Samuel Curson, a merchant on the Dutch Caribbean island of Sint Eustatius.[2] On the other side of this list is a letter, dated July 28, 1776, and, alternatively, Sunday, the 12th day of Menachem Av, in the year 5536 of the Hebrew calendar.

Jonas Phillips was born to an Ashkenazi Jewish family in Hesse and, as a young man, he came to British North America as an indentured servant to a Sephardic Jewish planter. He completed his contract in South Carolina and moved to New York, where he became a merchant. He married Rebecca Mendez Machado, the daughter of refugees from Portugal.[3] The couple moved to Philadelphia, and on July 28, 1775, Phillips put out an advertisement for his new store on Market Street.[4] Exactly one year later, Phillips wrote the letter on the back of the list of goods. His message was for a family member and fellow merchant in Amsterdam named Gumpel Samson. Phillips told Samson that he was sending his letter through Samuel Curson, his contact in the Dutch

Caribbean, because it was not always possible or safe to send mail directly from Philadelphia to Europe. Curson entrusted Phillips's letter to a ship headed for Amsterdam. But a British ship intercepted the vessel soon after it left Sint Eustatius, and Gumpel Samson never received the letter, or what it contained.[5]

Jonas Phillips had folded up and enclosed one of John Dunlap's broadsides of the Declaration of Independence in his letter to Gumpel Samson.[6] However, the broadside's connection to Phillips was not obvious.[7] When the broadside was deposited among the intercepted papers in the Colonial Office, it was separated from Phillips's letter. The letter had been written in Yiddish, adding an extra layer of concealment in case it was intercepted.[8] To a British officer in the middle of a war, looking at a letter written from Philadelphia in July 1776, the Judeo-German text probably seemed to have been written in code. To an archivist, there is nothing in English on the page that would suggest that this letter enclosed a Dunlap broadside. But a translation of the letter reveals that Phillips wanted to send Gumpel Samson the declaration of his new country, one that resembled the Dutch Republic, where Samson lived. Phillips did not know what would come of the United States. He was just grateful that, despite the war, his Philadelphia business was doing well.[9]

Statistically, it is astonishing that one of the surviving Dunlap broadsides of the Declaration of Independence belonged to a Jewish person. Jews numbered, at most, one in every thousand people in British North America in 1776.[10] But the fact that Jonas Phillips's Dunlap broadside ended up in the intercepted papers in the Colonial Office is much less surprising. Merchants with transatlantic communication networks between family members and commercial contacts tried to maintain these connections even when the war made regular correspondence more challenging.[11]

The letter that Phillips wrote on the back of a list of goods he wanted to sell was much more about family and business than it was about the Declaration of Independence. Phillips began his letter with a blessing for

Gumpel Samson, and he signed it as Jonas, son of Felbush of Buseck.[12] Phillips's father was deceased, but his mother was still living in Europe. He had tried to send her some money the previous year, but was not sure if she ever received it, so, alongside the Dunlap broadside, he enclosed a bill of exchange for ten pounds sterling and asked Samson to make sure it got to his mother. Phillips closed his letter with greetings and blessings from his wife, Rebecca, and their children.

Jonas Phillips wanted to share the Declaration of Independence with Gumpel Samson because it was news. In fact, by the time he wrote his letter on July 28, the Declaration had been news for a while. On the back of Phillips's Dunlap broadside there are circles of red, waxy residue in each corner. Before Phillips sent this broadside to Samson, it had been posted up somewhere in Philadelphia. It had a history before Phillips took it down, folded it up, and put it in the mail. Although he did not express a strong opinion about independence in his letter, Phillips understood what the Declaration meant.

The connection between the Phillips family and the Declaration of Independence would persist. Uriah Phillips Levy, Jonas and Rebecca's grandson, would later purchase Thomas Jefferson's Monticello plantation to preserve it, in part because of his admiration for the principal author of the Declaration.[13]

Wayward broadsides of the Declaration of Independence, including Jonas Phillips's Dunlap broadside, are a reminder of how the Continental Congress, for all their energetic efforts, had little control over how the news of independence circulated in 1776. The Committee of Secret Correspondence had sent a Dunlap broadside to France, where Silas Deane was trying to secure support for the united colonies. But unlike previous petitions to King George III, the Congress did not make plans to send the Declaration to anyone in the British government. The Declaration was not meant for the king—it was about the king. As the Congress focused on other audiences, they did not adequately prepare for the likelihood that British officials would send the Declaration to London themselves.

There are five known broadsides of the Declaration of Independence in the National Archives at Kew. Each one, including Jonas Phillips's broadside, ended up in the hands of a British official in the summer of 1776.[14]

On Monday, July 8, after John Hancock sent out Dunlap broadsides to civic and military leaders throughout the United States, the Committee of Secret Correspondence sent a broadside to Silas Deane. The committee enclosed the Declaration of Independence in a letter they entrusted to Peter Parker, captain of the *Dispatch* brigantine.[15] They instructed Parker to leave immediately for the French port of Bordeaux, where he was to deliver the letter to two sympathetic merchants.[16] The committee hoped that the *Dispatch* would be swift enough, and the winds and the weather good enough, for Parker to outrun enemy ships and cross the Atlantic quickly and safely. When he boarded the *Dispatch*, Parker attached a heavy weight to the committee's letter, "ready to throw overboard and sink" the parcel if his ship was "unfortunately taken by the Enemy."[17] The committee did not tell Parker why this letter was so important, or even who the intended recipient was, but they added a postscript explaining that Parker could talk to "Silas Deane Esqr. who lately went from this place for Bourdeaux," if he happened to run into him.

The Committee of Secret Correspondence was far more concerned with interception than reception when it came to the Declaration of Independence. They could have—and arguably should have—sent multiple Dunlap broadsides to Silas Deane, divided among various ships taking different routes across the Atlantic, to increase the odds that their message would reach Paris. The committee also could have prepared a French translation of the Declaration for Deane. By his own admission, Deane could read and understand French "tolerably well," but he could not write it, and he would have to find someone in Paris who was trustworthy and skilled enough to translate for him.[18] Instead, the committee relied on a single printed copy of the Declaration in English. A few days after the *Dispatch* left Philadelphia, a British vessel threatened the ship. Captain Peter Parker, following the committee's instructions, threw the letter for Deane—and the Declaration of Independence—overboard to prevent the British from intercepting the message.

There is no more evocative image of how messy the process of declaring independence was than the Dunlap broadside that was supposed to announce the news to France disintegrating in the ocean. This was almost literally the "Skiff made of Paper" that John Dickinson had envisioned in his speech to the Continental Congress on July 1. He had wanted his colleagues to put their trust in the abilities of their appointed agent in France and not undermine Silas Deane by declaring independence without his knowledge.[19]

In August, the Committee of Secret Correspondence sent another copy of the Declaration of Independence to Deane. The committee included a duplicate of the letter that they had written on July 8, and added the good news that, since then, the Declaration had received "universal approbation" in the United States and that the people seemed "more animated by it in defence of their Country."[20] This second attempt did not reach Deane until November. The broadside that was thrown overboard had cost the United States precious time. Allowing a copy of the Declaration to fall into British hands—even if it was enclosed in a letter of confidential information for the Congress's secret agent—would have been less harmful than failing to get a copy to the French government in a timely manner.

While Silas Deane's Dunlap broadside was disintegrating in the Atlantic, other copies of the Declaration of Independence were traveling safely on British mail ships. HMS *Mercury* was the packet boat that brought the news of independence to England. The *Mercury* offered the first opportunity to communicate with London after General William Howe and his troops arrived in New York. The boat was stuffed with thousands of pieces of mail, including the letters that Howe had written to the secretary of state for North America, Lord George Germain, on July 7 and 8. As the *Mercury* prepared to leave New York Harbor on July 10, Vice Admiral Molyneux Shuldham added one more letter to its load. It was addressed to John Montagu, 4th Earl of Sandwich and First Lord of the Admiralty, and contained "a Copy of the late Declaration of the Continental Congress, one Printed Copy of which arriv'd here last night."[21] Shuldham described the Declaration as "the first authentic confirmation of what has been so long suspected, the Establishment of Independence in America." A printed copy of the Declaration must have made its way to Shuldham's ship, HMS *Chatham*, on the night of July 9, perhaps in the same hours that saw the statue of George III toppled and beheaded. One of Shuldham's clerks had neatly copied the Declaration on three sheets of paper, front and back, to be enclosed in his letter and sent to the admiralty office in London.[22] Shuldham held onto the printed copy, perhaps to show to Vice Admiral Richard Howe when he sailed into the harbor.

In New York City, shortly after HMS *Mercury* left for England, Hugh Gaine printed broadsides of the Declaration of Independence that looked very similar to John Dunlap's broadside.[23] One of Gaine's broadsides traveled from his office—located on Hanover Square, named for George III's line of Hanoverian kings—to William Tryon on HMS *Duchess of Gordon*. Even after he was implicated in the Hickey Plot against the Continental Army, Tryon was still getting news from Manhattan. There is a name on the back of the broadside that fell into his hands, perhaps a clue as to the intended recipient of this copy of the Declaration.[24] Tryon enclosed this broadside in a letter to Lord Germain. "The Confederate Colonies have declared themselves independent States," Tryon wrote.[25] He explained that the Declaration had been "published through the Streets of New York"—a city in shambles, where the Anglican churches had been shuttered and the king's statue and "every Vistage of Royalty" had been destroyed by the "Rebels."

The King's Commissioners for Restoring Peace also sent broadsides of the Declaration to London. At Staten Island on August 11, Vice Admiral Richard Howe and General William Howe jointly wrote a letter to Lord George Germain, enclosing a copy of their declaration explaining their powers as commissioners. Though they assured Germain that it had been "very generally circulated," they neglected to mention that it was the Continental Congress that had circulated the text.[26] Although General Howe had shared the news of independence with Germain already, in one of the letters stuffed on the *Mercury* packet, the Howe brothers wrote: "it is our Duty to acquaint Your Lordship that, on the 4th. of July last, the General Congress came to a Resolution to declare, that the associated Colonies are, and of Right ought to be, free and independent States." They enclosed a printed copy of the Declaration, a Dunlap broadside that "came accidentally" into their hands shortly after the *Mercury* left.[27] And they quoted from the last paragraph of the Declaration, which explained that the colonies were "absolved from all Allegiance to the British Crown, and that all political Connection between them and the State of Great Britain is, and ought to be, totally dissolved."[28]

Before the Howe brothers' letter reached London, Lord George Germain received another letter with the news of independence from Virginia. On July 31, on board his eponymous ship anchored in the Potomac River, Lord Dunmore wrote to Germain, enclosing another Dunlap broadside. This copy of the Declaration looked a bit different, and Dunmore had acquired it through horrific circumstances.

Dunmore's flotilla of ships had been anchored at Gwynn's Island in the Chesapeake Bay, where they were joined by HMS *Roebuck* after Captain Andrew Snape Hamond was chased out of the Delaware River in May. Gwynn's Island, with its fresh air, livestock, and fish, could have been a respite for Dunmore's white soldiers, as well as the Black men and women who had run to Dunmore hoping to be freed from slavery.[29] Instead, the small, triangular island became a graveyard.

Lord Dunmore, the royal governor of Virginia, was convinced that the tide was turning toward reconciliation in his colony. On June 26, he sent Lord Germain a copy of the Virginia Convention's May 15 Resolution. Dunmore was "well pleased" with this resolution.[30] He believed that independence was "quite repugnant to the wish of most" Virginians, and that this resolution would convince the people to rise up against their provincial leaders. Dunmore also let Germain know that smallpox and fever had "carried off an incredible number" of the people who had sought refuge with him, "especially the blacks."[31] If his Black regiment had stayed healthy, Dunmore expected that it would have numbered 2,000 formerly enslaved men, capable of "penetrating into the heart of this Colony." Instead, Dunmore's forces were stuck in Chesapeake Bay, with the sick people quarantined on one side of Gwynn's Island. The situation deteriorated rapidly. On July 11, after enduring a few days of enemy fire, Dunmore abandoned the island under the cover of night.

The following week, the Declaration of Independence reached nearby Williamsburg, Virginia. But Alexander Purdie only had enough space in his *Virginia Gazette* to print the last few paragraphs of the Declaration.[32] Independence was important news, but so was an account—filling two columns of Purdie's newspaper—of what Lord Dunmore had left behind at Gwynn's Island. Smallpox and fever had taken "near 500 souls" since Dunmore had anchored at the island, and Purdie's correspondent personally "counted 130 graves (or rather holes loosely covered over with earth)."[33] Sickness was not the only cause of mass death. As the British forces made a hasty evacuation from the island, fire spread through the huts that had been built from brush. Dunmore had caused a "scene of misery, distress, and cruelty" on Gwynn's Island.

The day after Alexander Purdie printed the Declaration of Independence alongside this tragic account, William Dixon and John Hunter printed the Declaration in full in their competing *Virginia Gazette*, opposite an extract from the journal of an officer who had been to Gwynn's Island. The officer wrote that "the deplorable situation of the miserable wretches left behind is beyond description."[34] He described a young Black child "found sucking at the breast of its dead mother," a reminder that women and children had sought freedom with Dunmore, too. The governor's "neglect of those poor creatures" was cruel, perhaps "enough to discourage others from joining him." The gruesome details of Black people found dead and dying as the stench of putrefaction spread over the island were made all the more horrifying by their placement on the same pages of the *Virginia Gazette* as the Continental Congress's assertion of rights to life and liberty. When the accounts of the aftermath at Gwynn's Island circulated through Virginia and the rest of the United States, they would give readers the impression that enslaved people were worse off with Dunmore than they had been on their enslavers' plantations.

After Lord Dunmore abandoned Gwynn's Island and the bodies of the Black people who had looked to him for freedom, he learned about the Declaration of Independence. Dunmore's ships—carrying significantly fewer Black recruits than they had a few weeks earlier—moved to St. George Island on the Maryland side of the Potomac River, not far from Richard Henry Lee's Chantilly plantation on the Virginia side of the river. When Lee wrote to Thomas Jefferson to thank him for sending the committee draft of the Declaration of Independence to compare with the final version, he complained that "our African Hero," Dunmore, was "now disturbing us" in the Potomac.[35] Dunmore had sent more than 100 Black and white volunteers to a house on St. George Island, where, in his words, "about 300 of the Rebels" were assembled.[36] "We were no sooner landed than the Rebels fled on all quarters from the House, & Offices, all of which we burnt," Dunmore wrote to Lord George Germain. Dunmore and his men did "all the mischief" they could, including seizing papers from the house before they set it on fire. It seems that a Dunlap broadside of the Declaration was among these papers.

Lord Dunmore enclosed the looted Dunlap broadside in his July 31 letter to the British secretary of state, "lest your Ldp should not have seen the Resolutions of the Congress."[37] It was one of the broadsides that John Dunlap had created with an imprint reading Baltimore instead of Philadelphia.[38] Perhaps one of the "Rebels" purchased the broadside from Dunlap's Baltimore printing office and either brought it or sent it to the house on St. George Island. In his letter to Germain, Dunmore enclosed a few other papers "found whilst we were last on shore," including an account from one of the Williamsburg newspapers of "GLORIOUS NEWS" from Sullivan's Island.[39] At the end of this supplement to his weekly newspaper, Alexander Purdie had added a grateful toast to "*General* LEE, *and our brave Friends of*

SOUTH CAROLINA! HUZZA!"[40] Dunmore did not initially believe the report of British defeat. But before he sent Germain his letter containing the Dunlap broadside and this newspaper, he was forced to add a somber postscript. It turned out that Purdie's newspaper contained "too true an account of our loss before Charles Town." It was, on the whole, a disappointing update from Virginia.

Lord George Germain was undoubtedly one of the first people in Great Britain to receive the Declaration of Independence, sometime during the second week of August 1776. But, thanks to the royal governors and commissioners in North America, the news kept coming, and the secretary of state's office filled up with copies of the Declaration. The Dunlap broadside from Lord Dunmore reached Germain on September 3, and the broadsides from Governor Tryon and the Howe brothers arrived on September 28. Clerks working for Germain created manuscript duplicates of the broadsides that were sent to him.[41] Later that fall, Jonas Phillips's Dunlap broadside was added to the cache of intercepted letters to and from American colonists. Meanwhile, two copies of the Declaration—one manuscript, one printed—went to the admiralty office.[42] Unlike the Committee of Secret Correspondence's attempt to communicate with Silas Deane, there was redundancy in British transatlantic communication. The Continental Congress did not plan to send the Declaration of Independence to the British ministry, but British officials recognized the Declaration as news and wanted to make sure it reached London.

⊗⊗⊗

On August 8, HMS *Mercury* sailed into the port of Falmouth in southwest England, and the Continental Congress lost all control over the news of independence.[43] On Saturday, August 10, the first confirmed report of American independence appeared on the front page of the *London Gazette*, the official newspaper of the British government. Londoners knew that good news was printed in the *Gazette* quickly and bad news was printed at whatever speed and in as much detail as the secretaries of state wanted, if at all.[44] Most London newspapers were published three days a week, and some even six days a week (excepting Sundays). Three or four columns per page, four pages per issue—that was a lot of space that needed to be filled with information and advertisements. By contrast, the *London Gazette* was published only twice a week, on Tuesdays and Saturdays, leaving a conspicuous gap between official updates on the situation in the colonies that needed to be filled. The majority of London's newspapers at this time were anti-ministry, or biased toward the Opposition. This did not mean that they supported the independence of the colonies, but it did mean that they were highly critical of the secretary of state for North America, Lord George Germain. Anti-ministry publishers became increasingly suspicious that Lord Germain's office was concealing news from North America.

Readers of the *London Gazette* on August 10 learned about General William Howe's arrival at Staten Island and the Continental Congress's vote for independence from strategic extracts of four letters from the *Mercury*'s cargo: two from Howe to Lord George Germain, one from William Tryon to Germain, and one from Vice Admiral Molyneux Shuldham to the Earl of Sandwich.[45] In the *London Gazette*, the contents of Howe's letters of July 7 and 8 were woven together so that only half of the original content was made public. In his original July 8 letter, Howe explained that someone had brought him a newspaper, from which he learned that the Continental Congress had declared independence. But in the *London Gazette*, this part of the story was stripped out, and Howe was simply "informed" of this news.[46] Perhaps Howe reading a newspaper seemed like an unnecessary detail to include—or maybe Germain's office did not want to publicize the fact that Howe had learned about independence from the rebel press.

Over the next week, the news of independence spread to other London newspapers as different publishers reprinted the extracts from the *London Gazette*, as well as other letters that supposedly traveled by the *Mercury* packet. One letter, written from Staten Island, suggested that the delegates in the Continental Congress were so poor—"Hancock excepted"—that they could be bought off easily.[47] Surely Benjamin Franklin was particularly susceptible, "at a proper price," because his son, the royal governor of New Jersey, was in prison. Another letter claimed that Benjamin and William Franklin had taken to opposite sides of the war on purpose, "so that, let who will triumph, the doctor and his family will be on the right side."[48] A British officer wrote home with his hope that the troops on Staten Island would soon be joined "by great numbers of the Provincials, many of whom are become highly dissatisfied, from the late declaration of independence, published by the Congress."[49] He expected that a swift victory over the Continental Army in New York would "put an end to this hurlyburly touching Independence."

Londoners had anticipated that the colonies would declare independence, but they had also thought that independence would be contentious. A report in the *Morning Post* on Monday, August 12, confirmed this bias. The Continental Congress "at last carried their favorite point, in voting by a small majority the United Colonies free, and independent states."[50] The separation from Great Britain had "already driven most of the dispassionate members" from the colonial governments and "caused a general desertion" in the Continental Army. This was, of course, a great exaggeration. But the *Morning Post* made clear that, if the Congress had declared independence so that they could form alliances "with some powerful European nation," then "the absurdity of the idea" would "soon be made manifest." Before ever seeing the Declaration of Independence, the publisher of the *Morning Post* claimed that it was merely a "declaration of *dependency*" on some other European power.[51] Readers were primed to believe that the United States would not—could not—survive on their own.

Mary Say, the publisher of London's *Gazetteer and New Daily Advertiser*, cited a letter brought to England by the *Mercury* as evidence for three claims that would circulate for weeks, losing context and gaining authority with each reprinting. Beginning with one of the most common phrases a printer could use to deflect attribution—"we are informed"—the *Gazetteer* reported that "when the Congress resolved upon independence there were present several foreigners of different nations, amongst whom were some persons of distinction from the Courts of Versailles and Madrid."[52] Evidently, the Continental Congress had been keeping up a correspondence with Britons' "natural enemies the French and Spaniards," and only declared independence because France and Spain promised "every assistance in their power." According to the *Gazetteer*, "as soon as the Colonies declared themselves independent states, two foreign vessels, which were at Philadelphia, slipped their cables, and sailed with the intelligence to the above Courts." There is no way of knowing if this letter from the *Mercury* packet actually existed, who wrote it, or what exactly it said—or if this entire story was crafted in Mary Say's printing office. But that did not stop other newspapers from copying these claims.

According to the *Gazetteer and New Daily Advertiser*—and every other London newspaper that copied it—the independence and sovereignty of the United States were entangled with and legitimized by European powers. In three sentences, Say's newspaper suggested that the Continental Congress had ulterior motives for declaring independence, but also that the Congress had arranged to send copies of their declaration to France and Spain. A pseudonymous writer suggested that the leaders of the Congress must have made a deal with the devil in return for alliances with European powers.[53] But there were no ships waiting in the Delaware River to carry the Declaration of Independence to Versailles and Madrid. The one copy of the Declaration that the Continental Congress tried to send to France had to go in secret, and it did not make it very far. If there had been foreign envoys in Philadelphia and ships prepared to sail immediately for Europe with copies of the Declaration, the United States' entry onto the world stage would have looked very different.[54]

In the week following the August 10 issue of the *London Gazette*, when the Declaration of Independence was known in London but not yet published, two British secretaries of state met with an American who had recently returned from a suspicious trip to France. Dr. Edward Bancroft was on a very short list of men in Europe whom the Committee of Secret Correspondence thought that Silas Deane could trust. Years earlier, Bancroft had been Deane's student in Connecticut, and they could reconnect under the guise of "old acquaintance" without drawing too much attention.[55] But Paris was swarming with Britons. "My arrival here, my name, my lodgings, and many other particulars have been reported to the British administration," Deane complained.[56] Nevertheless, Bancroft traveled from his home in London to Paris at the beginning of July and spent three weeks with Deane before returning to London. After Paul Wentworth, the former colonial agent for New Hampshire, told Bancroft that the British ministry knew about this trip, Bancroft joined Wentworth for a pivotal meeting with Henry Howard, 12th Earl of Suffolk and secretary of state for the Northern Department, and Thomas Thynne, 3rd Viscount Weymouth and secretary of state for the Southern Department.[57]

Edward Bancroft's behavior over the years to come, as secretary to Silas Deane and the United States' diplomats in Paris, indicates that he was a double agent. If that is true, then Bancroft became a British spy the week that the news of the Declaration of Independence reached London, when he met with the British secretaries of state.[58] Bancroft provided intelligence that Deane had shared with him in confidence, including Deane's impressions of the Continental Congress when he left Philadelphia and the specifics of their instructions for him.[59] He also described meetings between Deane and French officials. Bancroft sat out of Deane's conversations at Versailles with Charles Gravier, the Comte de Vergennes and Minister of Foreign Affairs, but he assured the Earl of Suffolk and the Viscount Weymouth that Deane had given him a "minute" and "faithfull Relation of every Part" of his conversation with Vergennes."

Edward Bancroft's intelligence suggested that the Comte de Vergennes wanted to send formal aid to the colonies, but not until after the Continental Congress declared independence and the Continental Army proved that it could stand up to the British army. Bancroft later recalled that, after spending three weeks in Paris with Silas Deane, he had "returned to England, convinced, that the Government of France would endeavour to Promote an Absolute Separation, of the United Colonies, from Great Britain."[60] The timing of his meeting with the British secretaries of state mattered. "The Declaration of Independancy, was not then known in Europe," Bancroft recalled. He hoped that, given the threat of the French entering the war, the British ministry could prevent independence, "by some accommodation with the Colonies or by other means."

The Declaration of Independence was never printed in the *London Gazette*—not on August 10, not in the next issue on August 13, not ever. But though the British secretaries of state could keep the Declaration out of their official newspaper, they could not keep it from being "known in Europe." It was hard for other publishers to believe that, out of the thousands of pieces of mail brought from North America to England by the *Mercury* packet, the government had nothing more to publish. The daily newspapers were compelled to fill in the gaps, sometimes with fact, more often with speculation. Henry Sampson Woodfall's *Public Advertiser* claimed that, "were the other Papers prevented from printing the Truth," anyone who read the *London Gazette* would be left to believe "that Success attends our Arms" and that the leaders of the Continental Congress "were in a Dungeon."[61] Woodfall was particularly suspicious because the captain of the *Mercury* met with Lord George Germain for hours and had a special audience with King George III.[62] On August 16, Woodfall's *Public Advertiser* copied a paragraph from the *London Evening-Post* which speculated that the dispatches brought by the *Mercury* contained "much more than has been made public."[63] On the front page of that same issue, Woodfall made one piece of news from the *Mercury* public: he printed the Declaration of Independence in full for the first time in London.

⁂

The Atlantic Ocean was an unreliable space, and in the summer of 1776, letters and copies of the Declaration of Independence did not always reach their intended destinations. This worked to the detriment of Silas Deane, who was sitting in Paris for many weeks waiting for news, and to the advantage of Lord George Germain, who was inundated with copies of the Declaration. The British secretary of state for North America read the Declaration long before the Continental Congress's agent in France could do the same. On the other side of the ocean, the Continental Congress had no idea what was happening to the Declaration in London.

9

Pretended Acts

London Changes the Declaration

George III "betrayed not the least emotion" as Lord George Germain read aloud the Declaration of Independence, with its twenty-seven grievances leveled against the king. But when Germain reached the passage, "A Prince, whose Character is thus marked by every act which may define a Tyrant, is unfit to be the Ruler of a free People," the king "changed colour." He screamed, *"will my kingdoms hear this and not persist till such flagitious rebellion and licentiousness is punished."*[1] At least, this was the story in the London press. There is no actual record of exactly when or how George III learned about the Declaration. But this story was based on a fair premise—that, as secretary of state for North America, it was Lord Germain's unenviable responsibility to deliver the news of independence to the king. The rest of this story reveals an anxiety among some London newspaper publishers when it came to printing the Declaration. The text was less about independence from the king than about the king himself. If George III had remained stone-faced until the end of the list of grievances, then printing the grievances—not to mention the accusation of tyranny—was potentially dangerous.

In London, the Declaration of Independence changed. The text that appeared in London newspapers was excerpted, censored, manipulated, and accompanied by misinformation and rumor. And across Europe, from the middle of August through the fall, newspaper publishers translated the news of independence as it was printed in London. Some publishers did acknowledge that the British metropole might not be the most trustworthy source. For example, Claude-Isaac Peuch, the publisher of the *Gazette d'Utrecht* in the Dutch Republic, reminded his readers that it was impossible to know the exact details of the war between Great Britain and the colonies. But Peuch thought it was best to print all the news from London, even conflicting reports, and let time determine whether the information was true or not.[2] London newspaper publishers were political mediators who influenced the reception of the news of independence for many more people in many more languages than just their metropolitan, English-reading subscribers.

⁂

The Declaration of Independence first appeared in London newspapers on Friday, August 16. It was printed in two newspapers: the anti-ministry *Public Advertiser* and the pro-ministry *Lloyd's Evening Post*.[3] Henry Sampson Woodfall, the *Public Advertiser*'s publisher, somehow gained access to the Declaration before any other printer in London, and he had prepared his readers the previous day with a notice that the "Declaration by the *Representatives of the* United States of AMERICA *in* General Congress" would be in the paper's next issue.[4] *Lloyd's Evening Post* may have copied the *Public Advertiser*, or both publishers may have relied on the same copy of the Declaration—either one of the manuscript copies that had traveled across the Atlantic on HMS *Mercury* or a handwritten copy of a copy. The evidence is in the thirteenth grievance. In printings of the Declaration created in the United States, its final phrase says that the king assented to "Acts of pretended Legislation," but in the first two London newspaper printings of the Declaration and every other British printing that followed, the phrase was flipped around to "pretended Acts of Legislation"—presumably an error made in haste rather than a conscious alteration.[5]

John Laurens, who was born in South Carolina, read the Declaration of Independence in the August 16 issue of the *Public Advertiser*. He believed the text to be an "Authentic Copy" of the original, and, apart from the "pretended Acts of Legislation," he was right.[6] Laurens had moved with his father and brothers to London in 1771. By the summer of 1776, he had been studying law for almost two years and was desperate to return home. After the Declaration reached Charleston in early August, Laurens's father, Henry, was forced to admit that he should have granted his son's repeated requests to leave London a bit sooner.[7] Though the younger Laurens was glad to read the Declaration, he was frustrated by the rest of the news in the London press, from premature reports of battles around New York to incomplete intelligence from the Battle of Sullivan's Island. There was even a "foolish paragraph in some of the papers" that claimed that the British government was going to "seize the persons of all Americans in England, in order hereafter to make an advantageous Exchange of Prisoners."[8] But Laurens was not too worried about himself or his new country. He declared, "I think America in a fair way—and that we have no Reason to be so dreadfully apprehensive as some people would make us believe."

Henry Sampson Woodfall printed the Declaration of Independence in full in the *Public Advertiser*—from "In CONGRESS, July 4, 1776" through the names of the president and secretary of the Continental Congress—but in *Lloyd's Evening Post*, the words "king," "Prince," "Tyranny," and "Tyrant" were redacted and replaced with dashes.[9] Anyone who read the list of grievances would have understood that the "P—, whose character is thus marked by every act which may define a t—" was George III. This was self-censorship by the publisher, a strategy to avoid accusations of bias or, worse, sedition.

On August 17, the day after the *Public Advertiser* and *Lloyd's Evening Post*, the Declaration was printed in other London newspapers.[10] The publishers of the *London Chronicle*, the *Middlesex Journal*, and the *Morning Chronicle* printed the text in full.[11] But in Mary Say's *General Evening Post*, another handful of words were redacted, including "king," "Prince," and "ruler," as well as "Great Britain."[12]

Readers of any of these newspapers would have gotten a sense of the Declaration of Independence more or less as the Continental Congress had intended. But readers of other London newspapers had a very different experience. Some London publishers felt that it was necessary to extract or further edit the text.[13] The *Daily Advertiser* only included the "Substance" of the Declaration.[14] That meant summarizing the grievances as "a Number of Proceedings detrimental to the Colonies, most of which have been already mentioned, at different Times, from the Resolutions of their several Assemblies," and stating that the colonists blamed an unspecific "great Person, instead of the Ministry and Parliament." Printing only the "Substance" of the Declaration could be seen as a practical decision, since the full text typically required multiple columns. But the *Daily Advertiser*'s many subscribers—around 3,500 in 1776—would have had to look elsewhere if they wanted to know the colonists' grievances about the king.[15] The publisher also softened "History of the present King of Great Britain" to "History of the present Ruler," and the line about the king's tyrannical character—the one that other publishers had felt the need to censor—was edited out entirely. Mary Say made similar choices in her *Gazetteer and New Daily Advertiser*. Several key sentences were omitted, along with the list of grievances, "*the substance of which have repeatedly appeared in all the public prints.*"[16]

The publisher of the *St. James's Chronicle* chose a different tactic. The list of grievances appears in full, but the pronouns were changed from "He" to "It"—a bizarre glimpse at what the Declaration of Independence might have looked like if the Continental Congress had blamed Parliament, as in their previous petitions.[17] The first grievance, for example, was altered to: "It has refused its Assent to Laws the most wholesome and necessary for the public Good." The grievance that obliquely referred to Parliament proved tricky to twist around. "He has combined with others" turned into "It has combined," throwing off the structure of the sentence.[18] "The History of the present King of Great Britain" transformed into "The present History of Great Britain," and the tyrant prince became the tyranny of "Government." This manipulation of the text saved no space on the page and must have taken considerable effort and concentration. Perhaps this was an act of excessive self-censorship, or perhaps the publisher was trying to make an anti-ministry statement by shifting responsibility to the "Government."

Regardless, readers of the *St. James's Chronicle* would have assumed, as John Laurens had, that they were reading an authentic copy of the Declaration—unless they checked another newspaper.

After he printed the Declaration in his newspaper, Henry Sampson Woodfall called his readers' attention to the Continental Congress's timing. The *Public Advertiser* incorrectly asserted that the Congress had waited to declare independence until after General William Howe had arrived. Woodfall suggested that "nothing can be a greater proof of the resources and courage of the Americans, than reserving their Declaration of independency" until "the whole force of England" was assembling against them.[19] The Congress would not have declared independence "if they had not the *means* of defence, or were not *determined to fight*."[20] But other Londoners, from the king's ministers to newspaper readers, waited with bated breath for news of what had ensued following the arrival of Vice Admiral Richard Howe in New York to join his brother. For all that people in London knew, as they read the Declaration of Independence six weeks after the fact, it might be outdated and could already have been nullified, either by pardons and accommodations offered by the King's Commissioners for Restoring Peace or by the military might of the British fleet.

Once the Declaration was published in London, newspaper contributors could be more specific in their complaints about the text. Some writers immediately questioned whether the Declaration represented the sentiments of all the colonists or just the men sitting in the Continental Congress. Within days of the first newspaper printings of the Declaration in London, "Pacificus" wrote a series of essays about it for the *Morning Chronicle*. This author expected more from "men of education," who had "the appearance at least of reason," than a Declaration built entirely on falsehoods.[21] Pacificus argued that George III was a ruler who "none but the very worst of Rebels, and such alone as are fit to be Delegates in an American Congress, could ever think of stigmatizing with the name of *tyrant*."[22] Other news articles claimed that John Hancock, the president of the Continental Congress, did not support independence at all and had become a "melancholy picture of remorse" after July 4.[23] He had been misguided by the "*arch rebel* and crafty pettifogger, *Adams*."[24] Though John Adams had become more prominent in the Continental Congress as he pushed for independence, in London it was Samuel Adams who was still believed to be the architect of the rebellion, dragging his unwitting colleagues over the edge.[25]

The *Morning Post* printed "*A Reply to the Declaration of the Representatives of the* Disunited States *in* America, *in Congress assembled*," signed "X.Y."[26] This writer used the form of the Declaration to critique its content, writing that all men, "tho' *created equal*, are not intended to remain so,"[27] and that the history of the present king was the "establishment of peace, mercy, and good government." To this writer, the grievances were fallacies. In fact, the king had "nobly refused to pass laws for the accommodation of large districts of deluded people." With the consent of Parliament, he had "sent foreign auxiliaries among a distracted, fanatic, and *uncivil* people." X.Y. believed that the British colonists were a people who were made to be subdued. They had no sovereignty or authority, and they had turned against a king whose character was "great and merciful," not tyrannical. Like any parody, this "Reply" was only legible to someone who knew the true circumstances it was satirizing—in this case, someone who had read the full, unedited text of the Declaration of Independence.

In London, the most provocative thing about the Declaration of Independence was that it was so focused on King George III. Perhaps newspaper publishers in the imperial capital would have treated the Declaration differently if the Continental Congress had focused their ire on the British ministry, or more specifically on Lord George Germain, who was consistently one of the most unpopular men in the London press.[28] But because the Declaration was about the king, it was potentially dangerous to print. Years earlier, Henry Sampson Woodfall, the publisher of the *Public Advertiser*, had been charged with libel for printing pseudonymous letters that were critical of the king.[29] When John Almon published Thomas Paine's *Common Sense* in London in the spring of 1776, he had left long blank spaces in the text instead of daring to print phrases like "the Royal Brute of Great Britain."[30] The difference was that the Declaration was vital news, an update on the war that metropolitan readers needed to see. An essay written by "A true Friend to the Hanover Succession" for the *Gazetteer and New Daily Advertiser* speculated about whether printing the Declaration was a seditious act or not.[31] This writer determined that, although the Declaration might have had the power to unite the colonists, it could not have the same power over Britons. Publishers in London were totally "innocent" because the Declaration could not, "in common sense, be supposed to have any effect in the success of the war," and they could not be held culpable for their role in circulating the news.

The publishers of *The Crisis* already had tested whether they would be tried for sedition if they went a step further and openly supported the rebellion in the colonies. The third issue of this weekly London publication had been so provocative that Parliament ordered copies to be burned amid crowds of spectators.[32] Though Thomas William Shaw was the printer of *The Crisis*, according to the last page of every issue, Samuel Axtell was accused of being the real printer, and he was charged with sedition and fined. The authors, proprietors, and publishers behind *The Crisis* remained a mystery for its entire print run, from January 1775 to October 1776. When the Declaration of Independence appeared in the August 24 issue, it looked less like a piece of news and more like the essays denouncing the king that had made *The Crisis* so controversial. "The following is the Declaration of INDEPENDENCE of the BRAVE, FREE, and VIRTUOUS *Americans*, against the most dastardly, slavish, and vicious TYRANT, that ever disgraced a Nation," the publisher explained.[33] The Declaration was a model of writing against the king.[34] In stark contrast to the newspapers that printed the censored versions of the Declaration, *The Crisis* praised the Continental Congress for calling George III a tyrant.

An intriguing copy of the Declaration of Independence that was printed in London was folded up and inserted in a bound volume of issues of *The Crisis*. It is a broadside, with the text of the Declaration neatly arranged in two columns separated by a double line.[35] Above the title appears a portrait of John Hancock, a serene profile of the president

Figure 9.1 Broadside printed by unknown London printer. Courtesy of the John Carter Brown Library.

of the Continental Congress with a radiant liberty cap above and olive branches below.[36] Surrounded by symbols of liberty, this Hancock looks every bit the ruler of a free people that George III, according to the Declaration, had failed to be. This broadside bears the telltale mark of a London printing, the flipped-around "pretended acts of legislation" at the top of the second column. The back of the broadside is an inky mess of smudged fingerprints and offsetting from when it was originally printed and stacked with many more copies than survive today. After the broadside was folded up and bound with *The Crisis*, the residue from the text of the Declaration and the Hancock portrait transferred from one half of the paper to the other. The ink from the title of one of the issues of *The Crisis* also transferred to the broadside, upside down and mirrored on the ghostly offset portrait. But binding and ink residue might not be the only things connecting this broadside of the Declaration to *The Crisis*. There must have been some overlap between those who subscribed to *The Crisis* and those who purchased the broadsides of the Declaration bearing John Hancock's portrait. In other words, there were people who proudly supported the United States—and its presumed leader—within the British metropole.[37]

The changes that were made to the Declaration of Independence in London traveled to the rest of Great Britain and Europe. As was the case in London, readers' experiences differed depending on which newspaper they read. In the spa destination of Bath, west of London, there were two weekly newspapers, the *Bath Journal* on Mondays and the *Bath Chronicle* on Thursdays. The Declaration was printed in full in the *Journal* on Monday, August 19.[38] But on Thursday, August 22, the publisher of the *Chronicle* censored the word "King" and added a note to his subscribers: "*Our readers will observe that the recital of grievances in the above declaration differs little from those repeatedly published by the Provincial Assemblies; only in this, the Congress have thrown off the mask, and* now *attribute their oppressions to* the King himself."[39] The *Hampshire Chronicle*, in the port city of Southampton on the southern coast of England, copied the London *Daily Advertiser* and published the "substance" of the Declaration.[40] In the burgeoning industrial city of Birmingham, the publishers of the local gazette only printed the conclusion of the Declaration and explained that the Congress prefaced these final paragraphs with "a great many grievances which they say they have suffered."[41]

The Declaration of Independence quickly crossed the Irish Sea and found some sympathetic readers in Ireland.[42] The publisher of the *Hibernian Journal* in Dublin printed the Declaration in full and described it as "the best Explanation of the Rights of the people, which has been published this Age," because it "clearly points out the Duty of the Governor and Governed."[43] Someone writing for the *Hibernian Journal* under the name "Indignans" agreed with this sentiment, arguing that declaring independence was "certainly the wisest Step" that the Continental Congress "could have taken in their present Circumstances."[44] Indignans had harsh words for the king and all his ministers and wondered how the empire could have fallen so far since the death of George II and the ascension of George III. The writer hoped that the "Seperation of thirteen Provinces" would soon be followed by "a Separation of as many Heads" of the king's ministers, "too much fraught with Mischief to deserve to stand any longer on the Shoulders which bore them."

Four days after the Declaration of Independence was first printed in London, excerpts were printed in French and Dutch in newspapers in Utrecht, Leiden, and Haarlem. On August 20, the first and last paragraphs of the Declaration were printed in Dutch in the *Haerlemse Courant*.[45] The publisher, Johannes Enschedé, added a bracketed note explaining that the list of grievances was simply too long to include, which is why he focused on the beginning and the end of the text. But Enschedé's subscribers pushed back. In the next issue of the *Courant* on August 22, the translated list of grievances takes up an entire column on the front page.[46] Enschedé inserted another note, set in italics with a triangle of asterisks to catch readers' attention. Apparently, several subscribers were eager to read the middle of the Declaration in order to understand the reasons why the colonies wanted to separate from Great Britain. The grievances began, "Hy (*namely de K.*) heeft . . . ," or "He (namely the K.) has . . . ."[47] When Enschedé printed the excerpts of the Declaration on August 20, he substituted two asterisks for the word "king." This meant that, after he realized that people in Haarlem were interested in the Declaration, he had to explain the repetitive pronoun in the list of grievances. But he still redacted the words "Tyrant" and "prince." Perhaps it was Enschedé himself who censored the Declaration. More likely, he was copying from a London newspaper that had already obscured these words.

On the same day, August 20, Jean Luzac printed the last paragraph of the Declaration in French in his Leiden gazette, *Nouvelles Extraordinaires de Divers Endroits*.[48] He described the list of grievances—"*les griefs*"—as a summary of the Continental Congress's repeated but always fruitless complaints. The Declaration had been signed by "*le célèbre Jean Hancock*," the famous John Hancock. "*Célèbre*" might have been a reminder to readers of the Leiden gazette that Hancock was the president of the Continental Congress, the man whose name had been attached to many of the Congress's resolutions that had been printed in European newspapers over the previous year. Or Luzac might instead have been hinting at Hancock's more infamous past as a merchant.

The Leiden gazette was one of the most popular newspapers in Europe at this time.[49] It matters, then, that Jean Luzac combined his translation of the conclusion of the Declaration with another paragraph of news from London. On August 14—before the Declaration was printed in London newspapers—the *Morning Chronicle* claimed that:

> Copies of the Declarations of War by the Provincials are now in town, and are said to be couched in the strongest terms—that having now drawn the sword in defence of all that is dear to them, they are determined never to sheath it till a full compensation is made for the cruel oppressions they have sustained.[50]

When Luzac translated this paragraph into French and combined it with the final paragraph of the Declaration of Independence, he gave the impression that this evocative phrase about the "Provincials" drawing the sword originated in the Declaration itself.[51]

The paragraph in the *Morning Chronicle* calls into question whether the Declaration of Independence was a declaration of war. The concluding lines of the Declaration asserted that the United States had "full power to Levy War." But no one in the Continental Congress thought the document they approved on July 4 was a declaration of war. The Declaration came fifteen months into a war that had begun in earnest at Lexington and Concord. If the Congress ever had published a declaration of war, it was in July 1775, when they issued the Declaration of the Causes and Necessity of Taking Up Arms, in tandem with the Olive Branch Petition. That declaration had opposed "ambitious designs of separating from Great Britain" and implored George III to "relieve the Empire from the calamities of civil war."[52] For some colonists, it was the king and Parliament who had declared war through the proclamation of rebellion and the Prohibitory Act. The Declaration of Independence itself said that the king had waged war against his colonists.[53] But the clearest evidence that the Continental Congress did not think that the Declaration was a declaration of war is the fact that the delegates did not send a copy to King George III. The men who drafted, debated, and approved the text knew the law of nations well enough to understand that a declaration of war must "be known to the state against whom it is made."[54]

Jean Luzac helped to propagate the claim that the Declaration of Independence was a declaration of war by streamlining the news from

London into a single paragraph, blending true and imagined excerpts from the Declaration. This paragraph in the Leiden gazette was copied by printers across the European continent.[55] It was reprinted in the French-language *Courier du Bas-Rhin* in Cleves and translated into German in Augsburg and Münster, into Swedish in Stockholm, and into Italian in Bologna.[56] Luzac's description of the famous or "*célèbre*" John Hancock was translated, too: "dem berühmten Johann Hancock" in German, "den namnkunige Johan Hancock" in Swedish, "dal più volte citato Sig. Giovanni Hancock" in Italian, and so on.[57]

On August 30, ten days after he first reported the news of independence, Jean Luzac printed a French translation of the full text of the Declaration of Independence—save for an ellipsis in place of the word "king"—in the *Nouvelles Extraordinaires de Divers Endroits*.[58] Luzac did not explain why he had failed to publish a full translation sooner. The Leiden gazette had a much larger readership than the *Haerlemse Courant*, whose subscribers saw fit to complain that they did not get to read the whole Declaration, so perhaps Luzac's readers had made the same request. In the Leiden gazette, all the grievances were italicized, but a few other words and phrases were italicized as well, including the last part of the third sentence. Luzac drew his readers' attention to the Continental Congress's claim that mankind—"*le Genre humain*"—is more disposed to suffer under bad government than to abolish it altogether.[59] Only a few newspapers copied the full Declaration of Independence from the Leiden gazette. Most translated the misleading paragraph in Luzac's August 20 issue and never revisited the text.

When Jean Luzac printed the Declaration of Independence, he specified that this was a translation "telle qu'elle a été publiée en *Angleterre*"—as published in England.[60] This qualifier was repeated by the small number of printers who copied the full text from the Leiden gazette. But in Florence, for example, the version of the Declaration that was presented to the public was actually the Declaration as published in England, translated into French, and then translated into Italian.[61] Each instance of translation created more opportunities for the Continental Congress's words to lose their meaning. The phrase "merciless Indian Savages" that was approved in English in July became *"les impitoyables* Indiens *Sauvages"* in French in August, and *"I dispretati Indiani selvaggi"* in Italian in September.[62] "Savages" remained consistent, but "merciless" morphed into ruthless, and then despised. The European newspaper publishers that translated literally and directly from London newspapers came closer to what the Continental Congress had intended than the publishers who translated from the Leiden gazette or another non-English newspaper. In Altona, where the Declaration was translated directly from a London newspaper into German, the final phrase—the delegates' commitment of "our Lives, our Fortunes, and our sacred Honor"—reads "unserem Leben, unsern Güten und unsern geheiligten Ehrenworte."[63] But in Münster, the publisher worked from the French translation in Luzac's newspaper, and the phrase in French—"nos vies, nos biens, & notre honneur sacré, &c."—became "unser Gut, Blut, und geheiligte Ehre &c.," ampersand and all.[64]

From its earliest mention in London newspapers, the Declaration of Independence was a paradox. It was described as a declaration of war by "Provincials" rather than by an independent nation. It was a piece of important news that the British ministry neglected to print in the *London Gazette*, leaving other publishers to treat the text as they saw fit. It included a list of grievances that spoke to the king's tyrannical behavior, unless the publishers manipulated the text to erase those accusations. As these newspapers crossed the English Channel, the gap between the Declaration of Independence as originally printed and the one that the "candid World" was reading widened into a chasm that threatened the United States' ability to secure foreign alliances. Europeans read about the Declaration in their newspapers, under the "London" heading, excerpted and translated without any oversight from the Continental Congress. All the while, the Congress had no idea how the Declaration of Independence was being received in Europe or that their agent in Paris was becoming more frustrated by the day.

IO

An Old Storey

Silas Deane Waits for the Declaration

In mid-August 1776, as the news of the Declaration of Independence began to travel through Europe, the seven Lee siblings were spread around the Atlantic. Hannah Corbin and Thomas Ludwell Lee were in the family's home state of Virginia. Richard Henry Lee was leaving Virginia to return to the Continental Congress. Francis Lightfoot Lee and Alice Shippen were both in Philadelphia. William Lee was in London. And the youngest sibling, Arthur Lee, was traveling from London to Paris, much to Silas Deane's surprise.

Unlike Deane, who had just crossed the Atlantic for the first time, Arthur Lee had spent most of his adult life in Europe, studying medicine and law and then serving as a colonial agent. When the Continental Congress created the Committee of Secret Correspondence, they relied on Lee to collect and dispatch intelligence for them in London, with "great circumspection and impenetrable secrecy."[1] When the Congress decided to send Silas Deane to Paris, the committee instructed him to "correspond with Mr. Arthur Lee, agent of the Colonies in London."[2] Despite Lee's connection to the Committee of Secret Correspondence, and despite having a sister in Philadelphia and two brothers in the Continental Congress—including one who had pushed for the vote on independence—Lee probably found out about the Declaration of Independence from a London newspaper.

Arthur Lee left London the same week that the Declaration of Independence was printed in the city's newspapers.[3] On the morning of August 22, Silas Deane learned that Lee would soon be in Paris. He admitted to the French foreign minister, Charles Gravier, the Comte de Vergennes, that this trip was "surprising," since Lee was "the agent of the United Colonies in Great Britain and known to be such."[4] Thus, traveling was risky for him. The only explanation that came to Deane's mind was that Lee "had received some particular intelligence from the United Colonies." The timing of Lee's trip suggests that he wanted to talk to Deane about the Declaration of Independence and how their own roles, as agents of the United States rather than the united colonies, would change. Perhaps Lee believed the reports in London newspapers that the Congress had sent copies of their Declaration to the courts of Europe and thought that Deane might have more information than he did. But Deane, too, had to learn the news of independence through the London press.[5]

Silas Deane expected that he would receive a copy of the Declaration of Independence directly from the Continental Congress. Arthur Lee probably expected this as well. But odds are that both men would have heard the news of independence through British sources even if the Dunlap broadside that the Committee of Secret Correspondence had sent to Deane in July had survived its transatlantic journey. Still, Deane expected that the Congress would send him a special copy of their Declaration, a tool that he could use at the court of Versailles to formalize an alliance between the United States and France. Ideally, the Declaration would be accompanied by a proposed treaty that he could attempt to negotiate. Instead, Deane endured months of silence from the Committee of Secret Correspondence as the news of independence spread all around him.

⊗⊗⊗

"The declaration of independency made by the United Colonies, is announced in the English papers," Silas Deane wrote to Charles-Guillaume-Frédéric Dumas.[6] Deane had just started corresponding with

Dumas, a friend of Benjamin Franklin and the Continental Congress.[7] Dumas lived in the Dutch Republic, where William V, the Prince of Orange and stadtholder, was wary of the Declaration of Independence. It read to him like a poor copy of the 1581 Plakkaat van Verlatinghe, or Act of Abjuration, proclaimed by his ancestors against the Spanish King Philip II.[8] As Dumas and Deane began to write back and forth, Dumas hesitated to sign his name to his letters, for fear of being outed as a friend of the United States too quickly. Meanwhile, Deane wanted to visit Dumas at his home near The Hague, but he was not sure if it would be safe for him to travel in the Dutch Republic.[9] Nevertheless, the two men forged a connection. Deane had to put off his trip after he learned that the Congress had declared independence. He told Dumas that, although he had "received no despatches" from the Congress on the topic, he was "in daily expectation of them."[10] While Arthur Lee was in Paris with Deane, his brother, William, responded to a letter that Dumas had sent to London. Lee told Dumas that the Declaration had "totally changed the nature of the contest."[11] Great Britain could only succeed by "a scheme of conquest, which few imagine can succeed." The British ministry hoped that, before the opening of Parliament in October, they would hear the news of a victory in North America. "In the mean time," Lee wrote, "every effort is made to prevent France from taking any open or even private part with America."

After Arthur Lee left Silas Deane in Paris and returned to London, he found the city on edge, waiting "to hear of a decisive action at New York."[12] He sent a letter to Dumas and assured him that it was safe for him to openly support the United States in the Dutch Republic. The British would need to have a "certain and decisive" victory before they could "venture to attack the friends of America in Europe." "I flatter myself with being as much within the eye of their enmity as any man can be," Lee wrote. He thought that the "enmity of bad men" was a virtuous place to be. Like his brother, Lee could see the effect that the Declaration of Independence was having in London. There was a "publick torpor." The British people did not "seem to feel themselves at all interested in the vast consequences" that flowed from the Declaration. If France allied with the United States, Lee expected that it would be a "shock" that would wake up "a deluded prince and a deluded people."

Arthur Lee may have been in the "eye" of British "enmity" in London, but Silas Deane was drawing British ire in Paris, too, as the news of independence spread. The British ambassador to the court of Versailles was David Murray, the 2nd Earl of Mansfield and Viscount Stormont. At the end of September, Stormont wrote a letter from Paris to the British secretary of state for the Southern Department, Thomas Thynne, 3rd Viscount Weymouth, marked "Most Confidential."[13] Stormont told Weymouth about "Cyrus Deane," who sometimes called himself a native of Bermuda but was "well known" to be "a North American and a secret agent from the Congress." Stormont kept an eye on Deane as he worked to send supplies to North America and received enquiries from Frenchmen who wanted to join the fight for independence. The court of Versailles "cannot be a stranger to these Manœuvres of Deane," Stormont fumed, "and no doubt is glad to wink at them."

Lord Stormont had heard that Silas Deane wanted to be received at Versailles as a representative of the "Independent States of America."[14] The story around Paris, which Stormont shared with Viscount Weymouth, was that Deane had applied for such a reception to the Comte de Vergennes and to Jean Frédéric Phélypeaux, the Comte de Maurepas and first minister of state. But Vergennes and Maurepas had written a response to Deane explaining that they could not grant his request "in the <u>present moment</u>."[15] Stormont was not sure if he could trust this story. "I imagine M. de Maurepas & M. de Vergennes are too cautious to <u>write</u> upon such a subject," Stormont told Weymouth. Stormont knew that it would be "unwise" for the court of Versailles to acknowledge Deane. Such a step would be an "Insult," equal to a "Declaration of War" against Great Britain.

In October 1776, as Lord Stormont sent intelligence about "Cyrus Deane" to London, Silas Deane wrote a series of letters to the Committee of Secret Correspondence in Philadelphia, each one more bitter than the last. On October 1, Deane described how the Continental Congress's "absolute silence" had made the French ministry "extremely uneasy."[16] The situation was made worse by Stormont's "bold assertions" that the

Congress was going to reconcile with Great Britain. "For Heaven's sake," Deane told the Committee of Secret Correspondence, "if you mean to have any connections with this kingdom, be more assiduous in getting your letters here." Deane tried his best to dispute Stormont's claims. But misinformation about the United States continued to spread, and even Charles-Guillaume-Frédéric Dumas was unsure what to believe. He sent a number of questions to Deane about the current state of affairs, and Deane tried his best to respond. He explained that "a reconciliation between Great Britain and the United States of America is improbable ever to take place."[17] He also refuted the stories that had originated in the British press about Benjamin Franklin hedging his bets on independence. "I know what Dr. Franklin's sentiments were when I left America," Deane told Dumas, "and that nothing but a miracle could convert him to wish for an accommodation on other terms than the independence of the Colonies."

On October 8, Silas Deane began another letter to the Committee of Secret Correspondence with a blunt assessment. "Your Declaration of the Fourth of July last has given this court, as well as several others in Europe, reason to expect you would in form announce your independency to them and ask their friendship," Deane explained.[18] After all, the last paragraph of the Declaration—including the Congress's assertion that the United States had the power to contract alliances—was the part that had been reprinted and translated most often in European newspapers, thanks in part to Jean Luzac's Leiden gazette. The lag between the Congress's words and actions was giving Deane "inexpressible anxiety." A few days later, he wrote another letter to Dumas and complained that he was "still without intelligence of any kind from America."[19]

On October 17, Silas Deane "once more put pen to paper, not to attempt what is absolutely beyond the power of language to paint," his "distressed situation" in Paris, "totally destitute of intelligence or instructions."[20] No, he wrote to "plainly inform" the Committee of Secret Correspondence that a French alliance was at extreme risk. The "cause of the United Colonies or United States"—Deane did not know which name to use—had suffered at the court of Versailles for lack of communication from the Continental Congress. Deane had given the French court "every excuse" which his "barren invention could suggest." He had even pleaded what turned out to be the truth—that the Congress must have sent intelligence and instructions for him that had been intercepted. But King Louis XVI's ministers were unconvinced. Ships from North America were arriving at European ports every day. It seemed impossible that not one of them contained a letter for Silas Deane. The only bright spot for Deane was that Edward Bancroft had returned to Paris, and his arrival was well timed. Deane's assistant had just left for Amsterdam, and Bancroft immediately stepped in to help. Deane believed that Bancroft was his friend, though he was probably already a British spy.

In a postscript to the letter that Silas Deane wrote to the Committee of Secret Correspondence on October 17, he complained that the Declaration of Independence was only known in Europe through the newspapers, "on which a serious resolution can not be grounded."[21] If the United States wanted to be acknowledged "among the Powers of the Earth," as the Declaration said, then the courts of Europe needed to see a copy of the Declaration that came directly from the Continental Congress. The Declaration as published in England and translated in a European gazette would not suffice. The next week, Deane addressed the committee again, in "a state of anxiety and perplexity which no words can express."[22] Another week passed, and Deane was livid. He wondered, had the Congress decided against an alliance with France? Had they lost faith in his abilities? "If I am not the proper person to announce your independency and solicit in your behalf," Deane seethed, "let me entreat you to tell me so, and relieve me from an anxiety which is become so intolerable that my life is a burden."[23] Deane still had not heard anything from the Congress since June. He told the Committee of Secret Correspondence that "all Europe have their eyes on the States of America, and are astonished to find month after month rolling away without your applying to them in form."

Finally, in November 1776—four months after the Continental Congress declared independence—Silas Deane received a copy of the Declaration of Independence from the Committee of Secret Correspondence.[24] It was enclosed in a letter that the committee had written on August 7. But the committee also enclosed a copy of the letter they had written to Deane on July 8—just four days after the Congress had declared independence. Deane had spent months assuming, correctly, that the Congress had tried to communicate the Declaration to him but their message had not reached him. He berated the committee for sending a single letter and a single copy of the Declaration in the first place, insisting that duplicates of every message for him "should be lodged in every port, in the hands of faithful and attentive persons, to be forwarded by the first conveyance to any part of Europe."[25] The committee's fear that their message to Deane could end up in British hands had nearly brought the effort to secure an alliance with France to the point of "totally miscarrying for want of intelligence." Deane had waited for so long only to be rewarded with "what had been circulated through Europe": a printed copy of the Declaration.

Silas Deane had expected that the Continental Congress would send a more formal copy of the Declaration of Independence to France with an official seal or signatures. Instead, the Committee of Secret Correspondence more than likely sent him a Dunlap broadside, as they had tried to do in their first attempt to share the Declaration with him. "I certainly prefer simplicity of style, as well as manners," Deane wrote. But the Dunlap broadside was not particularly impressive or permanent, especially in the gilded halls of Versailles. If the Continental Congress wanted Deane to introduce the United States "among the established powers and rank with them," then a printed broadside would not suffice. Still, Deane tried to make the most of his long-awaited communication. He had clerks copy out the text by hand in English, and he had it translated into French.[26] Deane immediately requested an audience with the Comte de Vergennes, "having received Dispatches from America of very great importance."[27]

In late November 1776, Silas Deane went to the court of Versailles and formally presented the Declaration of Independence to the French ministry. He explained that the Continental Congress had "taken the earliest opportunity of informing this court of the declaration of their independency," but their July 8 letter and the copy of the Declaration it enclosed did not reach their destination.[28] Though Deane's belated announcement was "well received" by the French court, there was still much to be done before France could acknowledge the United States as an independent country and an ally.[29] Misinformation was still working against Deane's efforts. Versailles was buzzing with the report—attributed to a letter sent from Philadelphia to London—that Deane had advised the Congress to negotiate with King George III's Commissioners for Restoring Peace because he "could obtain no assistance from Europe." This incensed Deane. "You can hardly conceive how dangerous even such reports are," he told the Committee of Secret Correspondence, "and how prejudicial every step that looks like confirming them."[30] The Congress's inability to get a copy of the Declaration of Independence to Silas Deane, and their naïveté about the formality expected by European courts, hurt the United States. If Deane had received the committee's letter and the Dunlap broadside that had been sent to him on July 8, perhaps he would have been able to secure a treaty of alliance with France more quickly—or perhaps not. Regardless, Deane "presented the declaration of Independency" to the French court "after it had indeed become an Old Storey in every part of Europe."[31]

The persistent silence from Philadelphia had sent Silas Deane's mind in all different directions, collecting as much intelligence and repudiating as much misinformation from London as he possibly could. He thought up strategies to distract the British forces. In October, he suggested that the Continental Congress could instigate an uprising of enslaved laborers in the Caribbean colonies to draw British ships away from North America. He clarified that this plan was "not employing slaves," even though "the example of our enemy authorizes" such a strategy—a reference to Lord Dunmore's Black regiment.[32] Two months later, Deane still thought the idea was a good one and advised the Committee of Secret Correspondence that the United States could play Great Britain's "own game" against them through strategic insurrections on the islands of Saint Vincent and Jamaica.[33] Perhaps Deane had read reports from London of British authorities foiling a planned uprising in the parish of Hanover in Jamaica in July 1776. Half of the enslaved people who were brought to trial for their alleged role in this conspiracy were acquitted, but the other half were whipped, transported to other colonies, or executed.[34] Deane's anxious brainstorming of ideas to help the United States did not account for these kinds of casualties.

Silas Deane also continued thinking of ways to endear the United States to France. He pitched ideas for gifts that the Continental Congress could send to the French queen, who seemed sympathetic. Marie Antoinette loved horseback riding, and Deane wondered if she might enjoy "a fine Narragansett Horse or Two" or "a pair of Bay Horses."[35] Deane remembered the orrery, a beautiful mechanical model of the solar system that David Rittenhouse had built a few years earlier, and wondered if it could be shipped from Philadelphia to Versailles. Any "curious American productions" would, "though trifles in themselves, be of consequence rightly timed and placed."[36] Deane was desperate to improve the United States' image in France. And indeed help was on the way, in the form of the most famous American in the world. While Deane was writing about horses and other "trifles," Benjamin Franklin was sailing into the French port of Auray.[37]

In the fall of 1776, while Silas Deane waited for any sort of communication from the Committee of Secret Correspondence, the Continental Congress created the United States' first official diplomatic corps. On October 2, the committee wrote to let Deane know that the Congress had agreed on a draft treaty of commerce and alliance with France.[38] Deane's work would transition from secret to public as he was appointed a commissioner to negotiate the treaty. He was supposed to be joined by Benjamin Franklin and Thomas Jefferson. But Jefferson had returned home to Virginia in September.[39] He insisted on being with his ailing wife, Martha, who had miscarried while he was with the Congress in Philadelphia.[40] Jefferson brought his family to Williamsburg to stay in

George Wythe's house near the Capitol while he served in the Virginia Assembly. There, he received a letter from John Hancock with his commission and instructions to sail to France separately from Franklin, to increase the odds that at least one of them would arrive safely.[41] Jefferson spent three days debating whether to go or not. Ultimately, he refused the appointment, because felt he could not leave his family behind or safely bring them with him.[42] Jefferson was sure that there were many other men in the Congress who could take his place. Instead, the Congress decided that Arthur Lee would be the third commissioner.

Silas Deane was "most agreeably surprised" by Benjamin Franklin's arrival in France.[43] It had taken only thirty days for Franklin to sail from the capes of the Delaware River to Quiberon Bay, and when he reached land on December 4 he immediately wrote to Deane.[44] Franklin made sure that Deane knew about their commission and about the replacement of Thomas Jefferson by Arthur Lee. Until he could join Deane in Paris, Franklin hoped to travel incognito. But that proved to be impossible. As Deane wrote to the Comte de Vergennes, Franklin's arrival in France was the "common topic of conversation" in Paris and had "given birth to a thousand conjectures and reports."[45] Though Deane himself kept up the ruse, insisting that he was "ignorant" of Franklin's motives or business in France, he wrote to Charles-Guillaume-Frédéric Dumas, "here is the hero, and philosopher, and patriot, all united in this celebrated American, who at the age of seventy-four, risks all dangers for his country."[46] Deane also sent word to Arthur Lee in London to come to Paris "without delay, for the news of Mr. Franklin's arrival may occasion his friends being forbid coming from London to France." Lee wrote back that he would be gratified to serve the United States "in a public character"—glad to "bid adieu, perhaps forever," to his covert life in the imperial capital—and thrilled to join Deane and Franklin, "our Pater Patriae."[47]

⊗⊗⊗

The Continental Congress had high hopes for their Declaration of Independence in Europe. They needed the old powers to acknowledge the United States as a new power. But the courts of Europe needed to hear directly from the Congress, to see an authenticated copy of the Declaration, and to know what the United States intended to be. Instead, Europeans had learned about the Declaration in their newspapers and fallen into the trap of British misinformation. By the time Silas Deane heard directly from the Committee of Secret Correspondence and felt empowered to present the Declaration to the French court, independence was an "Old Storey." Deane's increasingly irate letters to the committee in the fall of 1776 would not reach the Congress until 1777, by which time the delegates had been forced to leave Philadelphia.

Conclusion

A Lasting Testimony

On June 28, 1776, Oliver Wolcott left Philadelphia. He had arrived in January, and had been anxious to leave. Life in the city, especially during wartime, was pricey, about six times more expensive than at his home in Litchfield, Connecticut. He had quickly tired of seeing unfamiliar faces around town and hearing the constant rumble of the streets, which was "farr from being musical."[1] Soon, the sweltering summer weather would make Philadelphia an even more unpleasant place to be. In addition, Wolcott's health had declined, from "a long Attention to Business of the Sedentary Kind"—sitting in the Continental Congress, day after day. "I do most sincerely Wish to return to the Pleasures of a domestick rural Life," Wolcott wrote to his wife, Laura. He had waited as his colleagues Roger Sherman and Samuel Huntington spent weeks at home, away from the Congress, until finally it was his turn.[2] On his way to Connecticut, Wolcott stopped in New York on July 1 and took stock of the Continental Army's preparations for the British fleet.[3] He arrived in Litchfield on July 4. Instead of spending that week sitting in the Pennsylvania State House debating independence, Oliver Wolcott got what so many of his colleagues in the Congress desperately wanted: fresh air and time with family.

Oliver Wolcott is remembered as a signer of the Declaration of Independence, but he did not vote for independence. Nor would he sign the parchment copy of the Declaration on August 2, when the majority of his fellow delegates did. Wolcott received the news of independence in Litchfield the week after July 4, around the same time that carts rolled into town carrying the dismembered statue of King George III.[4] A few pieces had been stolen on the 100-mile journey from Manhattan, but the carts still held more than one ton of lead.[5] This was unloaded at Wolcott's foundry in Litchfield, and his children and a few local women set to work melting down the "leaden George" into bullets. Eleven-year-old Mary Ann Wolcott produced more than 10,000 bullets, her fourteen-year-old sister Laura made over 8,000, and their eight-year-old brother Frederick added nearly 1,000 to a total of more than 42,000 bullets, ready to fire at the British forces.[6] Soon, Wolcott himself would be called to war.

Oliver Wolcott spent five weeks at home before taking to the road again, this time as a brigadier general in the Connecticut militia.[7] On August 27, he watched from Manhattan as the British forces that had been amassing at Staten Island for two months finally attacked. General George Washington was forced to retreat. By the end of September, Wolcott's brigade was so depleted that Washington discharged the remaining men, and Wolcott traveled south to Philadelphia and took his seat again in the Continental Congress.[8] Any improvement to his health during his time in Connecticut was wrecked by his service in New York. Wolcott told his wife that he planned to stay in Philadelphia "till the Expiration of my Delegation."[9] He did not expect to be reappointed to the Congress. He had already spent enough time away from his family, living a "Solicitous Life." He assured Laura that if anyone had ambitions to take his place in the Connecticut delegation, "I shall not quarrel." Wolcott did not know that, just a few days before he wrote those words, he had been reappointed for another year.[10]

By the time Oliver Wolcott returned to Philadelphia in October 1776, fifty-three delegates had signed the parchment copy of the Declaration of Independence.[11] Their experience of solemnly pledging their lives and fortunes to the cause of independence as a group before the British attacked New York must have been different from Wolcott's experience of signing alone after witnessing the battle in Manhattan firsthand. On August 2, the president of the Continental Congress, John Hancock, became the first to add his famous signature to the parchment. The rest of the delegates signed in state order, from north to south, in columns from right to left.[12] The first column on the right side of the parchment begins with Josiah Bartlett and William Whipple—whose smaller signatures started the trend that made Hancock's look disproportionately large—then Samuel Adams, John Adams, and Robert Treat Paine of Massachusetts. Elbridge Gerry had left Philadelphia in mid-July, as "worn out of Health, by the Fatigues of this station" as Wolcott.[13] He expected that the Declaration would be signed while he was away, and asked John Adams to sign his name by proxy.[14] Instead, the delegates kept a blank space between the Massachusetts signatures and Rhode Island delegate Stephen Hopkins's shaky signature until Gerry returned to the Congress in September and signed the parchment himself. After Hopkins's name was William Ellery, and then the Connecticut delegation: Roger Sherman, Samuel Huntington, and William Williams, who had joined the Congress during Wolcott's absence. When Wolcott signed the parchment Declaration in October, his name was at the bottom right corner, the last name in this column of New Englanders and the fifty-fourth signature on the parchment.

On July 4, Matthew Thornton was serving as president of the New Hampshire Provincial Assembly, and he would only be appointed to the Continental Congress in September 1776. Yet, when he arrived in Philadelphia on November 3, he became the fifty-fifth signer of the Declaration of Independence. Not all the other signers were members of the Congress on July 4, either. Charles Carroll of Carrollton had been appointed to the Maryland delegation on the day itself, and more than half of Pennsylvania's delegation had been replaced on July 20.[15] But the signature of Thornton, who had been appointed to the Congress months after independence was declared, feels out of place. In fact, his signature is physically out of place, at the bottom of the column of New Englanders, below Oliver Wolcott. Since Josiah Bartlett and William Whipple had not expected that any other New Hampshire delegates would sign the Declaration, there was no room left between their signatures and the first signature of the Massachusetts delegation.

The fifty-sixth signature on the parchment is the most mysterious. Thomas McKean had been instrumental in the vote for independence. The Delaware delegation had been divided on July 1—McKean in favor of independence and George Read against—and McKean had written hastily to Caesar Rodney, imploring him to come to Philadelphia to vote. But soon after July 4, McKean left the Congress to join the Pennsylvania Associators—military volunteers— in New Jersey. He did not sign the parchment copy of the Declaration on August 2 or for some time thereafter, as he sporadically attended the Congress's meetings. McKean may actually have signed as late as 1781, the year that he became president of the Continental Congress. For at least the first few months—if not the first few years—of its existence, the signed parchment Declaration only had fifty-five signatures.[16]

Looking at the parchment, it is a challenge to identify who signed the Declaration of Independence when. Unlike the United States Constitution, which sits alongside the Declaration in the rotunda of the National Archives in Washington, DC, the parchment was not signed on a single day.[17] And the state delegations were not labeled by state on the Declaration, as they would be on the Constitution.

The signatures of the men who signed after August 2 typically appear after the rest of those in their delegations. Matthew Thornton's lone signature at the bottom of the right-hand column, separate from his state's delegation, is one exception. Another exception is in the Virginia delegation, where the signatures follow this order: George Wythe, Richard Henry Lee, Thomas Jefferson, Benjamin Harrison, Thomas Nelson, Jr., Francis Lightfoot Lee, and Carter Braxton. But Jefferson was actually the first Virginian to sign. Wythe and Lee were still in Virginia on August 2. Jefferson exercised one last bit of influence over how the Declaration would look by intentionally leaving space above his name where his friends and mentors could sign when they returned to Philadelphia.[18] Though Jefferson would later insist that "Author of the Declaration of American Independence" should be inscribed at the top of the obelisk marking his grave, in 1776 he did not want his name to be at the top of the Virginia signers.[19]

The fifty-six men known and celebrated as the signers of the Declaration of Independence were never in the same room at the same time. The signatures are not a record of the delegates who approved the Declaration on July 4 or the men who were in the Pennsylvania State House on August 2, when the parchment copy was ready to be signed. Focusing on the signatures obscures the impact of the delegates who were part of the story but did not sign. Robert R. Livingston, who was a member of the Committee of Five that had drafted the Declaration, never signed the parchment. After petitioning the Congress multiple times, he had been allowed to return home to New York to work on the state's new constitution, and he would not return to the Congress for several years.[20] The collective memory of the United States takes the signers and the parchment copy of the Declaration of Independence for granted, without considering the contexts behind the individual signatures, or those, like Livingston's, that were never added to the document.

⊗⊗⊗

In December 1776, Charles Thomson packed up the signed parchment copy of the Declaration of Independence and the rest of the Continental Congress's papers. Seven months had passed since Philadelphia first felt threatened by HMS *Roebuck* and HMS *Liverpool* sailing up the Delaware River. By year's end, General William Howe was in Trenton, New Jersey, and General George Washington had been forced across the river to Pennsylvania. Philadelphia was at serious risk of a British invasion and the Congress was no longer safe. On December 11, Oliver Wolcott wrote to assure Laura that, "if the Enemy should drive us out of this City (which I do not really expect) you will soon hear to what Place I shall go."[21] The next day, the Congress decided that Baltimore was the place. Wolcott wrote another letter to his wife: "The present Scene it is true Appears somewhat gloomy," he confided.[22] But the words of the Declaration of Independence echoed in Wolcott's own declaration that Great Britain would soon learn the "Folly of attempting to Inslave a People who by the Tyes of Consanguinity and affection ever were desirous of promoting her truest Happiness."

The delegates made the frigid journey 100 miles southwest and reconvened at a spacious Baltimore tavern on December 20.[23] Wolcott found Baltimore to be "infinitely the most dirty Place" he had ever been, and he told his wife that "no One can Walk about here but in Boots."[24] And it was even more expensive than Philadelphia.[25] Still, Wolcott and his colleagues understood that the Congress could function only if they were at a safe distance from the theater of war.

A few delegates stayed behind in Philadelphia, including Robert Morris. On the day the Continental Congress convened in Baltimore, Morris "with a heavy heart" wrote to Silas Deane.[26] He could not give Deane an exact account of everything that had happened before the Congress had evacuated because he had sent the papers he would have referenced to the safety of the Pennsylvania countryside, along with his wife, Mary, and their four young children. But Morris summarized the dire situation for both the Continental Army and the Continental Congress. He told Deane that there were only "two Chances for relief—one is from you." If France declared war on Great Britain, it would "Change the fate of affairs." But Morris insisted, "they must do it Soon." If time was lost to "tedious negociations," then the only option left for the United States would be to "sue for peace from her oppressors." Morris asked Deane to show his hasty and emotional "scrawl" to Benjamin Franklin and Arthur Lee. Much of the fate of the United States was in the hands of the Continental Congress's new diplomatic corps in Paris.

"These are the times that try men's souls," Thomas Paine wrote in the first number of *The American Crisis,* printed in Philadelphia after the Continental Congress left.[27] The summer joy of independence had been chilled by successive British victories. But there were glimmers of hope from the Continental Army. On Christmas night, George Washington sailed from Pennsylvania across the Delaware River and his soldiers took control of Trenton. This was soon followed by another victory in nearby

Princeton. Because of the British ships that were a constant presence between Cape May and Cape Henlopen, Robert Morris still had not sent his December 20 letter to Silas Deane. So he added to his letter an account of how Washington had surprised the German soldiers in Trenton and made strategic moves in New Jersey that had caused many more casualties for the British than for the Continental Army. Morris told Deane that it was the perfect time for France to join the war, "whilst we have strength."[28] Finally, at the end of January, Morris saw an opportunity to send his message to Deane safely down the Delaware River and, hopefully, on to France. Though the army's recent victories had boosted morale, Morris's tone remained nervous and he was insistent that the United States needed immediate support from France.[29]

On January 18, 1777, in Baltimore, the Continental Congress ordered a new printing of the Declaration of Independence, an "authenticated copy" including the names of the delegates who had signed the parchment.[30] Perhaps the Continental Army's recent victories in New Jersey had inspired the Continental Congress. Or maybe the Congress's evacuation from Philadelphia had convinced the delegates that they needed to create a public record of what was on the parchment. The job of printing authenticated broadside copies of the Declaration went to Mary Katharine Goddard. A printer and postmaster, Goddard had become one of the busiest people in Baltimore upon the Congress's relocation. In July, she had printed the Declaration in her *Maryland Journal*, relying on one of the first printings of the Declaration, either one of John Dunlap's broadsides or the version printed in Benjamin Towne's *Pennsylvania Evening Post*.[31] In January, Goddard relied on the signed parchment copy.

The Goddard broadsides marked a transition for the Declaration of Independence from news to archival treasure. These were the first printed copies of the Declaration to include the title approved on July 19, 1776: "THE UNANIMOUS DECLARATION OF THE Thirteen United States of AMERICA."[32] Goddard organized the text in two columns separated by a line of typographical ornaments. She emphasized with capital letters the religious invocations in the text, including

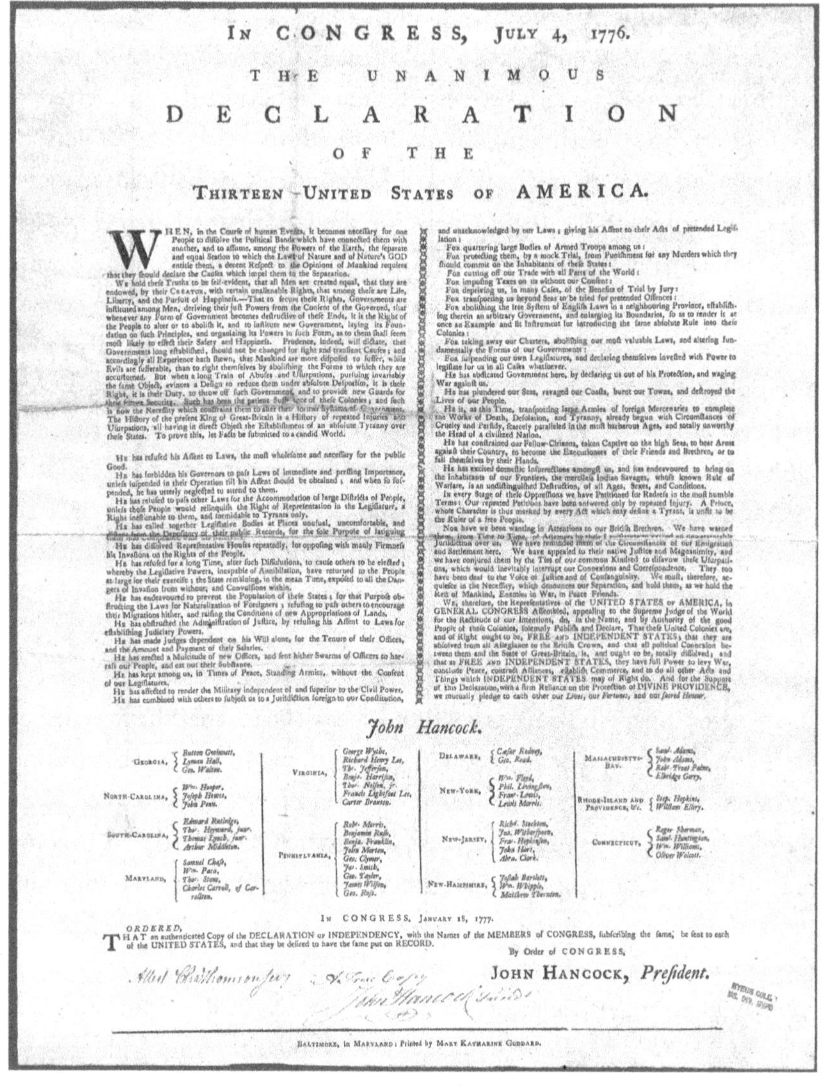

Figure C.1 Broadside printed by Mary Katharine Goddard. The New York Public Library.

"Nature's GOD" and "DIVINE PROVIDENCE."[33] Goddard also italicized the delegates' pledge of their "*Lives*," "*Fortunes*," and "*sacred Honour*."[34] Below the text sits John Hancock's name, in large italics; the rest of the delegates' names are grouped and labeled by delegation. (Matthew Thornton's name appears with the other New Hampshire signers.) But she misunderstood the organization of the delegations on the parchment, reading the names from left to right instead of from right to left, and organizing the states in four columns instead of five. The north-south order was thereby lost, as North Carolina was listed after Georgia, and so on across the page.

There are only fifty-five printed names in the list of signers on Mary Katharine Goddard's broadside. The Delaware delegation is missing Thomas McKean, who had not yet signed the parchment. But each Goddard broadside bears another printed name, as well as two signatures. The imprint at the bottom of the broadside announced that these copies of the Declaration had been printed in "Baltimore, in Maryland" by Mary Katharine Goddard, not "M. K. Goddard" as she typically abbreviated her name in the colophon of the *Maryland Journal*. Above her name, she included the Continental Congress's January 18 order and left space for John Hancock and Charles Thomson to authenticate each broadside with their signatures, so that each state would know that the broadside they received was an authenticated "true copy" of the signed parchment. The two names that had accompanied the Declaration of Independence from John Dunlap's first printing—John Hancock and Charles Thomson— were finally rendered as handwritten signatures, Hancock's more famous name alongside Thomson's less famous but no less important one.[35]

The Continental Congress did not need hundreds of Goddard broadsides in the way they had needed hundreds of Dunlap broadsides. They only required thirteen broadsides, one authenticated copy of the Declaration for each of the thirteen states. It took about two weeks for Goddard's printing office to complete this work. On January 31, John Hancock wrote a circular letter to the state governments. He explained that "there is not a more distinguished Event in the History of America, than the Declaration of her Independence—nor any that in all Probability, will so much excite the Attention of future Ages."[36] The Continental Congress wanted these broadsides of the Declaration to be "preserved in the most careful Manner that can be devised," so that the United States would remember why the Congress had decided to declare independence from Great Britain. Hancock sent his letter and a Goddard broadside to each state, to "remain a lasting Testimony of your approbation of that necessary & important Measure." These broadsides would lay the foundations of the various states' archives.[37]

The broadside that John Hancock sent to Rhode Island is still in the state archives in Providence, the town where Mary Katharine Goddard had learned the printing trade alongside her mother, Sarah, and her brother, William.[38] But Rhode Island's Goddard broadside was not preserved in the most careful manner. Over time, tears that resembled lightning bolts cracked the brittle paper. The famous second sentence of the Declaration was split in half, and another tear ruptured the final paragraph. Conservators have hydrated and carefully mended the paper so that it looks like a complete sheet again.[39] But at the bottom of the broadside, there is damage that cannot be undone. A thick black ink line pierces through the imprint where, sometime after January 1777, someone blotted out Goddard's name from the broadside she had printed. Rhode Island's copy of the Declaration of Independence has survived in the state archives as "a lasting Testimony," but Goddard's name has been erased, for reasons unknown.

In July 1776 and January 1777, the Continental Congress wanted to disseminate copies of the Declaration of Independence. But their reasons were different in each moment. On July 4, 1776, the Declaration was news. It was information that needed to travel quickly. Six months later, the Declaration was no longer news. The Goddard broadsides were not designed to be read publicly or privately. They were instead an authenticated, printed record of the Congress's commitment to securing the independence of the United States. In July 1776, the Congress had depended on public celebrations of the Declaration across the colonies-turned-states to foster a sense of unified identity in a contentious moment. In January 1777, however, the Congress wanted to bring the state archives into alignment with one another, in expectation that "future Ages" would look to the Declaration as the defining moment in the history of the United States.

Six months after the Continental Congress declared independence, the future of the United States was still uncertain. New York City was under British control and, although British forces did not invade Philadelphia in December 1776 as was feared, in September 1777 General William Howe would march into the city. The Continental Army found some success in New Jersey in the winter of 1776, but the following winter in Valley Forge would prove bleak.

Across the United States, couples honored John Hancock by naming their children after him. Meanwhile, John and Dorothy Hancock's own daughter, Lydia, born in Philadelphia in October 1776, would die in infancy. The Continental Congress had empowered Silas Deane, Benjamin Franklin, and Arthur Lee to negotiate an alliance between France and the United States. But the treaty would not be agreed to until 1778, and it would take years for other European powers to recognize the independence and sovereignty of the United States. Though the Massachusetts Council agreed to a treaty of alliance with the Mi'kmaq and Wolostaqiyik in July 1776, the first formal treaty between the United States and Native powers would not come about until September 1778 at Fort Pitt. The work of forming new state governments and a confederation among the states would drag on, too. The Articles of Confederation, the third product of the Lee Resolutions, are not on display in the rotunda of the National Archives alongside the Declaration because they did not last and were ultimately replaced by the United States Constitution.

In the crucial months between John Dunlap's broadside and Mary Katharine Goddard's broadside, when the Declaration of Independence was news, it was a story in a steady stream of information and misinformation. The likelihood that the Declaration would be successful—that the United States would survive—rose and fell with the news of military victories and defeats, new plans of government, and commercial opportunities and embargos. Nevertheless, in January 1777, John Hancock was confident that the Continental Congress's decision to declare independence would be the most "distinguished Event in the history of America."[40]

Appendix

Transcription of the Dunlap Broadside of the Declaration of Independence

In CONGRESS, July 4, 1776.
A DECLARATION
By the REPRESENTATIVES of the
UNITED STATES OF AMERICA,
In GENERAL CONGRESS assembled.

WHEN in the Course of human Events, it becomes necessary for one People to dissolve the Political Bands which have connected them with another, and to assume among the Powers of the Earth, the separate and equal Station to which the Laws of Nature and of Nature's God entitle them, a decent Respect to the Opinions of Mankind requires that they should declare the causes which impel them to the Separation.

We hold these Truths to be self-evident, that all Men are created equal, that they are endowed by their Creator with certain unalienable Rights, that among these are Life, Liberty, and the Pursuit of Happiness— –That to secure these Rights, Governments are instituted among Men, deriving their just Powers from the Consent of the Governed, that whenever any Form of Government becomes destructive of these Ends, it is the Right of the People to alter or to abolish it, and to institute new Government, laying its Foundation on such Principles, and organizing its Powers in such Form, as to them shall seem most likely to effect their Safety and Happiness. Prudence, indeed, will dictate that Governments long established should not be changed for light and transient Causes; and accordingly all Experience hath shewn, that Mankind are more disposed to suffer, while Evils are sufferable, than to right themselves by abolishing the Forms to which they are accustomed. But when a long Train of Abuses and Usurpations, pursuing invariably the same Object, evinces a Design to reduce them under absolute Despotism, it is their Right, it is their Duty, to throw off such Government, and to provide new Guards for their future Security. Such has been the patient Sufferance of these Colonies; and such is now the Necessity which constrains them to alter their former Systems of Government. The History of the present King of Great-Britain is a History of repeated Injuries and Usurpations, all having in direct Object the Establishment of an absolute Tyranny over these States. To prove this, let Facts be submitted to a candid World.

He has refused his Assent to Laws, the most wholesome and necessary for the public Good.

He has forbidden his Governors to pass Laws of immediate and pressing Importance, unless suspended in their Operation till his Assent should be obtained; and when so suspended, he has utterly neglected to attend to them.

He has refused to pass other Laws for the Accommodation of large Districts of People, unless those People would relinquish the Right of Representation in the Legislature, a Right inestimable to them, and formidable to Tyrants only.

He has called together Legislative Bodies at Places unusual, uncomfortable, and distant from the Depository of their public Records, for the sole Purpose of fatiguing them into Compliance with his Measures.

He has dissolved Representative Houses repeatedly, for opposing with manly Firmness his Invasions on the Rights of the People.

He has refused for a long Time, after such Dissolutions, to cause others to be elected; whereby the Legislative Powers, incapable of Annihilation, have returned to the People at large for their exercise; the State remaining in the mean time exposed to all the Dangers of Invasion from without, and Convulsions within.

He has endeavoured to prevent the Population of these States; for that Purpose obstructing the Laws for Naturalization of Foreigners; refusing to pass others to encourage their Migrations hither, and raising the Conditions of new Appropriations of Lands.

He has obstructed the Administration of Justice, by refusing his Assent to Laws for establishing Judiciary Powers.

He has made Judges dependent on his Will alone, for the Tenure of their Offices, and the Amount and Payment of their Salaries.

He has erected a Multitude of new Offices, and sent hither Swarms of Officers to harrass our People, and eat out their Substance.

He has kept among us, in Times of Peace, Standing Armies, without the consent of our Legislatures.

He has affected to render the Military independent of and superior to the Civil Power.

He has combined with others to subject us to a Jurisdiction foreign to our Constitution, and unacknowledged by our Laws; giving his Assent to their Acts of pretended Legislation:

For quartering large Bodies of Armed Troops among us:

For protecting them, by a mock Trial, from Punishment for any Murders which they should commit on the Inhabitants of these States:

For cutting off our Trade with all Parts of the World:

For imposing Taxes on us without our Consent:

For depriving us, in many Cases, of the Benefits of Trial by Jury:

For transporting us beyond Seas to be tried for pretended Offences:

For abolishing the free System of English Laws in a neighbouring Province, establishing therein an arbitrary Government, and enlarging its Boundaries, so as to render it at once an Example and fit Instrument for introducing the same absolute Rule into these Colonies:

For taking away our Charters, abolishing our most valuable Laws, and altering fundamentally the Forms of our Governments:

For suspending our own Legislatures, and declaring themselves invested with Power to legislate for us in all Cases whatsoever.

He has abdicated Government here, by declaring us out of his Protection and waging War against.

He has plundered our Seas, ravaged our Coasts, burnt our Towns, and destroyed the Lives of our People.

He is, at this Time, transporting large Armies of foreign Mercenaries to compleat the Works of Death, Desolation, and Tyranny, already begun with circumstances of Cruelty and Perfidy, scarcely paralleled in the most barbarous Ages, and totally unworthy the Head of a civilized Nation.

He has constrained our fellow Citizens taken Captive on the high Seas to bear Arms against their Country, to become the Executioners of their Friends and Brethren, or to fall themselves by their Hands.

He has excited domestic Insurrections amongst us, and has endeavoured to bring on the Inhabitants of our Frontiers, the merciless Indian Savages, whose known Rule of Warfare, is an undistinguished Destruction, of all Ages, Sexes and Conditions.

In every stage of these Oppressions we have Petitioned for Redress in the most humble Terms: Our repeated Petitions have been answered only by repeated Injury. A Prince, whose Character is thus marked by every act which may define a Tyrant, is unfit to be the Ruler of a free People.

Nor have we been wanting in Attentions to our British Brethren. We have warned them from Time to Time of Attempts by their Legislature to extend an unwarrantable Jurisdiction over us. We have reminded them of the Circumstances of our Emigration and Settlement here. We have appealed to their native Justice and Magnanimity, and we have conjured them by the Ties of our common Kindred to disavow these Usurpations, which, would inevitably interrupt our Connections and Correspondence. They too have been deaf to the Voice of Justice and of Consanguinity. We must, therefore, acquiesce in the Necessity, which denounces our Separation, and hold them, as we hold the rest of Mankind, Enemies in War, in Peace, Friends.

We, therefore, the Representatives of the UNITED STATES OF AMERICA, in General Congress, Assembled, appealing to the Supreme Judge of the World for the Rectitude of our Intentions, do, in the Name, and by Authority of the good People of these Colonies, solemnly Publish and Declare, That these United Colonies are, and of Right ought to be, Free and Independent States; that they are absolved from all Allegiance to the British Crown, and that all political Connection between them and the State of Great-Britain, is and ought to be totally dissolved; and that as Free and Independent States, they have full Power to levy War, conclude Peace, contract Alliances, establish Commerce, and to do all other Acts and Things which Independent States may of right do. And for the support of this Declaration, with a firm Reliance on the Protection of divine Providence, we mutually pledge to each other our Lives, our Fortunes, and our sacred Honor.

Signed by Order *and in* Behalf *of the* Congress,
JOHN HANCOCK, President.

Attest.
CHARLES THOMSON, Secretary.

Philadelphia: Printed by John Dunlap.

Notes

ABBREVIATIONS

AFC   Adams Family Correspondence

CO   National Archives (UK), Colonial Office Papers

CSC   Committee of Secret Correspondence

DJA   *Diary and Autobiography of John Adams*

GL   Gilder Lehrman Institute of American History

JCC   *Journals of the Continental Congress*

LDC   *Letters of Delegates to the Continental Congress*

NDAR   *Naval Documents of the American Revolution*

PBSA   *Papers of the Bibliographical Society of America*

PMHB   *Pennsylvania Magazine of History and Biography*

PGW   *Papers of George Washington*

PJJ   *Papers of John Jay*

PTJ   *Papers of Thomas Jefferson*

RDC   *The Revolutionary Diplomatic Correspondence of the United States*

SP   National Archives (UK), State Papers

WMQ   *William and Mary Quarterly*

INTRODUCTION

1. Mary [Polly] Palmer to John Adams, August 4, 1776, *AFC*, vol. 2, 76–78.
2. Frederick Tupper and Helen Tyler Brown, eds., *Grandmother Tyler's Book: The Recollections of Mary Palmer Tyler (Mrs. Royall Tyler) 1775–1866* (G. P. Putnam's Sons, 1925), 23.
3. Abigail [Smith] Adams's sister, Mary, was married to Richard Cranch, who was Polly Palmer's father Joseph's brother-in-law. John Adams knew Joseph Palmer—who was often called "Deacon Palmer" in this period of the Adams family's correspondence—but made no mention of Polly in his correspondence until his courtship with Abigail began.
4. Tupper and Brown, *Grandmother Tyler's Book*, 23–24.
5. John Adams to Abigail Smith [Adams], April 7–9, 1764, *AFC*, vol. 1, 16–19.
6. John Adams to Abigail Smith [Adams], May 4, 1764, *AFC*, vol. 1, 43.
7. Tupper and Brown, *Grandmother Tyler's Book*, 23–25. The family friend was Colonel Josiah Quincy.
8. Mary [Polly] Palmer to John Adams, June 15–17, 1776, *AFC*, vol. 2, 9–12.
9. Ibid.

10. John Adams to Samuel Cooper, July 2, 1776, *PJA*, vol. 4, 357–58.

11. John Adams to Mary [Polly] Palmer, July 5, 1776, *AFC*, vol. 2, 34–35.

12. John Adams to Abigail [Smith] Adams, July 3, 1776, *AFC*, vol. 2, 27–29.

13. John Adams to William Gordon, May 26, 1780, *PJA*, vol. 9, 342–44.

14. John Adams to Benjamin Rush, April 4, 1790, *PJA*, vol. 20, 304–308.

15. John Adams to Mary [Polly] Palmer, July 5, 1776, *AFC*, vol. 2, 34–35.

16. My thanks to Sara Georgini for confirming the *PJA* editors' position that the copy of the Declaration of Independence enclosed in John Adams's letter was more than likely a Dunlap broadside.

17. John Adams to Mary [Polly] Palmer, July 5, 1776, *AFC*, vol. 2, 34–35.

18. Mary [Polly] Palmer to John Adams, August 4, 1776, *AFC*, vol. 2, 76–78.

19. Polly Palmer, her mother, and her sister moved to Peacefield after her father's death in 1788.

20. Mary [Polly] Palmer to John Adams, November 25, 1789, *PJA*, vol. 20, 185–86. The book was Thomas Prince's *Chronological History of New-England*.

21. Mary [Polly] Palmer to Abigail [Smith] Adams, December 11, 1785, *AFC*, vol. 6, 489–92.

22. Mary [Polly] Palmer to John Adams, November 25, 1789, *PJA*, vol. 20, 185–86. Twenty-year-old William Cranch was Polly Palmer's cousin and John and Abigail Adams's nephew. A few months later, Palmer wrote to Abigail Adams to suggest that her letter might have been lost, implying that she never received a reply from John Adams. Mary [Polly] Palmer to Abigail [Smith] Adams, March 17–20, 1790, *AFC*, vol. 9, 27–29.

23. Sometime before 1841, Israel K. Tefft collected the letter, and it is now in the Dreer Collection at the Historical Society of Pennsylvania. John Adams to Mary [Polly] Palmer, July 5, 1776, *AFC*, vol. 2, 35, nn. 1, 3.

24. Tupper and Brown, *Grandmother Tyler's Book*, 23.

25. The extensive and interdisciplinary literature on the Declaration of Independence includes: Danielle Allen, *Our Declaration: A Reading of the Declaration of Independence in Defense of Equality* (Liveright, 2014); David Armitage, *The Declaration of Independence: A Global History* (Harvard University Press, 2007); Carl Becker, *The Declaration of Independence: A Study on the History of Political Ideas* (Harcourt, Brace, 1922); Richard R. Beeman, *Our Lives, Our Fortunes, and Our Sacred Honor: The Forging of American Independence, 1774–1776* (Basic, 2013); John Bidwell, *The Declaration in Script and Print: A Visual History of America's Founding Document* (Pennsylvania State University Press, 2024); Julian P. Boyd, *The Declaration of Independence: The Evolution of the Text as Shown in Facsimiles of Various Drafts by Its Author, Thomas Jefferson* (Library of Congress, 1943); Philip F. Detweiler, "The Changing Reputation of the Declaration of Independence: The First Fifty Years," *WMQ* 19, no. 4 (1962): 557–74; Sydney George Fisher, "The Twenty-Eight Charges Against the King in the Declaration of Independence," *PMHB* 31, no. 3 (1907): 257–303; Jay Fliegelman, *Declaring Independence: Jefferson, Natural Language & the Culture of Performance* (Stanford University Press, 1993); Herbert Friedenwald, *The Declaration of Independence: An Interpretation and an Analysis* (Macmillan, 1904); Frederick R. Goff, *The John Dunlap Broadside: The First Printing of the Declaration of Independence* (Library of Congress, 1976); John H. Hazelton, *The Declaration of Independence: Its History* (Dodd, Mead, 1906); Wilbur Samuel Howell, "The Declaration of Independence and Eighteenth-Century Logic," *WMQ* 18, no. 4 (1961): 463–84; James H. Hutson, "The Partition Treaty and the Declaration of American Independence," *Journal of American History* 58, no. 4 (1972): 877–96; Stephen E. Lucas, "The Rhetorical Ancestry of the Declaration of

Independence," *Rhetoric and Public Affairs* 1, no. 2 (1998): 143–84; Donald S. Lutz, "The Declaration of Independence as Part of an American National Compact," *Publius* 19, no. 1 (1989): 41–58; Allen Jayne, *Jefferson's Declaration of Independence: Origins, Philosophy, and Theology* (University Press of Kentucky, 1998); Pauline Maier, *American Scripture: Making the Declaration of Independence* (Knopf, 1997); Dumas Malone, *The Story of the Declaration of Independence* (Oxford University Press, 1954); Robert M. S. McDonald, "Thomas Jefferson's Changing Reputation as Author of the Declaration of Independence: The First Fifty Years," *Journal of the Early Republic* 19, no. 2 (1999): 169–95; Peter S. Onuf, "A Declaration of Independence for Diplomatic Historians," *Diplomatic History* 22, no. 1 (1998): 71–83; William Pencak, "The Declaration of Independence: Changing Interpretations and a New Hypothesis," *Pennsylvania History* 57, no. 3 (1990): 225–35; Steve Pincus, *The Heart of the Declaration: The Founders' Case for an Activist Government* (Yale University Press, 2016); Jack N. Rakove, *The Annotated U.S. Constitution and Declaration of Independence* (Belknap Press of Harvard University Press, 2009); Wilfred J. Ritz, "From the *Here* of Jefferson's Handwritten Rough Draft of the Declaration of Independence to the *There* of the Printed Dunlap Broadside," *PMHB* 116, no. 4 (1992): 499–512; Steven Sarson, *The Course of Human Events: The Declaration of Independence and the Historical Origins of the United States* (University of Virginia Press, 2025); Eric Slauter, "The Declaration of Independence and the New Nation," in *The Cambridge Companion to Thomas Jefferson,* ed. Frank Shuffelton (Cambridge University Press, 2009), 12–34; Thomas Starr, "Separated at Birth: Text and Context of the Declaration of Independence," *Proceedings of the American Antiquarian Society* 110, no. 1 (2000): 153–99; Mary E. Stuckey, ed. *Used, Abused, and Sidelined: Debating the Declaration* (Pennsylvania State University Press, 2025); Alexander Tsesis, *For Liberty and Equality: The Life and Times of the Declaration of Independence* (Oxford University Press, 2012); Moses Coit Tyler, "The Declaration of Independence in the Light of Modern Criticism," *The North American Review* 163, no. 4 (July 1896): 1–16; Richard Wendorf, "Declaring, Drafting, and Composing American Independence," *PBSA* 108, no. 3 (2014): 307–24; Garry Wills, *Inventing America: Jefferson's Declaration of Independence,* rev. ed. (Doubleday, 2002); John R. Wunder, "'Merciless Indian Savages' and the Declaration of Independence: Native Americans Translate the Ecunnaunuxulgee Document," *American Indian Law Review* 25, no. 1 (2000/1): 65–92; and Michael P. Zuckert, "Self-Evident Truth and the Declaration of Independence," *Review of Politics* 49, no. 3 (1987): 319–39. It is noteworthy that male authors predominate in this literature, with the relatively recent exceptions of Allen and Maier.

26. For models that trace the confluence of news and the impact of copying and paraphrasing during the American Revolution, see Will Slauter, "News and Diplomacy in the Age of the American Revolution," Ph.D. diss. (Princeton University, 2007); Robert G. Parkinson, *The Common Cause: Creating Race and Nation in the American Revolution* (Omohundro Institute and University of North Carolina Press, 2016). On printed objects and communication during the American Revolution more broadly, see Joseph M. Adelman, *Revolutionary Networks: The Business and Politics of Printing the News, 1763–1789* (Johns Hopkins University Press, 2019); Bernard Bailyn and John B. Hench, eds., *The Press and the American Revolution* (American Antiquarian Society, 1980); Carol Sue Humphrey, *The American Revolution and the Press: The Promise of Independence* (Northwestern University Press, 2013); Jordan E. Taylor, *Misinformation Nation: Foreign News and the Politics of Truth in Revolutionary America* (Johns Hopkins University Press, 2022);

Michael Warner, *The Letters of the Republic: Publication and the Public Sphere in Eighteenth-Century America* (Harvard University Press, 1990); and William B. Warner, *Protocols of Liberty: Communication Innovation and the American Revolution* (University of Chicago Press, 2013).

27. The Dunlap broadside, transcribed in Appendix 1, is the source for all quotations from the Declaration of Independence unless otherwise noted. This word count corresponds to the Dunlap broadside but is approximate for all other copies of the Declaration, because words were added, removed, and changed as the text was copied.

28. John Adams to Hezekiah Niles, February 13, 1818, *Founders Online*.

29. John Adams to Benjamin Kent, June 22, 1776, *PJA*, vol. 4, 326.

30. Eli Merritt, *Disunion Among Ourselves: The Perilous Politics of the American Revolution* (University of Missouri Press, 2023), 3.

31. As William Hogeland writes, "nobody who was there on those days, let alone those who weren't, could ever agree on all that happened during them." Hogeland, *Declaration: The Nine Tumultuous Weeks When America Became Independent, May 1–July 4, 1776* (Simon & Schuster, 2010), 168.

32. *DJA*, vol. 3, 335–37; John Adams to Timothy Pickering, August 6, 1822, *Founders Online*; *PTJ*, vol. 1, 299–329.

33. John Adams to Caesar Augustus Rodney, April 30, 1823, *Founders Online*; Notes of Proceedings in the Continental Congress, June 7–August 1, 1776, *PTJ*, vol. 1, 299–329. Julian Boyd, the first *PTJ* editor, wrote a thorough editorial note about Thomas Jefferson's claim and offered nine pieces of datable evidence as "overwhelming proof that Jefferson was mistaken." On the myth of the July 4 signing, see Mellen Chamberlain, "The Alleged Signing of the Declaration of Independence, July 4, 1776," *Proceedings of the Massachusetts Historical Society* 1 (1884–85): 272–98; Friedenwald, *The Declaration of Independence*, 121–51; Hazelton, *The Declaration of Independence*, 193–219; and Charles Warren, "Fourth of July Myths," *WMQ* 2, no. 3 (July 1945): 242–48.

34. National Archives and Records Administration (emphasis in original). The introduction of Pauline Maier's *American Scripture* is an exceptional critical examination of the outsized role the signed parchment has held in the public memory and civic culture of the United States. To her thoughtful desacralization of the parchment, I would add that one consequence of generations of Americans treating the parchment as the definitive copy of the Declaration of Independence is that copies that look different from the parchment—especially in libraries and archives outside of the United States—may be overlooked or under-analyzed. For example, a guide to American Revolution materials in European archives produced in anticipation of the Bicentennial records a copy of the Declaration in the Vatican Archives, but the manuscript is actually a copy of the Articles of Confederation. My thanks to Elizabeth McCahill and Gianfranco Armando for their assistance in clarifying this error. For the original reference, see W. J. Koenig and S. L. Mayer, eds., *European Manuscript Sources of the American Revolution* (Bowker, 1974), 305.

35. Historians tend to breeze through the weeks following July 4 with little consideration of the dissemination of the Declaration of Independence. The most frequently mentioned episodes are the printing (though rarely the distribution) of the Dunlap broadside and the reading for the Continental Army in New York on July 9. See Adelman, *Revolutionary Networks*, 155; Allen, *Our Declaration*, 99; Armitage, *The Declaration of Independence*, 12–16, 69–75, 81–82; George Bancroft, *History of the United States, From the Discovery of*

the American Continent, vol. IX, 3rd ed. (Little, Brown, 1873), 32–37; Whitfield J. Bell, Jr., *The Declaration of Independence: Four 1776 Versions* (American Philosophical Society, 1976); Carl Berger, *Broadsides and Bayonets: The Propaganda War of the American Revolution*, rev. ed. (Presidio Press, 1976), 198–200; Russ Castronovo, *Propaganda 1776: Secrets, Leaks, and Revolutionary Communications in Early America* (Oxford University Press, 2014), 4–5; Charles D. Deshler, "How the Declaration Was Received in the Old Thirteen," *Harper's New Monthly Magazine* 85, no. 506 (1892): 165–87; Detweiler, "The Changing Reputation of the Declaration of Independence," 558; Joseph J. Ellis, *Revolutionary Summer: The Birth of American Independence* (Knopf, 2013), 71–72; Fliegelman, *Declaring Independence*, 25–26; Hazelton, *The Declaration of Independence*, 232–34, 240–81; Benjamin H. Irvin, *Clothed in Robes of Sovereignty: The Continental Congress and the People Out of Doors* (Oxford University Press, 2011), 136–37; Maier, *American Scripture*, 154–60; Parkinson, *The Common Cause*, 255–56, 259–62; Starr, "Separated at Birth," 159–61; Tsesis, *For Liberty and Equality*, 24–31, 33 [note that several of Tsesis's examples of public readings are misdated]; David Waldstreicher, *In the Midst of Perpetual Fetes: The Making of American Nationalism, 1776–1820* (Omohundro Institute and University of North Carolina Press, 1997), 30–35; and Warner, *Protocols of Liberty*, 227–29. Michael J. Walsh, "Contemporary Broadside Editions of the Declaration of Independence," *Harvard Library Bulletin* 3, no. 1 (1949): 31–43. Though outdated, Walsh's catalog is still a good reference for extant contemporary broadsides.

36. The national and international identities that the Continental Congress hoped the Declaration of Independence would create are best understood through two concepts: Benedict Anderson's "imagined community" and Eliga Gould's "treaty-worthiness." Anderson, *Imagined Communities: Reflections on the Origin and Spread of Nationalism*, rev. ed. (Verso, 2006); Gould, *Among the Powers of the Earth: The American Revolution and the Making of a New World Empire* (Harvard University Press, 2012).

37. Robert Parkinson notes that the two most important words in the Declaration of Independence are "he" and "we": "these pronouns are mighty weapons, rhetorically and conceptually. They are independence." Parkinson, *The Common Cause*, 254–55.

38. David Armitage contends that the Declaration of Independence was "a document of state-making, not of nation formation." Armitage, *The Declaration of Independence*, 17. On the early diplomatic history of the United States, see Samuel Flagg Bemis, *The Diplomacy of the American Revolution* (American Historical Association, 1935); Jonathan R. Dull, *A Diplomatic History of the American Revolution* (Yale University Press, 1985); Larrie D. Ferreiro, *Brothers at Arms: American Independence and the Men of France & Spain Who Saved It* (Knopf, 2016); Leonard J. Sadosky, *Revolutionary Negotiations: Indians, Empires, and Diplomats in the Founding of America* (University of Virginia Press, 2009). On European perceptions of the American Revolution, see Horst Dippel, *Germany and the American Revolution, 1770–1800: A Sociohistorical Investigation of Late Eighteenth-Century Political Thinking*, trans. Bernard A. Uhlendorf (University of North Carolina Press, 1977); Jonathan Singerton, *The American Revolution and the Habsburg Monarchy* (University of Virginia Press, 2022).

39. As Eliga Gould argues, "what we sometimes forget—though people at the time knew it—is that the United States could not become the nation that Americans imagined without the consent of other nations and people." Gould, *Among the Powers of the Earth*, 2.

40. Sadosky, *Revolutionary Negotiations*, 82–84.

41. This approach draws on Thomas R. Adams and Nicolas Barker's adaptation of Robert Darnton's communications circuit, which accounts for the publication, manufacture, distribution, reception, and preservation of a text, and acknowledges the humans (as well as the potential for certain decisions and errors) involved in each part of the circuit. Adams and Barker, "A New Model for the Study of the Book," in *A Potencie of Life*, ed. Nicolas Barker (British Library, 1993); Darnton, "What Is the History of Books?," *Daedalus* 111, no. 3 (1982): 65–83.

42. Allen, *Our Declaration*, 75–77; Becker, *The Declaration of Independence*, 5, n. 1.

43. Elizabeth Eisenstein argues that "having a printed text serve as the 'original' of a manuscript is something of an oddity," and she describes the Declaration of Independence as "perhaps the most celebrated instance of such an inversion." This is an oversimplification of the publication process. The Continental Congress must have provided John Dunlap with an unsigned manuscript "original" in order to produce his broadside. Eisenstein, *The Printing Revolution in Early Modern Europe*, 2nd ed. (Cambridge University Press, 2005), 342; Julian P. Boyd, "The Declaration of Independence: The Mystery of the Lost Original," *PMHB* 100, no. 4 (1976): 438–67.

44. In the fifth grievance, Timothy Matlack wrote "Represtative," inserted a caret between the "s" and "t," and added "en" above the line. Matlack also interlineated the word "only" in the phrase "Our repeated Petitions have been answered only by repeated injury."

45. Armitage, *The Declaration of Independence*, 70–71. Both Thomas Jefferson and Charles Thomson knew enough French to supervise a translation, which could have been made by one of the many Francophone engineers and other émigrés who had come to Philadelphia to help the united colonies.

46. On the framing of circum-Atlantic history, see Armitage, "Three Concepts of Atlantic History," in *The British Atlantic World, 1500–1800*, ed. David Armitage and Michael J. Braddick (Macmillan, 2002), 16–18.

47. For example, a few weeks before and after he printed the Declaration of Independence, John Dunlap was forced to print his Philadelphia newspaper on blue cartridge paper. *Dunlap's Pennsylvania Packet or the General Advertiser*, June 17, 1776; August 13, 1776.

48. John Lacey Journal, Fort Ticonderoga Museum, 2016.5.1-2.

49. *Public Register: Or, Freeman's Journal*, August 20–22, 1776, 1; August 22–24, 1776, 2; Hazelton, *The Declaration of Independence*, 485, n. 58; Malone, *The Story of the Declaration of Independence*, 4.

50. *New-England Chronicle*, September 5, 1776, 3; Armitage, *The Declaration of Independence*, 74–75.

51. Sadosky, *Revolutionary Negotiations*, 3.

52. Gould, *Among the Powers of the Earth*, 2.

53. Armitage, *The Declaration of Independence*, 26.

54. Mary [Polly] Palmer to John Adams, *AFC*, vol. 2, 76–78.

55. John Adams to Abigail [Smith] Adams, July 3, 1776, *AFC*, vol. 2, 29–33.

CHAPTER 1

1. Enclosure in Robert Walpole to Weymouth, July 6, 1776, SP 89/82, 181 (emphasis in original). My thanks to Lauren Michalak for photographing Walpole's papers. This printed copy of the May 15 Resolution does not seem to match any other known contemporary printing. On the May 15 Resolution, see Willi Paul Adams, *The First American Constitutions: Republican Ideology and the Making of the State Constitutions in the Revolutionary Era*, trans. Rita Kimber and Robert Kimber, rev. ed. (Rowan & Littlefield,

2001), 59–62; Joseph J. Ellis, *Revolutionary Summer: The Birth of American Independence* (New York: Knopf, 2013), 17–19; William Hogeland, *Declaration: The Nine Tumultuous Weeks When America Became Independent, May 1–July 4, 1776* (Simon & Schuster, 2010), 46–48, 91–101; Jerrilyn Greene Marston, *King and Congress: The Transfer of Political Legitimacy, 1774–1776* (Princeton University Press, 1987), 281–96; Jack N. Rakove, *The Beginnings of National Politics: An Interpretive History of the Continental Congress*, rev. ed. (Johns Hopkins University Press, 2019), 96–98; Richard Alan Ryerson, *The Revolution Is Now Begun: The Radical Committees of Philadelphia, 1765–1776* (University of Pennsylvania Press, 1978), 211–23; Gordon S. Wood, *The Creation of the American Republic, 1776–1787*, rev. ed. (Omohundro Institute and University of North Carolina Press, 1998), 131–32. Because the Continental Congress approved the resolution itself on May 10, some historians use "May 10 resolution" to refer to this text.

2. *JCC*, vol. 4, 341–47. Willi Paul Adams notes that "new structures of political authority developed simultaneously on both state and continental levels," and "both spheres of political activity were obviously dependent on each other and influenced each other reciprocally." None of the colonies adopted new constitutions without an explicit recommendation from the Continental Congress, whether on a case-by-case basis or through the May 15 Resolution. Adams, *The First American Constitutions*, 49–50.

3. This language echoed the Continental Congress's instructions to New Hampshire, South Carolina, and Virginia in November and December 1775. The Congress gave these colonies permission to form new governments that would "best produce the happiness of the people, and most effectually secure peace and good order…during the continuance of the present dispute." *JCC*, vol. 3, 319–27, 402–405.

4. *DJA*, vol. 3, 382–84.

5. *JCC*, vol. 2, 158–62.

6. "By the King, A Proclamation, For Suppressing Rebellion and Sedition" (London: Charles Eyre and William Strahan, 1775). The Continental Congress formally responded to the king's proclamation on December 6, 1775, but agreed that, despite "the name of Majesty," the allegations against the Congress had come from Parliament and had "no foundation in the royal authority." *JCC*, vol. 3, 408–13.

7. *Dunlap's Pennsylvania Packet or the General Advertiser*, January 15, 1776, 1.

8. Samuel Ward to [Ward's daughter], January 8, 1776, *LDC*, vol. 3, 61.

9. On *Common Sense*, see Joseph M. Adelman, *Revolutionary Networks: The Business and Politics of Printing the News, 1763–1789* (Johns Hopkins University Press, 2019), 151–54; Trish Loughran, *The Republic in Print: Print Culture in the Age of U.S. Nation Building, 1770–1870* (Columbia University Press, 2007), chap. 2; Pauline Maier, *American Scripture: Making the Declaration of Independence* (Knopf, 1997), 33–34.

10. [Thomas Paine], *Common Sense* (R. Bell [Philadelphia], 1776), 25.

11. [Paine], *Common Sense*, 79; David Armitage, *The Declaration of Independence: A Global History* (Harvard University Press, 2007), 52.

12. John Adams to Abigail [Smith] Adams, March 19, 1776, *AFC*, vol. 1, 362–64.

13. [John Adams], *Thoughts on Government*, in *PJA*, vol. 4, 65–93; Hogeland, *Declaration*, 138–39.

14. John Adams to Horatio Gates, March 23, 1776, *PJA*, vol. 4, 58–60. The Continental Congress fought the embargo by empowering privateers to attack and seize goods from British ships. They tasked John Jay, James Wilson, and George Wythe with drafting a response to the Prohibitory Act. *JCC*, vol. 4, 227–33.

15. John Adams to Horatio Gates, March 23, 1776, *PJA*, vol. 4, 58–60.

16. James Duane to Robert R. Livingston, March 20, 1776, *LDC*, vol. 3, 413–16.

17. John Adams to James Warren, May 18, 1776, *PJA*, vol. 4, 192–94.

18. *JCC*, vol. 3, 389–92. The initial members were John Dickinson, Benjamin Franklin, Benjamin Harrison, John Jay, and Thomas Johnson.

19. CSC to Silas Deane, March 3, 1776, *RDC*, vol. 2, 78–80.

20. Ibid.

21. Sir James Jay, John's older brother, had developed the recipe for the ink. In September 1776, John Jay revealed to Robert Morris that, "when Mr. Deane went to France I communicated to him a Mode of invisible writing unknown to any but the inventor and myself." John Jay to Robert Morris, September 15, 1776, *PJJ*, vol. 1, 294–97.

22. Instructions for Silas Deane, March 2, 1776, *LDC*, vol. 3, 320–23.

23. Edmund Pendleton to Thomas Jefferson, May 24, 1776, *PTJ*, vol. 1, 296–97.

24. In her biography of John Dickinson, Jane Calvert writes that "his were the politics of conscience, a civics lesson to future generations to stand on principle without regard for self or party." Calvert, *Penman of the Founding: A Biography of John Dickinson* (Oxford University Press, 2024).

25. John Langdon to George Washington, May 10, 1776, *PGW*, vol. 4, 255–57. George Merchant arrived in Philadelphia by the evening of May 20.

26. On the German soldiers, see Friederike Baer, *Hessians: German Soldiers in the American Revolutionary War* (Oxford University Press, 2022), especially chap. 1; Carl Berger, *Broadsides and Bayonets: The Propaganda War of the American Revolution*, rev. ed. (Presidio Press, 1976), chap. 5; Robert G. Parkinson, *The Common Cause: Creating Race and Nation in the American Revolution* (Omohundro Institute and University of North Carolina Press, 2016), 216–24.

27. *Dunlap's Pennsylvania Packet*, January 15, 1776, 1.

28. As Friederike Baer argues, "the plan to use foreign troops against the colonists helped shape a narrative that depicted the king as the one who had rejected his American subjects, rather than the other way around." Baer, *Hessians*, 24.

29. *Dunlap's Pennsylvania Packet*, May 6, 1776, supplement (emphasis in original).

30. *Pennsylvanischer Staatsbote*, May 7, 1776, 2; Baer, *Hessians*, 205–206; Parkinson, *The Common Cause*, 219.

31. *JCC*, vol. 4, 328–30.

32. On May 10, after adjourning the Committee of the Whole, the Continental Congress requested that the committee present their proceedings on the following Monday, May 13, "withholding the names of the persons they have employed, or with whom they have corresponded." *JCC*, vol. 4, 341–47.

33. Copy of Samuel Graves to Andrew Snape Hamond, December 25, 1775, enclosed in Richard Howe, 1st Earl Howe to Lord George Germain, May 16, 1777, CO 5/126, 350. Hamond's goals were "to prevent any Supplies getting to the Rebels," "to annoy them," and "to protect and defend the persons and property of His Majesty's Loyal and Obedient Subjects wherever they can be distinguished." These instructions predate Graves's knowledge of the Prohibitory Act. Silas Deane left Philadelphia on March 8, 1776, but there was a problem with the ship that he was supposed to take directly to Bordeaux. Robert Morris prepared a new ship, the *Betsey*, "with a cargo of Provisions for Bermuda in order to send Silas Deane Esqr. on that Island." Deane was supposed to decide whether the *Betsey* should continue to Bordeaux, or if he should charter another

vessel from Bermuda. CSC Minutes of Proceedings, March 27, 1776, *LDC*, vol. 3, 453–54; Robert Morris to Silas Deane, March 30, 1776, *LDC*, vol. 3, 466–68.

34. Copy of Andrew Snape Hamond to Henry Bellew, May 15, 1776, enclosed in Richard Howe, 1st Earl Howe to Lord George Germain, May 16, 1777, CO 5/126, 378.

35. *Minutes of the Provincial Council of Pennsylvania, From the Organization to the Termination of the Proprietary Government*, vol. 10 (Theo. Fenn, 1852), 557–58.

36. *Dunlap's Pennsylvania Packet*, May 13, 1776, 3.

37. On the British strategy for New York, see Rohit T. Aggarwala, "'I want a Packet to arrive': Making New York City the Headquarters of British America, 1696–1783," *New York History* 98, no. 1 (2017): 7–39.

38. *Dunlap's Pennsylvania Packet*, June 3, 1776, 2. A letter from New York shared the report of this captain, who had sailed from the Caribbean island of Saint Croix to Salem, Massachusetts, and connected with the captain of a British brigantine on May 10.

39. David Hawke and other historians argue that the preamble of the May 15 Resolution was "unquestionably aimed at Pennsylvania." Hawke, *In the Midst of a Revolution* (University of Pennsylvania Press, 1961), 121.

40. Charlene Mires, *Independence Hall in American Memory* (University of Pennsylvania Press, 2002), 20–21.

41. Hogeland, *Declaration*, chap. 1.

42. *JCC*, vol. 4, 357–58.

43. Adams, *The First American Constitutions*, 61; Wood, *The Creation of the American Republic*, 132.

44. *JCC*, vol. 4, 357–58.

45. *DJA*, vol. 2, 238–41.

46. Ibid.

47. Ibid. Benjamin H. Irvin, *Clothed in Robes of Sovereignty: The Continental Congress and the People Out of Doors* (Oxford University Press, 2011), 138.

48. John Dickinson, who was absent from this debate, used the same analogy in the notes he prepared for his speech on July 1.

49. Thomas Stone to [James Hollyday?], May 20, 1776, *LDC*, vol. 4, 46–54.

50. Caesar Rodney to Thomas Rodney, May 17, 1776, *LDC*, vol. 4, 30.

51. Thomas Jefferson to Thomas Nelson, Jr., May 16, 1776, *PTJ*, vol. 1, 292–93.

52. John Adams to James Warren, May 15, 1776, *PJA*, vol. 4, 186–87.

53. John Adams to Abigail [Smith] Adams, May 17, 1776, *AFC*, vol. 1, 410–12.

54. *JCC*, vol. 4, 367–69.

55. *DJA*, vol. 3, 385–86; Julian P. Boyd, *The Declaration of Independence: The Evolution of the Text as Shown in Facsimiles of Various Drafts by Its Author, Thomas Jefferson* (Library of Congress, 1943), 14–15.

56. Enclosure in Sebastião José de Carvalho e Melo, Marquês de Pombal to Luis Pinto de Souza, July 2, 1776, Arquivo Nacional da Torre do Tombo, PT–TT–MNE–LL–1–L123. The correspondence between Walpole and Pombal is in French. On Pombal, see Dauril Alden, "The Marquis of Pombal and the American Revolution," *The Americas* 17, no. 4 (1961): 369–76.

57. Robert Walpole to Sebastião José de Carvalho e Melo, Marquês de Pombal, July 2, 1776, with enclosure, Arquivo Nacional da Torre do Tombo, PT–TT–MNE–LL–1–L123.

58. "Dom José por graça de Deos rey de Portugal, e dos Algarves, daquém, e dalém mar,…não só se declaráram inteiramente apartadas de sujeição á Coroa da Grão Bretanha" (July 5, 1776).

59. Fabrício Prado, "Anglo-Portuguese Cooperation in Eighteenth-Century Atlantic South America," in *The Río de la Plata from Colony to Nations, Commerce, Society, and Politics*, ed. Fabricio Prado, Viviana L. Greco, and Alex Borucki (Palgrave Macmillan, 2022), 106–10.

60. "Dom José por graça de Deos rey de Portugal."

61. The edict bears the printed signature of the Conde de Azambuja, head of the Conselho da Fazenda.

62. *General Evening Post*, July 27–30, 1776, 4.

63. Robert Walpole to Thomas Thynne, 3rd Viscount Weymouth, July 6, 1776, with enclosures (handbill of May 15 Resolution [in English]; copy of July 4 edict [in Portuguese]; copy of July 4 edict [in English]; copy of Walpole to John Hort, July 2, 1776 [in English]; and copy of Hort to Walpole, July 3, 1776 [in English]), SP 89/82, 179–95.

64. Copy of Robert Walpole to John Hort, July 2, 1776, enclosed in Walpole to Thomas Thynne, 3rd Viscount Weymouth, July 6, 1776, SP 89/82, 192–93.

65. Copy of John Hort to Robert Walpole, July 3, 1776, enclosed in Walpole to Thomas Thynne, 3rd Viscount Weymouth, July 6, 1776, SP 89/82, 194–95.

66. John Hort to Thomas Thynne, 3rd Viscount Weymouth, July 6, 1776, SP 89/82, 194–95.

67. Charles-Jean Garnier to Joseph-Matthias Gérard de Rayneval, August 13, 1776, Archives Diplomatiques, microfilm reel 517, 282–85.

68. Robert Walpole to Thomas Thynne, 3rd Viscount Weymouth, July 20, 1776, SP 89/82, 202–204.

69. *Lloyd's Evening Post*, July 10–12, 1776, 7.

70. Journal of the Massachusetts Council, June 1, 1776, *NDAR*, vol. 5, 334–36.

71. *New-England Chronicle*, May 30, 1776, 1 (emphasis in original).

72. Printers across the northern colonies, including Samuel Hall, copied the May 15 Resolution from the *Constitutional Gazette*, which contained several typographical errors. The text as approved by the Continental Congress referred to "petitions" which became a singular "petition" in this newspaper. The last phrase of the preamble also shifted from third-person plural to first-person plural—from "their lives" and "their enemies" to "our lives" and "our enemies." In British newspapers, "our lives" became "ourselves." *Constitutional Gazette*, May 18, 1776, 4.

73. Silas Deane spent most of June in Bordeaux and left on June 30. Silas Deane to CSC, August 18, 1776, *RDC*, vol. 2, 112–22.

74. Archives Diplomatiques, États-Unis, vol. 1, 88.

75. Archives Diplomatiques, États-Unis, vol. 1, 88. The easiest portions of the cross-out to identify are "d'indépend[…]," "Amérique," "Gr.," and "1776."

76. Silas Deane to CSC, August 18, 1776, *RDC*, vol. 2, 112–22.

77. Ibid. In William Shakespeare's *Othello*, Iago explains that "there are many events in the womb of time which will be delivered." From Deane's report of the meeting it is unclear whether the Comte de Vergennes quoted Shakespeare himself or Deane used a Shakespeare quotation to summarize Vergennes's sentiments.

78. Carter Braxton to Landon Carter, May 17, 1776, *LDC*, vol. 4, 18–21.

79. "Diary of Col. Landon Carter," *WMQ* 18, no. 1 (July 1909): 37–38; Parkinson, *The Common Cause*, 224.

CHAPTER 2

1. *Virginia Gazette*, May 17, 1776, 1.
2. Ibid., 3 (emphasis in original).
3. Ibid., 3; Danielle Allen, *Our Declaration: A Reading of the Declaration of Independence in Defense of Equality* (Liveright, 2014), 61–64. The Virginia Convention's resolution spread through newspapers, but it seems that Edmund Pendleton also sent a copy of the resolution to every provincial assembly. See *Journals of the House of Representatives of Massachusetts, 1776*, vol. 52 (Massachusetts Historical Society, 1985), 30; *Journals of the Provincial Congress, Provincial Convention, Committee of Safety and Council of Safety of the State of New-York, 1775–1776*, vol. 1 (Thurlow Weed, 1842), 474–75; *Minutes of the Provincial Congress and the Council of Safety of the State of New Jersey* (Naar, Day & Naar, 1879), 449–52.
4. Note that Thomas Jefferson used the language of "piratical warfare" to describe the transatlantic slave trade in the final grievance in the draft Declaration of Independence. Robert G. Parkinson, *The Common Cause: Creating Race and Nation in the American Revolution* (Omohundro Institute and University of North Carolina Press, 2016), 228–29.
5. *Virginia Gazette*, May 17, 1776, 3 (emphasis in original).
6. Danielle Allen notes that "a 'colony' identifies a social group whose affairs are organized by someone else. A 'state' identifies a social group that organizes its own affairs." Allen, *Our Declaration*, 121.
7. *JCC*, vol. 4, 358–62.
8. This child was a daughter, born in October 1776 and named for John's aunt and surrogate mother, Lydia Henchman Hancock, who died suddenly in April 1776. Her death was widely reported in newspapers. See, for example, *Public Advertiser*, August 6, 1776, 2.
9. Thomas Jefferson to Thomas Nelson, May 16, 1776, *PTJ*, vol. 1, 292–93.
10. Memorandum Books, 1776, *PTJ*, vol. 1, 412–37.
11. *JCC*, vol. 4, 390–96. The committee included Benjamin Harrison (VA), possibly in his role as chair of the Committee of the Whole, plus William Whipple (NH), John Adams (MA), Samuel Hopkins (RI), Roger Sherman (CT), Robert R. Livingston (NY), William Livingston (NJ), James Wilson (PA), George Read (DE), Tench Tilghman (MD), Richard Henry Lee (VA), Joseph Hewes (NC), Arthur Middleton (SC), and Lyman Hall (GA). Major Generals Horatio Gates and Thomas Mifflin joined George Washington for these meetings.
12. *JCC*, vol. 4, 409–11.
13. *JCC*, vol. 4, 411–14. The 6,000 militiamen intended for Canada included 3,000 (four battalions) from Massachusetts, 1,500 (two battalions) from Connecticut, and 750 (one battalion) each from New Hampshire and New York. The 13,800 militiamen intended for New York included 2,000 from Massachusetts, 5,500 from Connecticut, 3,000 from New York, and 3,300 from New Jersey. For the flying camp, the Congress requested 6,000 men from Pennsylvania, 3,400 from Maryland, and 600 from Delaware. They also agreed that George Washington could "employ in Canada a number of Indians," not exceeding 2,000 men.

14. John Adams to Abigail [Smith] Adams, June 3, 1776, *AFC*, vol. 2, 5.

15. Ibid., 5–6.

16. Charles Willson Peale, *George Washington*, 1776, Brooklyn Museum, 34.1178; Lillian B. Miller, ed., *The Selected Papers of Charles Willson Peale and His Family*, Vol. I: *Charles Willson Peale: Artist in Revolutionary America, 1735–1791* (Yale University Press, 1983), 182–83. John Hancock made arrangements with Peale on May 19, after he had invited George Washington to Philadelphia but before Washington had responded.

17. John Parke Custis to George Washington, June 10, 1776, *PGW*, vol. 4, 484–86.

18. George Washington to John Augustine Washington, May 31–June 4, 1776, *PGW*, vol. 4, 411–14.

19. Ibid. John Augustine Washington filled in for Richard Henry Lee as a Westmoreland County delegate at the Virginia Convention and may have enclosed the convention's May 15 Resolution in a letter written to George Washington on May 18 that has been lost.

20. *AA*, series 4, vol. 5, 859–60. This text is known as the Halifax Resolves.

21. David T. Morgan and William J. Schmidt, "From Economic Sanctions to Political Separation: The North Carolina Delegation to the Continental Congress, 1774–1776," *North Carolina Historical Review* 52, no. 3 (1975): 230–31. It took about ten days for mail to travel from Williamsburg to Philadelphia.

22. Joseph Hewes thought that the only cure for his illness would be to leave the Congress. He wrote that he would not do so until his colleagues returned, even if he was forced to "crawl to the Congress Chamber." Joseph Hewes to James Iredell, May 17, 1776, *LDC*, vol. 4, 26–27.

23. *AA*, series 4, vol. 5, 859–60.

24. Parkinson, *The Common Cause*, 241.

25. Their colleague, Thomas Nelson, Jr., returned to Philadelphia from Williamsburg just after George Washington left.

26. *Pennsylvania Evening Post*, June 6, 1776, 1–2. The Declaration of Rights was printed under the heading "Williamsburg, May 24." Purdie printed the *Virginia Gazette* on that date, but the text does not appear in that or any other issue of his newspaper. The drafting committee included George Mason, Thomas Ludwell Lee (Richard Henry and Francis Lightfoot Lee's older brother), Robert Carter Nicholas, and James Madison. It is possible that Thomas Ludwell Lee enclosed a copy of the draft in a letter to one of his brothers, perhaps dated May 24. Edmund Pendleton sent a letter to Thomas Jefferson on May 24 but did not mention the Declaration of Rights in the letter.

27. National Archives and Records Administration. The Lee Resolutions are typically treated as a singular "Lee Resolution," and the focus in the historiography is on the first resolution about a declaration of independence. I prefer the plural, so as to emphasize that the Declaration of Independence, the Model Treaty, and the Articles of Confederation were interconnected documents, undertaken simultaneously because of the Virginia Convention's instructions.

28. *JCC*, vol. 5, 424–27. John Dickinson sent a note to one of his Pennsylvania colleagues on Saturday morning to let him know "that the public Business in a very particular Manner demands his Attendance this Morning, as a Matter of the last Importance is to be determined." John Dickinson to Thomas Willing, [June 8, 1776], *LDC*, vol. 4, 169.

29. Edward Rutledge to John Jay, [June 8, 1776], *PJJ*, vol. 1, 249–50.

30. *JCC*, vol. 4, 427–29.

31. New Hampshire Delegates to Meshech Weare, May 28, 1776, *LDC*, vol. 4, 93–94.

32. Ibid., 194.

33. *Documents and Records Relating to the State of New-Hampshire During the Period of the American Revolution, from 1776 to 1783,* vol. 8 (Edward A. Jenks, 1874), 149–50.

34. Josiah Bartlett to Nathaniel Folsom, July 1, 1776, *LDC*, vol. 4, 348–50.

35. On New Jersey, see Maxine N. Lurie, *Taking Sides in Revolutionary New Jersey: Caught in the Crossfire* (Rutgers University Press, 2022).

36. The provincial congress intended to meet on Monday, June 10, but they did not have a quorum until six o'clock in the evening on Tuesday, June 11. *Minutes of the Provincial Congress and the Council of Safety of the State of New Jersey,* 446–48.

37. Kieran J. O'Keefe, "Mass Incarceration as Revolutionary Policy: The Imprisonment of the Hudson Valley Loyalists," *Early American Studies* 19, no. 3 (2021): 495–527.

38. *Minutes of the Provincial Congress and the Council of Safety of the State of New Jersey,* 472–74.

39. *JCC*, vol. 4, 417–20. The five-member committee included John Adams, Thomas Jefferson, Edward Rutledge, James Wilson, and Robert R. Livingston. On treason, see Carlton F. W. Larson, *The Trials of Allegiance: Treason, Juries, and the American Revolution* (Oxford University Press, 2019).

40. *JCC*, vol. 5, 473–77.

41. John Hancock to George Washington, June 25, 1776, *PGW*, vol. 5, 102–104.

42. Curtis P. Nettels, "A Link in the Chain of Events Leading to American Independence," *WMQ* 3, no. 1 (1946): 36–47.

43. General Orders, March 11, *PGW*, vol. 3, 448–49.

44. Court Martial for the Trial of Thomas Hickey and Others, June 26, 1776, *AA*, series 4, vol. 6, 1084–85.

45. William Whipple to Joshua Brackett, June 23, 1776, *LDC*, vol. 3, 300–301; *Pennsylvania Evening Post,* June 25, 1776, 2.

46. American Loyalist Claims, 1776–1835, Evidence, New York, 1783–1784, 291–300; Arrest Warrant from a Secret Committee [Philip Livingston, John Jay, Gouverneur Morris] of the New York Provincial Congress, June 21, 1776, *PGW*, vol. 5, 72–74.

47. American Loyalist Claims, 1776–1835, Evidence, New York, 1783–1784, 351–52. David King's enslaver was William Kippon. King said that he had "gained his Liberty by the war," but clarified that Kippon had promised to grant his freedom "long ago." On the Black community in Manhattan, see Leslie M. Harris, *In the Shadow of Slavery: African Americans in New York City, 1626–1863* (University of Chicago Press, 2003).

48. American Loyalist Claims, 1776–1835, Temporary Assistance F–K, New York, 689. David Mathews recommended that David King apply for compensation.

49. General Orders, June 27, 1776, *PGW*, vol. 5, 112–13.

50. Court Martial for the Trial of Thomas Hickey and Others, June 26, 1776, *AA*, series 4, vol. 6, 1084–85.

51. General Orders, June 28, 1776, *PGW*, vol. 5, 129–30; *Constitutional Gazette,* June 29, 1776, 3–4.

52. *JCC*, vol. 5, 427–29.

53. *JCC*, vol. 5, 429–31.

54. As Jane Calvert notes, if John Dickinson had been in favor of independence, "there is little doubt he would have been the lead draftsman" of the Declaration, "as he had been for most other congressional documents." Calvert, *Penman of the Founding: A Biography of John Dickinson* (Oxford University Press, 2024), 262.

55. Richard Henry Lee left Philadelphia on June 13. Richard Henry Lee to George Washington, June 13, 1776, *PGW*, vol. 4, 514–15.

56. On the drafting of the Declaration of Independence, see Pauline Maier, *American Scripture: Making the Declaration of Independence* (Knopf, 1997), chap. 3. Other analyses of the drafting include: Danielle Allen, *Our Declaration*, especially Part 2; Carl Becker, *The Declaration of Independence: A Study on the History of Political Ideas* (Harcourt, Brace, 1922); Julian P. Boyd, *The Declaration of Independence: The Evolution of the Text as Shown in Facsimiles of Various Drafts by Its Author, Thomas Jefferson* (Library of Congress, 1943); John H. Hazelton, *The Declaration of Independence: Its History* (Dodd, Mead, 1906); Garry Wills, *Inventing America: Jefferson's Declaration of Independence*, rev. ed. (Houghton Mifflin Company, 2002).

57. *PTJ*, vol. 1, 299–329. The *PTJ* editors explain that these notes were a loose insertion in Jefferson's manuscript autobiography, and that "a one- or two-page account of the Declaration would have conformed to the plan of the whole, but the 20-page insertion of the Notes threw it greatly out of scale."

58. *DJA*, vol. 3, 335–37.

59. [Timothy Pickering], *Col. Pickering's Observations Introductory to Reading the Declaration of Independence, at Salem, July 4, 1823* (Warwick Palfray, Jr., 1823); John Adams to Timothy Pickering, August 6, 1822, *Founders Online*; Maier, *American Scripture*, 99–100, 104.

60. Thomas Jefferson to James Madison, August 30, 1823, in *The Papers of James Madison, Retirement Series*, Vol. 2: *1 March 1823–24 February 1826*, ed. David B. Mattern et al. (University of Virginia Press, 2016), 114–16.

61. Pauline Maier vividly compares the work of reconstructing the drafting process to "assembling an immensely complex jigsaw puzzle in which some pieces are 'teases,' serving only to mislead, while others necessary to complete the picture have probably been lost forever." Maier, *American Scripture*, 97. The most notable document that is not known to survive is the manuscript copy of the approved text of the Declaration of Independence that must have been John Dunlap's source for the first broadside printings.

62. *PTJ*, vol. 1, 420–23. It was so much a scrap of paper that it went unnoticed by Julian Boyd, the first *PTJ* editor.

63. As Danielle Allen notes, by June 13 Thomas Jefferson had "written not one but three draft constitutions for Virginia. Congress's writer was at work but not, or at least not directly, for Congress," though not for long. Allen, *Our Declaration*, 65. Dumas Malone writes that "there was nothing on earth that Jefferson would have so liked to be as the author of the first Virginia Constitution." Malone, *The Story of the Declaration of Independence* (Oxford University Press, 1954), 60.

64. Carl Becker argues that Thomas Jefferson recognized how important the publication of this declaration would be, and therefore the rough draft "bears ample evidence of his search for the right word, the right phrasing." *The Declaration of Independence*, 197–98.

65. Carl Becker writes that, although the list of grievances occupies "a subordinate place in the logical structure," it is "of the highest importance in respect to the total effect which the Declaration aims to produce." *The Declaration of Independence*, 7, 205.

66. Danielle Allen describes each grievance as "a story in miniature." Robbed of "names, dates, and places," each grievance "becomes more like a myth or fable." Allen, *Our Declaration*, 218.

67. David Armitage, *The Declaration of Independence: A Global History* (Harvard University Press, 2007), 55; Maier, *American Scripture*, 105–23; Parkinson, *The Common Cause*, 250–58.

68. *PTJ*, vol. 1, 423–28 (emphasis in original). As Alexander Boulton notes, the grievance about the transatlantic slave trade was "clearly meant to be the rhetorical and emotional climax of the document," and "the only orthographical device it lacks is exclamation points!!!" Boulton, "The Declaration of Independence and the Language of Slavery," *Journal of the Early Republic* 44, no. 1 (2024): 21.

69. *PTJ*, vol. 1, 423–28.

70. Massachusetts Historical Society, Adams Family Papers; Abigail [Smith] Adams to John Adams, July 13–14, 1776, *AFC*, vol. 2, 48–49, n. 8.

71. Thomas Jefferson to Benjamin Franklin, [June 21, 1776], *PTJ*, vol. 1, 404–406; *PBF*, vol. 22, 485–86. This is the first recorded correspondence between the two men. The note is not explicit and is only dated "Friday morn." I. Minis Hays was the first to suggest that the enclosure was a draft of the Declaration, and the *PTJ* and *PBF* editors concur.

72. Benjamin Franklin to George Washington, June 21, 1776, *PBF*, vol. 22, 484–85.

73. Pauline Maier describes the draft that the Committee of Five presented to the Congress as "a mixture of beautifully crafted passages, some of which had begun with previously written prose, and others that remained overstated or overlong and so gave evidence of both its draftsman's feelings and the 'haste' with which the draft had been written." Maier, *American Scripture*, 142–43.

74. Josiah Bartlett to John Langdon, July 1, 1776, *LDC*, vol. 4, 350–51.

75. Edmund Randolph to Thomas Jefferson, June 23, 1776, *PTJ*, vol. 1, 407–408; William Fleming to Thomas Jefferson, June 27, 1776, *PTJ*, vol. 1, 474–76.

76. Thomas Jefferson to William Fleming, July 1, 1776, *PTJ*, vol. 1, 411–13.

77. Ibid. Thomas Jefferson and others referred to their home colony as their "country."

78. Edward Rutledge to John Jay, June 29, 1776, *PJJ*, vol. 1, 260–62.

79. John Jay to Edward Rutledge, July 6, 1776, *PJJ*, vol. 1, 263–65.

80. John Hancock to Certain Colonies, June 25, 1776, *LDC*, vol. 4, 317–19.

81. John Adams to Samuel Chase, July 1, 1776, *PJA*, vol. 4, 353–54.

82. On John Dickinson's July 1 speech, see Calvert, *Penman of the Founding*, 265–69.

83. Silas Deane had left Bermuda on May 3.

84. J. H. Powell, "Speech of John Dickinson Opposing the Declaration of Independence, 1 July 1776," *PMHB* 65, no. 4 (October 1941): 478; Robert Treat Paine's Diary, *LDC*, vol. 4, 386–88.

85. *DJA*, vol. 3, 395–98.

86. *DJA*, vol. 3, 395–98. Unlike John Dickinson, John Adams "made no Preparation beforehand and never committed any minutes" to paper. But twenty-nine years after the fact, Adams believed that, if he had a copy of Dickinson's speech in front of him, he would be able to reconstruct his own speech.

87. John Adams remembered that Richard Stockton, John Witherspoon, and Francis Hopkinson (actually Abraham Clark) had arrived on July 1, just "before the final Question was put," and "expressed a great desire to hear the Arguments." *DJA*, vol. 3, 395–98.

88. Caesar Rodney to Thomas Rodney, July 4, 1776, *LDC*, vol. 4, 388.

89. New York Delegates to the New York Provincial Congress, July 2, 1776, *LDC*, vol. 4, 371–72. This letter does not survive.

90. Becker, *The Declaration of Independence*, 3; Maier, *American Scripture*, 45.

91. *JCC*, vol. 5, 506–507.

92. Jane Calvert cites John Dickinson's experience with the Quaker process of dissent to explain his decision to abstain from the July 2 vote. She argues that "removing one's

objection is a tacit endorsement of the action to be taken," and that, "if patriotism means placing country before self, Dickinson suppressed every sentiment of foreboding in his heart and threw himself entirely behind the American cause." Calvert, *Penman of the Founding*, 269–70.

93. Henry Wisner to the New York Provincial Congress, July 2, 1776, *LDC*, vol. 4, 373. This letter does not survive.

94. *PTJ*, vol. 1, 423–28; Maier, *American Scripture*, 143–50. Danielle Allen notes that, "if you measure by word count, Congress reduced the Declaration by about 25 percent. Yet most of the argument structure initially provided by Jefferson survived." Allen, *Our Declaration*, 72.

95. Friederike Baer, *Hessians: German Soldiers in the American Revolutionary War* (Oxford University Press, 2022), 24–25; Sidney Kaplan, "The 'Domestic Insurrections' of the Declaration of Independence," *Journal of Negro History* 61, no. 3 (1976): 243–55; Parkinson, *The Common Cause*, chap. 3.

96. Armitage, *The Declaration of Independence*, 57–60; Boulton, "The Declaration of Independence and the Language of Slavery," 15–25. Carl Becker writes about being "glad" that the Continental Congress cut this grievance: "here the discrepancy between the fact and the representation is too flagrant," and, "even assuming the charges against the king to be true, it is the part of the Declaration in which Jefferson conspicuously failed to achieve literary excellence." Becker argues that, with this grievance, "Jefferson attempted something which he was temperamentally unfitted to achieve." Becker, *Declaration of Independence*, 213–14.

97. Danielle Allen notes that Thomas Jefferson had not intended to use "Lee's actual words," but "those words were, after all, the reason Jefferson had a declaration to write." Allen, *Our Declaration*, 264.

98. Carl Becker describes the closing sentence in Thomas Jefferson's rough draft as "perfection itself" before the Committee of the Whole added the supplication to providence. *Declaration of Independence*, 196.

99. *JCC*, vol. 5, 509–18. On July 4, a committee of New York, New Jersey, and Pennsylvania delegates wrote to the Lancaster Associators that the Continental Congress had directed them "this morning" to determine the best means of defending New Jersey and Pennsylvania. This order is recorded in the *JCC* after the Declaration of Independence was approved, which means that the Congress passed the Declaration earlier in the morning. The Committee of Congress to the Lancaster Associators, July 4, 1776, *LDC*, vol. 4, 379–83.

100. *JCC*, vol. 5, 509–18; Benjamin H. Irvin, *Clothed in Robes of Sovereignty: The Continental Congress and the People Out of Doors* (Oxford University Press, 2011), 1–2, 128–33.

101. John Adams to Samuel Chase, July 9, 1776, *PJA*, vol. 4, 372–73.

102. Silas Deane to CSC, November 28, 1776, *RDC*, vol. 2, 196–200; Irvin, *Clothed in Robes of Sovereignty*, 131–32.

CHAPTER 3

1. [Demophilus], *The Genuine Principles of the Ancient Saxon, or English Constitution* (Robert Bell, 1776), 41–46.

2. Julian Boyd suggests that Thomas Jefferson went to John Dunlap's printing office. He argues that "surely this proclamation to the world announcing one of the most decisive events in history would not have been entrusted to an ordinary messenger when the

charge had been specifically given to a committee of which Jefferson was head," and "no American of the day, not even Franklin, was so aware of the power of the printing press." This second point may stretch too far. But it does seem reasonable that Jefferson would have a vested interest, and perhaps Charles Thomson also helped to superintend the process. Boyd, "The Declaration of Independence: The Mystery of the Lost Original," *PMHB* 100, no. 4 (1976): 451–52. See also Wilfred J. Ritz, "From the *Here* of Jefferson's Handwritten Rough Draft of the Declaration of Independence to the *There* of the Printed Dunlap Broadside," *PMHB* 116, no. 4 (1992): 501–502.

3. For example: "'' that all Men are created equal, ''…" Historical Society of Pennsylvania, Ab-1776-25. This copy is often referred to as a proof copy. Julian Boyd argues that "it is incredible to suppose that a compositor of the competence to be expected in a leading printery such as Dunlap's would have placed them there if they, or something comparable to them, had not been present in the manuscript used as copy." Boyd, "The Declaration of Independence," 455. There are similar marks in a portion of Thomas Jefferson's rough draft. Wilfred J. Ritz argues that "the HSP fragment is not a proof copy of the *Dunlap Broadside*; rather it is a distinct printing of the Declaration that was made between the (now lost) first printing of Jefferson's draft Declaration and the final printing known as the *Dunlap Broadside*." Ritz, "From the *Here* of Jefferson's Handwritten Rough Draft," 504 (emphasis in original). I agree that the fragment should be treated as a distinct printing of the Declaration of Independence. See also Jay Fliegelman, *Declaring Independence: Jefferson, Natural Language & the Culture of Performance* (Stanford University Press, 1993), chap. 1; Frederick R. Goff, *The John Dunlap Broadside: The First Printing of the Declaration of Independence* (Library of Congress, 1976).

4. Thomas Starr, "Separated at Birth: Text and Context of the Declaration of Independence," *Proceedings of the American Antiquarian Society* 110, no. 1 (2000): 181.

5. John Dunlap broadside (emphasis in original).

6. Carl Becker, *The Declaration of Independence: A Study on the History of Political Ideas* (Harcourt, Brace, 1922), 206.

7. John Dunlap broadside (emphasis in original). David Armitage, *The Declaration of Independence: A Global History* (Harvard University Press, 2007), 22.

8. The surviving Dunlap broadsides have watermarks of Dutch papermakers, including Lubertus van Gerrevink, Dirk and Cornelius Blauw, and J. Honig and Zoonen. Goff, *The John Dunlap Broadside*.

9. Julian Boyd argues that it was "extremely unlikely that such an epochal manifesto, destined to be distributed from New Hampshire to Georgia, would have been issued in less than one or two hundred copies." Boyd, "The Declaration of Independence," 453.

10. Beinecke Rare Book and Manuscript Library, Yale University, 1977 Folio 13.

11. Goff, *The John Dunlap Broadside*. The broadside in the National Archives is an example of the first state, where the "P" in "Philadelphia" is directly below the comma in the attestation, and the broadside in the Library of Congress is an example of the second state, where the "P" is directly below the "N" in "THOMSON."

12. CO 5/1353, 399. There are, in short, surviving examples of five different states of the Dunlap broadside, all printed within days of July 4: the marked fragment (Historical Society of Pennsylvania); the first and second states identified by Goff, the second state missing the "our" (Beinecke Library); and the Baltimore imprint (National Archives [UK]). There is also a separate Dunlap printing on parchment (American Philosophical Society).

13. See, for example, the offsetting on the Dunlap broadside at the Albert H. Small Library, University of Virginia.

14. Morgan Browning, "Preserving the Dunlap Broadside of the Declaration of Independence," Pieces of History: A Blog of the U.S. National Archives, https://prologue.blogs.archives.gov/2021/07/02/preserving-the-dunlap-broadside-of-the-declaration-of-independence/.

15. Jacob Rush was the younger brother of Benjamin Rush, who was elected to the new Pennsylvania delegation on July 20. On Hancock's responsibility for distributing copies of the Declaration, see Pauline Maier, *American Scripture: Making the Declaration of Independence* (Knopf, 1997), 154–55, 159.

16. John Hancock to George Washington, July 6, 1776, *PGW*, vol. 5, 219–21; John Hancock to Artemas Ward, July 6, 1776, Houghton Library, Harvard University. Hancock also sent a letter to Major General Philip Schuyler on July 6 but did not mention the Declaration of Independence.

17. See, for example, John Hancock to the Pennsylvania Committee of Safety, July 5, 1776, *LDC*, vol. 4, 393. David Waldstreicher notes that, "on sending out the printed Declaration, the Congress did not recommend fasting, mourning, bell ringing, or any other observance," but instead expected people to celebrate "spontaneously." Waldstreicher, *In the Midst of Perpetual Fetes: The Making of American Nationalism, 1776–1820* (Omohundro Institute and University of North Carolina Press, 1997), 30.

18. John Hancock to William Cooper, July 6, 1776, *LDC*, vol. 4, 394–95.

19. John Adams to Mary [Polly] Palmer, July 5, 1776, *AFC*, vol. 2, 34–35; Elbridge Gerry to James Warren, July 5, 1776, *LDC*, vol. 4, 391–92.

20. Abraham Clark to William Livingston, July 5, 1776, *LDC*, vol. 4, 391. Livingston was elected governor of New Jersey in August 1776.

21. Chapin Library Special Collections, Williams College.

22. See, for example, Solomon Southwick broadside, John Carter Brown Library, bDB. U58 1776 DW7; Ezekiel Russell broadside, American Antiquarian Society, BDSDS.1776.

23. *Dunlap's Maryland Gazette; or, the Baltimore General Advertiser*, July 2, 1776, 3.

24. Whitfield Bell, Jr., *The Declaration of Independence: Four 1776 Versions* (American Philosophical Society, 1976); I. Minis Hays, "A Note on the History of the Jefferson Manuscript Draught of the Declaration of Independence in the Library of the American Philosophical Society," *Proceedings of the American Philosophical Society* 157 (July 1898).

25. Copy of Thomas Jefferson to Richard Henry Lee, July 8, 1776, *PTJ*, vol. 1, 455–56. Jefferson probably paired his fair copy with a printed copy of the Declaration "as agreed to by the house," either one of John Dunlap's broadsides or one of the first Philadelphia newspaper printings.

26. Richard Henry Lee to Thomas Jefferson, July 21, 1776, *PTJ*, vol. 1, 471.

27. Edmund Pendleton to Thomas Jefferson, August 10, 1776, *PTJ*, vol. 1, 488–91.

28. Richard Henry Lee to Thomas Jefferson, July 21, 1776, *PTJ*, vol. 1, 471. "Thing" is underlined in the original letter in the Thomas Jefferson Papers at the American Philosophical Society.

29. This manuscript was later owned by Cassius Francis Lee, Jr., and is now in the New York Public Library.

30. *Minutes of the Provincial Council of Pennsylvania, From the Organization to the Termination of the Proprietary Government*, vol. 10 (Harrisburg: Theo. Fenn, 1852), 633; John H. Hazelton, *The Declaration of Independence: Its History* (Dodd, Mead, 1906), 240–43; Maier, *American Scripture*, 158.

31. David Freeman Hawke, *In the Midst of a Revolution* (University of Pennsylvania Press, 1961), 161; Richard Alan Ryerson, *The Revolution Is Now Begun: The Radical Committees of Philadelphia, 1765–1776* (University of Pennsylvania Press, 1978), 82.

32. *Pennsylvania Evening Post*, June 27, 1776, 1.

33. The receipt for Michael Kuhn's payment passed down in the family of Owen Biddle, a member of the Committee of Safety, and was sold at auction in 2023.

34. *Dunlap's Pennsylvania Packet or the General Advertiser*, July 8, 1776, 3 (emphasis in original).

35. Christopher Marshall Diary, Historical Society of Pennsylvania.

36. The Dunlap broadside from which John Nixon read is believed to be the one in the collections of Independence National Historical Park. The fragment Dunlap broadside at the Historical Society of Pennsylvania was endorsed by a collector as "found among the papers of John Nixon of Phila. & supposed to be the original from which he read the Declaration in public," but this was not correct. Goff, *The John Dunlap Broadside*, 32; Hazelton, *The Declaration of Independence*, 553; Ritz, "From the *Here* of Jefferson's Handwritten Rough Draft of the Declaration of Independence to the *There* of the Printed Dunlap Broadside," 509.

37. John Adams to Samuel Chase, July 9, 1776, *PJA*, vol. 4, 372–73. Though the stage was long assumed to be the platform that the American Philosophical Society had built to observe the 1769 transit of Venus, evidence suggests it was a stage constructed for a public meeting on May 20, 1776, to discuss the May 15 Resolution. John Adams to James Warren, May 20, 1776, *PJA*, vol. 4, 195–97; *Pennsylvanischer Staatsbote*, July 9, 1776, 3.

38. John Adams to Abigail [Smith] Adams, July 3, 1776, *AFC*, vol. 2, 29–33.

39. John Adams to Samuel Chase, July 9, 1776, *PJA*, vol. 4, 372–73.

40. *Pennsylvania Journal; and the Weekly Advertiser*, July 10, 1776, 2. Diarist Christopher Marshall worried that creating a bonfire on an election day was risky, but what he witnessed on the night of July 8 was a "fine Star light" over bonfires, ringing bells, and "unanimity & agreement" about the Declaration of Independence. Christopher Marshall Diary, Historical Society of Pennsylvania.

41. Julie Winch, *A Gentleman of Color: The Life of James Forten* (Oxford University Press, 2002), 4, 30–31.

42. William Whipple to Joshua Brackett, July 8, 1776, *LDC*, vol. 4, 412–13.

43. *New-Hampshire Gazette; or, State Journal and General Advertiser* (Portsmouth), July 15, 1780, 1.

44. *Pennsylvania Evening Post*, July 11, 1776, 2; Francis S. Fox, *Sweet Land of Liberty: The Ordeal of the American Revolution in Northampton County, Pennsylvania* (Penn State University Press, 2000), 17.

45. *Pennsylvania Evening Post*, July 11, 1776, 2 (emphasis in original).

46. *New-York Gazette; and the Weekly Mercury*, July 22, 1776, 3.

47. New Jersey State Constitution, July 2, 1776, 9, New Jersey State Archives.

48. John Adams to Jonathan Dickinson Sergeant, July 21, 1776, *PJA*, vol. 4, 397–98.

49. Waldstreicher, *In the Midst of Perpetual Fetes*, 32–33.

50. *Dunlap's Pennsylvania Packet*, July 15, 1776, 3; August 5, 1776, 2; September 17, 1776, 2.

51. The Committee of Secret of Correspondence to Silas Deane, August 7, 1776, *PBF*, vol. 22, 553–55.

52. *Dunlap's Pennsylvania Packet*, July 15, 1776, 3; *Newport Mercury*, July 22, 1776, 4; *Virginia Gazette*, August 10, 1776, 6.

53. *Essex Journal and New-Hampshire Packet*, August 9, 1776, 3; *New-York Journal*, August 15, 1776, 3.

54. Benedict Anderson, *Imagined Communities: Reflections on the Origin and Spread of Nationalism*, rev. ed. (Verso, 2006).

55. C. L. Bragg, *Crescent Moon over Carolina: William Moultrie & American Liberty* (University of South Carolina Press, 2013), chaps. 8–10.

56. The pilot of HMS *Actaeon*, an enslaved man named Sampson, was considered so valuable that when the fighting began, he was sent below deck for safety. William Moultrie, *Memoirs of the American Revolution, So Far as It Related to the States of North and South Carolina, and Georgia*, vol. 1 (David Longworth, 1802), 170–71.

57. William Tennent III Journal, 62–63, South Caroliniana Library, University of South Carolina.

58. *AA*, series 5, vol. 1, 882.

59. *New-York Journal*, August 8, 1776, 3; Benjamin H. Irvin, *Clothed in Robes of Sovereignty: The Continental Congress and the People Out of Doors* (Oxford University Press, 2011), 141; Maier, *American Scripture*, 157–58; Robert G. Parkinson, *The Common Cause: Creating Race and Nation in the American Revolution* (Omohundro Institute and University of North Carolina Press, 2016), 259–61, 272; Waldstreicher, *In the Midst of Perpetual Fetes*, 31. This effigy was the physical manifestation of the British "proxies" that are the focus of Parkinson's book.

60. *New-York Journal*, August 8, 1776, 3 (emphasis in original).

61. *Journal and Correspondence of the Maryland Council of Safety*, Archives of Maryland Online, vol. 12, 55.

62. The substitute reader was William Aisquith.

63. *Dunlap's Maryland Gazette*, July 30, 1776, 3; Brendan McConville, *The King's Three Faces: The Rise and Fall of Royal America, 1688–1776* (Omohundro Institute and University of North Carolina Press, 2006), 307–308; Waldstreicher, *In the Midst of Perpetual Fetes*, 31.

64. Robert Christie to Daniel of St. Thomas Jenifer, December 10, 1776, *AA*, series 5, vol. 3, 1147–48.

65. American Loyalist Claims, 1776–1835, Evidence, Maryland 1783–1786, 73–78. Robert Christie hid in "some remote corner of the Province" until July 1777. He joined the British in New York and traveled with them to Philadelphia, back to New York, then to the West Indies, and finally to London.

66. As part of his argument that there was an informal public reading of the Declaration of Independence on July 4, Wilfred J. Ritz argues—I think unnecessarily—that "the publication of the Declaration in *The Pennsylvania Evening Post* issue of July 6 deprives the later ceremonial reading on July of any significance in terms of 'publishing' the Declaration." Ritz, "From the *Here* of Jefferson's Handwritten Rough Draft," 510.

67. *Pennsylvania Evening Post*, July 2, 1776, 4. This short paragraph was next to an advertisement offering a three-dollar reward for the return of a twenty-five-year-old man named Ishmael who had self-emancipated from his enslaver, William Thomas, in Southwark. On printers' complicity in the institution of slavery, see Jordan E. Taylor, "Enquire of the Printer: Newspaper Advertising and the Moral Economy of the North American Slave Trade, 1704–1807," *Early American Studies* 18, no. 3 (2020): 287–323.

68. *Pennsylvanischer Staatsbote*, July 5, 1776, 2; Willi Paul Adams, "German Translations of the American Declaration of Independence," *Journal of American History* 85, no. 4 (1999): 1327.

69. Karl J. R. Arndt, "The First Translation and Printing in German of the American Declaration of Independence," *Monatshefte* 77, no. 2 (1985): 138.

70. The newspaper and broadside present slightly different translations, even though Charles Cist probably helped with the translation for Henry Miller's newspaper. Arndt, "The First Translation and Printing in German of the American Declaration of Independence," 138–40. Like the English-language press in the thirteen colonies, "the German-language press was an integrating force, essential to the process of nation-building." Willi Paul Adams, "The Colonial-German Language Press and the American Revolution," in *The Press and the American Revolution*, ed. Bernard Bailyn and John B. Hench (American Antiquarian Society, 1980), 153.

71. *Reichspostreuter* (Altona), August 26, 1776, 2–3.

72. The *Germantowner Zeitung* and *North-Carolina Gazette* may have been active at this time, but no extant issues with the Declaration of Independence are known.

73. *New-York Journal; or, the General Advertiser* (New York: John Holt), July 11, 1776, 4; *Freeman's Journal, or New-Hampshire Gazette*, July 20, 1776, 4.

74. *New-York Journal*, July 11, 1776, 2 (emphasis in original).

75. John Holt broadside, New York Public Library.

76. *Connecticut Journal*, July 10, 1776, 2 (emphasis in original).

77. *Connecticut Journal*, July 3, 1776, 2.

78. Thomas and Samuel Green broadside, Boston Public Library.

79. As Danielle Allen has shown, the punctuation following the phrase "Life, Liberty, and the pursuit of Happiness" had a significant impact on comprehension of the sentence. Allen, *Our Declaration: A Reading of the Declaration of Independence in Defense of Equality*, epilogue.

80. *Maryland Gazette*, July 11, 1776, 2; *Providence Gazette; and Country Journal*, July 13, 1776, 3.

81. Someone added the "n" missing in "Hancock" to the margin of a broadside at the American Antiquarian Society. The donor of this broadside, Simon Greenleaf, noted that the error "shews the great haste to announce that great event." He claimed that the broadside had been posted up in Newburyport, Massachusetts, and preserved by his grandfather.

82. *Maryland Journal and the Baltimore Advertiser*, July 10, 1776, 1. The missing sentence is: "We have reminded them of the Circumstances of our Emigration and Settlement here."

83. *Maryland Journal*, July 10, 1776, 1 (emphasis in original).

84. *Essex Journal*, July 19, 1776, 1; *Freeman's Journal*, July 20, 1776, 4; *New Hampshire Gazette, or, Exeter Morning Chronicle*, July 16, 1776, 1. An unattributed broadside matches the newspapers in these and other anomalies, which is evidence that it may have been the work of one of these printers.

85. *New-Hampshire Gazette*, July 16, 1776, 1.

86. Isaiah Thomas, *The History of Printing in America, With a Biography of Printers, and an Account of Newspapers*, vol. 1 (Isaac Sturtevant, 1810), lxviii–lxix.

87. Thomas, *The History of Printing in America*, vol. 1, lxviii–lxix.

88. *Massachusetts Spy Or, American Oracle of Liberty*, July 17, 1776, 1.

89. *Massachusetts Spy*, July 17, 1776, 1 (emphasis in original).

90. The first issue of *Freeman's Journal* in Portsmouth, New Hampshire, appeared on May 25, and the first issue of the *American Gazette* in Salem, Massachusetts, appeared on June 18.

91. Parkinson, *The Common Cause*, Appendix A.

CHAPTER 4

1. George Washington to John Hancock, July 12, 1776, *PGW*, vol. 5, 283–85.

2. Edward H. Tatum, Jr., ed., *The American Journal of Ambrose Serle, Secretary to Lord Howe, 1776–1778* (Huntington Library, 1940), 28–30.

3. Tatum, *The American Journal of Ambrose Serle*, 30–31.

4. Ibid., 31 (emphasis in original).

5. In his book on the fire that destroyed New York City that fall, Benjamin Carp argues that "the year that Americans declared their independence was transitional, chaotic, and uncertain in ways that are not easy to resolve." Carp, *The Great New York Fire of 1776: A Lost Story of the American Revolution* (Yale University Press, 2023), 4.

6. George Washington to John Hancock, March 24, 1776, *PGW*, vol. 3, 522–25.

7. George Washington to Artemas Ward, July 1, 1776, *PGW*, vol. 5, 178–79.

8. Andrew Jackson O'Shaughnessy, *The Men Who Lost America: British Leadership, the American Revolution, and the Fate of the Empire* (Yale University Press, 2013), 91.

9. General Orders, July 2, 1776, *PGW*, vol. 5, 179–82. Joseph J. Ellis describes these orders as "Washington's own declaration, rendered pressingly relevant by the recognition" that the Declaration of Independence "would be quickly forgotten if the war was lost that same summer." Ellis, *Revolutionary Summer: The Birth of American Independence* (Knopf, 2013), 42.

10. Hezekiah Hayden to Nathaniel Hayden, July 4, 1776, Connecticut Digital Archive. On soldiers' appropriations of orders, see John A. Ruddiman, "'A record in the hands of thousands': Power and Negotiation in the Orderly Books of the Continental Army," *WMQ* 67, no. 4 (October 2010): 747–74, especially 767.

11. Francis Hutcheson to Frederick Haldimand, July 10, 1776, *NDAR*, vol. 5, 1010–13; Phillip Papas, *That Ever Loyal Island: Staten Island and the American Revolution* (New York University Press, 2007), 69–70.

12. Papas, *That Ever Loyal Island*, 9, 12. For a scathing prediction of this plan, see *Constitutional Gazette*, July 3, 1776, 3.

13. George Washington to Nathaniel Woodhull, June 27, 1776, *PGW*, vol. 5, 128–29.

14. Papas, *That Ever Loyal Island*, 61.

15. Ibid., 71.

16. Ibid., 67.

17. William Tryon to Lord George Germain, July 8, 1776, CO 5/1107, 368–69.

18. Abraham Clark to Elias Dayton, July 14, 1776, *LDC*, vol. 4, 451–53; Examination of James Macfarlan, July 5, 1776, *NDAR*, vol. 5, 936–37.

19. Hugh Mercer to George Washington, July 16, 1776, *PGW*, vol. 5, 341–42.

20. Worthington Chauncey Ford, ed., *Correspondence and Journals of Samuel Blachley Webb*, vol. 1 (1893), 150–51.

21. Ford, *Correspondence and Journals of Samuel Blachley Webb*, vol. 1, 160–62. Samuel, Sarah, their older brother Joseph, and their younger siblings Mehitable, John, and Abigail were the stepchildren of Silas Deane, the Continental Congress's agent in France. Lisa Wilson argues that Deane "used politics to escape his family obligations after the death of his first wife," the Webbs' mother, Mehitable. Wilson, *A History of Stepfamilies in Early America* (University of North Carolina Press, 2014), chap. 1, quote 36.

22. Ford, *Correspondence and Journals of Samuel Blachley Webb*, vol. 1, 151–52.

23. John Maitland to James Maitland, 7th Earl of Lauderdale, July 8, 1776, GL.

24. George Washington to John Hancock, July 4–5, 1776, *PGW*, vol. 5, 199–203; Ford, *Correspondence and Journals of Samuel Blachley Webb*, vol. 1, 152–53.

25. Joseph Reed to Esther [DeBerdt] Reed, July 4, 1776, New York Historical.

26. Baby Lucy Knox was born on February 26, 1776, outside of Boston, and she was baptized at Trinity Church in Boston after the British evacuation. Lucy Knox and baby Lucy were accompanied to Connecticut by "Mrs. Pollard," "Miss Airey," and Nathanael Greene's wife ("Betty"), but Henry Knox later complained to his brother that "Mrs Green…has like a Child Return'd again to New York." While Airey was gone, someone robbed her home on Dock Street. Lucy [Flucker] Knox to Henry Knox, ca. July 1776, GL; Henry Knox to William Knox, July 11, 1776, GL; *Constitutional Gazette*, July 10, 1776, 4.

27. Lucy [Flucker] Knox to Henry Knox, ca. July 1776, GL.

28. Henry Knox to Lucy [Flucker] Knox, July 4, 1776, GL.

29. Henry Knox to Lucy [Flucker] Knox, July 4, 1776, GL.

30. Ebenezer Hazard to Horatio Gates, July 5, 1776, *AA*, series 5, vol. 1, 20.

31. Isaac Bangs Journal, Massachusetts Historical Society, 89.

32. *Constitutional Gazette*, July 6, 1776, 3.

33. William Howe to Lord George Germain, July 7, 1776, *AA*, series 5, vol. 1, 105–106.

34. William Howe to Lord George Germain, July 8, 1776, *AA*, series 5, vol. 1, 121–22.

35. John Hancock to George Washington, July 6, 1776, *PGW*, vol. 5, 219–21.

36. Benjamin Franklin to George Washington, June 21, 1776, *PGW*, vol. 5, 64–65.

37. On June 10, John Hancock mentioned the meetings of the Committee of the Whole in letters to George Washington, but more to explain why his letters were brief than to let Washington know what the committee was discussing. On July 1, Hancock teased that his next letter would inform Washington of "some very decisive Measures." John Hancock to George Washington, June 10, 1776, *PGW*, vol. 4, 489–90; John Hancock to George Washington, June 21, 1776, *PGW*, vol. 5, 64–65.

38. John Hancock to George Washington, July 6, 1776, *PGW*, vol. 5, 219–21.

39. Ibid. Hancock's letter probably reached Washington late in the day on July 8. Washington first used "States" instead of "Colonies" in his correspondence on that day. George Washington to Thomas Seymour, July 8, 1776, *PGW*, vol. 5, 244–45. Some historians have conflated "ordered to read" with "read," however, there is no evidence to suggest that Washington personally read the Declaration aloud to his troops.

40. Library of Congress, MSS 44693. The text cuts off after the grievance that begins "He has constrained our fellow Citizens…." The University of Virginia has a Dunlap broadside that is also believed to have been part of George Washington's papers, but was taken by Tobias Lear after Washington's death. Albert H. Small Library, University of Virginia, KF4506.AQ 1776.

41. "The Brigade Majors, are to receive, at the Adjutant Generals Office, several of the Declarations to be delivered to the Brigadiers General, and the Colonels of regiments." General Orders, July 9, 1776, *PGW*, vol. 5, 245–47. There were four brigades in Manhattan at this time, led by Brigadier Generals William Heath, John Morin Scott, Joseph Spencer, and William Alexander, who was known as Lord Stirling.

42. George Washington to Philip Schuyler, July 11, 1776, *PGW*, vol. 5, 273–75; George Washington to Artemas Ward, July 9, 1776, *PGW*, vol. 5, 254–56.

43. George Washington to the Massachusetts General Court, July 9, 1776, *PGW*, vol. 5, 250. Washington repeated some of this language in his July 11 letter to Philip Schuyler.

44. General Order, July 9, 1776, *PGW*, vol. 5, 245–47.

45. Samuel Hovey to Ivory Hovey, July 10, 1776, New England Historic Genealogical Society, Mss 68; Solomon Nash Diary, New York Historical; Isaac Bangs Journal, Massachusetts Historical Society, 91.

46. General Orders, July 9, 1776, *PGW*, vol. 5, 245–47.

47. George Washington to John Hancock, July 10, 1776, *PGW*, vol. 5, 258–61.

48. George Washington to Adam Stephen, July 20, 1776, *PGW*, vol. 5, 408–409. On Braddock's Defeat, see David L. Preston, *Braddock's Defeat: The Battle of the Monongahela and the Road to Revolution* (Oxford University Press, 2015).

49. *New-York Journal; or, the General Advertiser*, July 11, 1776, 2 (emphasis in original). On the destruction of the statue within a broader context of memory and reiterative iconoclasm, see Wendy Bellion, *Iconoclasm in New York: Revolution to Reenactment* (Penn State University Press, 2019); Arthur S. Marks, "The Statue of King George III in New York and the Iconology of Regicide," *American Art Journal* 13, no. 3 (1981): 61–82.

50. Isaac Bangs Journal, Massachusetts Historical Society, 27–28.

51. Ford, *Correspondence and Journals of Samuel Blachley Webb*, vol. 1, 153.

52. Isaac Bangs Journal, Massachusetts Historical Society, 27–28.

53. *New-York Journal*, July 11, 1776, 2.

54. Ford, *Correspondence and Journals of Samuel Blachley Webb*, vol. 1, 153.

55. General Orders, July 10, 1776, *PGW*, vol. 5, 256–57.

56. *New-York Journal*, July 11, 1776, 2. Hugh Gaine's account in the July 15 *New-York Gazette* was not as sensational as Holt's, and John Anderson did not describe the destruction of the statue at all, perhaps because of space restrictions in his *Constitutional Gazette*.

57. Isaac Bangs Journal, Massachusetts Historical Society, 27–28 (strikethroughs in original).

58. Ebenezer Hazard to Horatio Gates, July 12, 1776, *AA*, series 5, vol. 1, 227–28.

59. "A Plan for Attacking Staten Island," ca. July 12, 1776, *PGW*, vol. 5, 280–83. The plan is in Lord Stirling's handwriting. In attendance at this meeting were Nathanael Greene, Nathaniel Heard, William Heath, Israel Putnam, John Morin Scott, Joseph Spencer, James Wadsworth, Stirling, and George Washington.

60. General Orders, July 13, 1776, *PGW*, vol. 5, 290–91.

61. Henry Knox to Lucy [Flucker] Knox, July 13, 1776, GL. Isaac Bangs recorded hearsay that several of the men who were killed "were drunk & neglected to Spunge, Worm, & Stop the Vent, and the Cartridges took fire while they were ranting them down." Isaac Bangs Journal, Massachusetts Historical Society, 93–97.

62. Henry Knox to Lucy [Flucker] Knox, July 13, 1776, GL.

63. *JCC*, vol. 5, 558–59; George Read to Gertrude Read, July 14, 1776, *LDC*, vol. 4, 455–56; Josiah Bartlett to Mary Bartlett, July 14, 1776, *LDC*, vol. 4, 449–50.

64. Richard Howe, 1st Earl Howe, Proclamation, June 20, 1776. The Howe brothers jointly issued a new version of this declaration dated July 14. The only substantive changes to the text were the addition of William Howe's name, along with plural rather than singular pronouns.

65. As of late June and early July 1776, John Murray, 4th Earl of Dunmore (VA), was near Gwynn's Island; Robert Eden (MD) was on his way back to England; John Wentworth (NH) had fled to Halifax and then sailed to New York with General William Howe; William Tryon (NY) was in New York Harbor; Josiah Martin (NC) and William Campbell (SC) were off the coast of Charleston; and James Wright (GA) was off the coast of Savannah.

66. Nicholas Cooke was deputy governor of Rhode Island under Joseph Wanton, and replaced Wanton as governor from November 1775 to May 1776, when Cooke was elected outright.

67. Lieutenant Samuel Reeve went south to Perth Amboy, New Jersey, and Lieutenant Richard Calcott went north, to Newport, Rhode Island. The Howe brothers enclosed a copy of the declaration in a separate letter to William Tryon, dated July 14.

68. Richard Howe, 1st Earl Howe to George Washington, July 13, 1776, *PGW*, vol. 5, 296–97.

69. Henry Knox to Lucy [Flucker] Knox, July 15, 1776, GL. The previous summer, General William Howe had addressed a letter to "George Washington Esqr. Cambridge," and Washington had responded with a letter addressed to "The Hon. W. Howe Esqr." William Howe to George Washington, August 22, 1775, *PGW*, vol. 1, 349; George Washington to William Howe, August 23, 1775, *PGW*, vol. 1, 352.

70. Henry Knox to Lucy [Flucker] Knox, July 15, 1776, GL; Ford, *Correspondence and Journals of Samuel Blachley Webb*, vol. 1, 155.

71. George Washington to John Hancock, July 14, 1776, *PGW*, vol. 5, 304–309.

72. Joseph Reed to Charles Pettit, July 15, 1776, New York Historical.

73. Henry Knox to Lucy [Flucker] Knox, July 15, 1776, GL.

74. George Washington to John Hancock, July 14, 1776, *PGW*, vol. 5, 304–309. This episode is frequently recounted in biographies of George Washington, beginning with Mason Weems and John Marshall, as an example of Washington's humble leadership.

75. George Washington to William Howe, July 15, 1776, *PGW*, vol. 5, 327. The Continental Congress directed George Washington to share the same message with General John Burgoyne in Canada.

76. William Howe to George Washington, July 16, 1776, *PGW*, vol. 5, 341–42. The attempted delivery of the letter took place on July 17.

77. Memorandum of an Interview with Lieutenant Colonel James Paterson, July 20, 1776, *PGW*, vol. 5, 398–403.

78. Joseph Reed to Esther [DeBerdt] Reed, July 20–21, 1776, New York Historical.

79. Margaret Moncrieffe had been living in the home of Continental Army Major General Israel Putnam. Later in life, she recalled going to the top of the house on Broadway to gaze through a telescope at the British ships at Staten Island. Moncrieffe fell deeply in love, at the age of thirteen, with twenty-year-old Aaron Burr, who replaced Samuel Blachley Webb as Putnam's aide-de-camp when Webb was promoted to George Washington's military family. Moncrieffe claimed that Burr proposed marriage, and she wanted to accept, but Putnam cautioned her not to marry her father's enemy. After Moncrieffe reunited with her father, he encouraged her to marry a British officer. *Memoirs of Mrs. Coghlan, (Daughter of the late Major Moncrieffe), Written By Herself and Dedicated to the British Nation*, vol. 1 (C. and G. Kearsley, [1794]).

80. Lucy [Flucker] Knox to Henry Knox, July 18, 1776, GL. Hannah Flucker married James Urquhart a few months after Lucy Flucker married Henry Knox. While Henry was transporting artillery for the Continental Army, James was the town major of British-occupied Boston. Lucy and Hannah's father, Thomas Flucker, was in London and her mother, Hannah, insisted on staying in Halifax until Thomas joined her. William Knox to Lucy [Flucker] Knox, July 11, 1776, GL.

81. Ford, *Correspondence and Journals of Samuel Blachley Webb*, vol. 1, 160–62. Whether it was the British adjutant general, Lieutenant Colonel James Paterson's fault or not, Sarah Simpson never received the letter.

82. On colonial agents, see Michael G. Kammen, *A Rope of Sand: The Colonial Agents, British Politics, and the American Revolution* (Cornell University Press, 1968).

83. Copy of Dennis DeBerdt to Joseph Reed, May 3, 1776, enclosed in Joseph Reed to Esther [DeBerdt] Reed, July 20–21, 1776, New York Historical (emphasis in original). It

seems that Arthur Lee found out about this meeting or had reason otherwise to be suspicious. He warned the committee about the king's commissioners and the "efficacy of money and promises" in negotiations, and he specifically cautioned them, "beware of Joseph Reed." Arthur Lee to the CSC, June 3, 1776, *RDC*, vol. 2, 95–96.

84. Joseph Reed to Esther [DeBerdt] Reed, July 16, 1776, New York Historical.

85. Joseph Reed to Esther [DeBerdt] Reed, July 22, 1776, New York Historical.

86. Lieutenant Samuel Reeve sailed to Perth Amboy, New Jersey on July 14 and had breakfast with Brigadier General Hugh Mercer, commander of the Continental Army's flying camp in New Jersey. Reeve gave Mercer the copies of Howe's declaration, as well as a letter that Howe had written to Benjamin Franklin, and Mercer sent these papers to George Washington, who forwarded them to John Hancock. Every letter in the packet remained sealed as it traveled except for Howe's letter to Franklin's son, New Jersey Governor William Franklin, which was unsealed when it reached Washington's hands. Hugh Mercer to George Washington, July 14, 1776, *PGW*, vol. 5, 309–10; George Washington to John Hancock, July 15, 1776, *PGW*, vol. 5, 325–26.

87. *JCC*, vol. 5, 574–90. Charles Carroll of Carrollton was also appointed to the Board of War.

88. *JCC*, vol. 5, 590–93.

89. Charles Carroll of Carrollton to Charles Carroll, Sr., July 29, 1776, *LDC*, vol. 4, 558–60.

90. Robert G. Parkinson, *The Common Cause: Creating Race and Nation in the American Revolution* (Omohundro Institute and University of North Carolina Press, 2016), 266–69.

91. *Pennsylvania Ledger Or the Virginia, Maryland, Pennsylvania, and New-Jersey Weekly Advertiser*, July 20, 1776, 2–3.

92. *JCC*, vol. 5, 590–93; Thomas Starr, "Separated at Birth: Text and Context of the Declaration of Independence," *Proceedings of the American Antiquarian Society* 110, no. 1 (2000), 161, 172.

93. George Bancroft made the connection between the Howe declaration and the order for a parchment copy of the Declaration of Independence, but most historians since Bancroft have focused on New York's approbation. Bancroft, *History of the United States, From the Discovery of the American Continent*, 3rd ed., vol. 9 (Little, Brown, 1873), 41.

94. John Adams to Abigail [Smith] Adams, July 20, 1776, *AFC*, vol. 2, 52–53.

95. William Whipple to Joshua Brackett, July 23, 1776, *LDC*, vol. 4, 531–32.

96. Charles Carroll of Carrollton to Charles Carroll, Sr., 20 Jul 1776, *LDC*, vol. 4, 495–97. Carroll enclosed the July 20 issue of the *Pennsylvania Ledger* so that his father could read Howe's declaration as well as the news from South Carolina.

97. *Pennsylvania Ledger*, July 20, 1776, 2–3; *Pennsylvania Evening Post*, July 20, 1776, 1–2.

98. As David Armitage describes it, the "first American civil war" ended and the "first Anglo-American war" began. Armitage, *Civil Wars: A History in Ideas* (Yale University Press, 2017), 143.

99. Richard Howe, 1st Earl Howe to Lord George Germain, August 11, 1776, CO 5/177, 14–15; William Howe to Lord George Germain, August 6, 1776, CO 5/93 Part 2, 228–29.

CHAPTER 5

1. John Adams to Abigail [Smith] Adams, July 20, 1776, *AFC*, vol. 2, 53–54.

2. The *AFC* editors note that, "so far as we know, [John Adams] had said nothing to [Abigail Adams] about the actual authorship of the Declaration, and since the copy of the draft that he had evidently sent on is *in his hand*, [Abigail Adams] would very natu-

rally have inferred that he was the author, and would, characteristically, have resented alterations by Congress in her husband's work." Abigail [Smith] Adams to John Adams, July 13–4, 1776, *AFC*, vol. 2, 48–9, n. 8 (emphasis in original).

3. John Adams to Abigail [Smith] Adams, July 16, 1776, *AFC*, vol. 2, 50–51. John Adams first learned about his family's inoculation through letters from Abigail's uncle, Isaac Smith, Sr., dated July 8, and Jonathan Mason, Jr., dated July 9.

4. Abigail Adams wrote to John Adams on June 17 and did not write again until July 13. By comparison, during those weeks John wrote to Abigail on June 26, July 3 (two letters), July 7 (two letters), July 10, and July 11.

5. In their correspondence at this time, John and Abigail Adams called their children "Nabby," "Johnny," "Charly," and "Tommy." Abigail's brother-in-law Richard Cranch wrote to John Adams that he had been inoculated at the same time as Charles on July 11, and that Abigail and the other three children were inoculated on July 12. But on July 13, Abigail wrote that "I yesterday arrived and was with all 4 of our Little ones inoculated." Abigail [Smith] Adams to John Adams, July 13–14, 1776, *AFC*, vol. 2, 45–49.

6. Ibid.

7. The mail from New York that arrived on July 13 brought John Adams's letters of July 3 and multiple copies of the Declaration of Independence. John Rowe Diaries, Massachusetts Historical Society, vol. 13, 2194.

8. Abigail [Smith] Adams to John Adams, July 13–4, 1776, *AFC*, vol. 2, 45–49.

9. On July 7, John Adams sent Abigail "an Evening Post," presumably the *Pennsylvania Evening Post* of July 6, the first newspaper printing of the Declaration of Independence. There is no clear evidence of whether he also sent her a Dunlap broadside. John Adams to Abigail [Smith] Adams, July 7, 1776, *AFC*, vol. 2, 37–38.

10. Abigail [Smith] Adams to John Adams, July 13–14, 1776, *AFC*, vol. 2, 45–49; Andrew M. Wehrman, *The Contagion of Liberty: The Politics of Smallpox in the American Revolution* (Johns Hopkins University Press, 2022), 183–84.

11. William Whipple to Josiah Bartlett, May 24, 1776, *LDC*, vol. 3, 435–36.

12. John Adams to Abigail [Smith] Adams, March 29, 1776, *AFC*, vol. 1, 366. Samuel Ward died on March 26 and his public funeral took place the next day.

13. John Adams to Samuel Cooper, July 2, 1776, *PJA*, vol. 4, 357–58; John Adams to Abigail [Smith] Adams, June 26, 1776, *AFC*, vol. 2, 23–24.

14. George Washington to the Massachusetts General Court, March 21, 1776, *PGW*, vol. 3, 505–507. On smallpox in the Continental Army, see Ann M. Becker, *Smallpox in Washington's Army: Disease, War, and Society During the Revolutionary War* (Lexington, 2023); Wehrman, *The Contagion of Liberty*.

15. Benedict Arnold to George Washington, February 27, 1776, *PGW*, vol. 3, 381–82.

16. John Adams to Abigail [Smith] Adams, June 16, 1776, *AFC*, vol. 2, 12–13.

17. Abigail [Smith] Adams to John Adams, June 17, 1776, *AFC*, vol. 2, 13–16.

18. John Adams believed (though the *PJA* editors suggest that he was only "half-serious") that one of the reasons Massachusetts sent him to the Continental Congress was that he had been inoculated for smallpox already. He wondered whether he might "Stand a Chance to be relieved" once other political figures were inoculated. John Adams to James Warren, July 24, 1776, *PJA*, vol. 4, 407–408; Wehrman, *The Contagion of Liberty*, chap. 2.

19. John Adams to Abigail Smith [Adams], April 26, 1764, *AFC*, vol. 1, 39–41. Abigail's letters from this time do not explain why her parents allowed her brother, William, to be inoculated but not her.

20. Abigail [Smith] Adams to John Adams, September 8, 1775, *AFC*, vol. 1, 276–78.

21. Abigail [Smith] Adams to John Adams, October 1, 1775, *AFC*, vol. 1, 288–89.

22. John Adams to Abigail [Smith] Adams, October 19, 1775, *AFC*, vol. 1, 302–304. John repeated this request six weeks later and offered to bring both Abigail and John Quincy back to Philadelphia with him when he returned home for the Continental Congress's winter break. John Adams to Abigail Adams, December 3, 1775, *AFC*, vol. 1, 331–33. It is worth noting that, although John suggested that their eldest son should be inoculated, Abigail made the decision that all four of her children, including her daughter, would be inoculated.

23. Abigail [Smith] Adams to John Adams, November 12, 1775, *AFC*, vol. 1, 324–26.

24. Abigail [Smith] Adams to John Adams, April 14, 1776, *AFC*, vol. 1, 378–81.

25. Isaac Smith, Sr., to John Adams, April 6–8, 1776, *AFC*, vol. 1, 372–74.

26. Isaac Smith, Sr., to John Adams, April 6–8, 1776, *AFC*, vol. 1, 372–74; Abigail [Smith] Adams to John Adams, June 17, 1776, *AFC*, vol. 2, 13–16.

27. Isaac Smith, Sr., to John Adams, July 8, 1776, *AFC*, vol. 1, 41–42.

28. Abigail Adams made her decision to come to Boston sometime before July 7, when she invited the tutor, John Thaxter, Jr., to join them. Abigail mentioned "a maid who has had the Distemper," "my old Nurse," "A Boy," her "unkle's maid," and a "Negro man." Abigail [Smith] Adams to John Thaxter, Jr., July 7, 1776, *AFC*, vol. 2, 37; Abigail [Smith] Adams to John Adams, July 13–14, 1776, *AFC*, vol. 2, 45–49.

29. John Hancock to John Adams, July 16, 1776, enclosed in John Adams to Abigail [Smith] Adams, July 16, 1776, *AFC*, vol. 2, 50–52. John Adams told Abigail that he would turn Hancock down because the "Kindness" of Isaac Smith, Sr., had "rendered it unnecessary, as well as improper" for them to accept Hancock's offer.

30. Abigail [Smith] Adams to John Adams, July 30, 1776, *AFC*, vol. 2, 69–70.

31. Artemas Ward to George Washington, July 4, 1776, *PGW*, vol. 5, 210–11.

32. George Washington to Artemas Ward, July 11, 1776, *PGW*, vol. 5, 276–78.

33. Artemas Ward to George Washington, July 15, 1776, *PGW*, vol. 5, 332.

34. George Washington to Artemas Ward, July 9, 1776, *PGW*, vol. 5, 254–56.

35. James Warren to John Adams, July 17, 1776, *PJA*, vol. 4, 389–91. As of July 10, the Warrens were still in Plymouth, and James wrote that "the Small Pox prevails," and "in Boston they have given up all thoughts of stopping it, and every Body is Inoculating." James Warren to John Adams, July 10, 1776, *PJA*, vol. 4, 378–80.

36. James Warren to John Adams, July 17, 1776, *PJA*, vol. 4, 389–91. Hannah Winthrop also described smallpox as the "reigning Subject" in a letter she wrote from Cambridge to Warren's wife. Hannah Winthrop to Mercy Otis Warren, July 8, 1776, Massachusetts Historical Society.

37. James Warren to John Adams, July 17, 1776, *PJA*, vol. 4, 389–91.

38. Elizabeth Fenn suggests that Abigail Adams was being irresponsible when she spent time in public as her smallpox symptoms took hold. Although she notes that there is no evidence that Adams "infected anyone as a result of her actions," Fenn writes that "wealthy individuals" such as Adams might have infected anyone who stayed in Boston but could not afford the financial cost of inoculation. Fenn, *Pox Americana: The Great Smallpox Epidemic of 1775–82* (Hill and Wang, 2001), 37. It is important to consider how wealth disparities intersected with public health access, but at this moment Boston was an intentionally infectious environment. Abigail Adams was far from the only person spending time in public spaces while symptomatic, since fresh air was encouraged as

treatment. My thanks to Andrew Wehrman for sharing his thoughts on Fenn's argument.

39. Cotton Tufts to John Adams, August 6–7, 1776, *AFC*, vol. 2, 81–83. Tufts's son, who was staying in the Smiths' house with the Adamses, was inoculated five times in twenty days before he finally erupted, probably as a result of the fourth attempt. Tufts complained that "there never was in any Place or among such Physicians such Doubts and Uncertainties with respect to the Eruptions or the Operations of Inoculation."

40. Abigail [Smith] Adams to John Adams, July 21–22, *AFC*, vol. 2, 55–57; Richard Cranch to John Adams, July 22, 1776, *AFC*, vol. 2, 57–58.

41. Daniel Greenleaf recalled that his father, William Greenleaf, read a line of the Declaration and Thomas Crafts repeated it, and they proceeded in this way until the end of the text. But none of the contemporary descriptions of this public reading, in newspapers or private letters, mentioned this arrangement. Crafts was the memorable reader. J. L. Bell, "Sheriff Greenleaf and Col. Crafts Read the Declaration," Boston 1775, July 2007, https://boston1775.blogspot.com/2007/07/sheriff-greenleaf-and-col-crafts-read.html.

42. Abigail [Smith] Adams to John Adams, July 21–22, 1776, *AFC*, vol. 2, 55–57.

43. *New-England Chronicle*, July 25, 1776, 3; Abigail [Smith] Adams to John Adams, July 21–22, 1776, *AFC*, vol. 2, 55–57.

44. In April 1775, there were four active newspapers in Boston: Benjamin Edes and John Gill's *Boston-Gazette*, Mills and Hicks's *Massachusetts Gazette*, Thomas and John Fleet's *Boston Evening-Post*, and Isaiah Thomas's *Massachusetts Spy*.

45. Isaiah Thomas, *The History of Printing in America, With a Biography of Printers, and an Account of Newspapers*, vol. 1 (Isaac Sturtevant, 1810), 136–40; Joseph M. Adelman, *Revolutionary Networks: The Business and Politics of Printing the News, 1762–1789* (Johns Hopkins University Press, 2019), 146.

46. Massachusetts Historical Society, The Annotated Newspapers of Harbottle Dorr, Jr., vol. 4, front matter (emphasis in original).

47. On collaboration among colonial printers, see Adelman, *Revolutionary Networks*, 39–41.

48. Gill, Powars and Willis broadside (emphasis in original).

49. Benjamin Gould to George Washington, June 21, 1776, *PGW*, vol. 5, 65; National Archives, Revolutionary War Pension and Bounty Land Warrant Applications, File W 1166. Benjamin Gould and Daniel Gould were both from Topsfield and may have been related.

50. Gill, Powars and Willis broadside, John Carter Brown Library.

51. Artemas Ward to George Washington, August 19, 1776, *PGW*, vol. 5, 81–82.

52. For example, when Martha Washington was inoculated in May 1776, she refused to write a letter to her sister-in-law. George Washington explained her excuse, "notwithstanding there could be but little danger in conveying the Infection in this Manner." George Washington to John Augustine Washington, May 31–June 4, 1776, *PGW*, vol. 4, 411–14. On this misconception and the domestic context for smallpox, see Sarah Schuetze, "Carrying Home the Enemy: Smallpox and Revolution in American Love and Letters, 1775–76," *Early American Literature* 53, no. 1 (2018): 97–125.

53. Abigail [Smith] Adams to John Adams, August 1, 1776, *AFC*, vol. 2, 72–73. Wehrman, *The Contagion of Liberty*, 98.

54. Timothy Pickering, Jr., to Richard Derby, July 18, 1776, *AA*, series 5, vol. 1, 426–27.

55. Ezekiel Russell broadside.

56. Ibid. (emphasis in original).

57. *American Gazette: or, the Constitutional Journal* (J. Rogers), July 16, 1776, 1, 4; John Rogers broadside. The broadside may predate the newspaper by a few days.

58. *American Gazette,* July 23, 1776, 2.

59. While the type was still set for this broadside, Ezekiel Russell condensed the title and added a woodcut of two facing portraits, possibly of George Washington and Artemas Ward. John D. Cushing writes that, "more than any other printer of his time, Russell used such primitive ornamentation frequently, although the cuts did not always bear a relationship to the substance of the works they adorned." John D. Cushing, "Ezekiel Russell's Edition of Jonathan Mitchell Sewall's 'War and Washington': A Bibliographical Note," *Proceedings of the Massachusetts Historical Society* 93 (1981): 112.

60. John Avery to William Greenleaf, August 5, 1776, *AA*, series 5, vol. 1, 778.

61. Ezekiel Russell broadside (emphasis in original).

62. Ezekiel Russell broadside, private collection (sold by Sotheby's, 2022).

63. Ezekiel Russell broadside, private collection (sold by Historical Auctions, 2016).

64. Ezekiel Russell broadside, private collection (sold by Sotheby's, 2018).

65. Ezekiel Russell broadside, American Antiquarian Society, BDSDS.1776.

66. Ezekiel Russell broadside, State Library of Massachusetts.

67. Ezekiel Russell broadside, Boston Public Library, RARE BKS H.766, Un3Ds pb.

68. Ezekiel Russell broadside, Massachusetts Historical Society.

69. Dexter, Franklin Bowditch, ed., *The Literary Diary of Ezra Stiles, D.D., LL.D.,* Vol. II: *March 14, 1776–December 1, 1781* (Charles Scribner, 1901), 21, 41.

70. Despite Ezra Stiles's connections to Brown University and Yale University, his copy of the Ezekiel Russell broadside is in the Houghton Library at Harvard University.

71. Gideon Hawley to William Phillips, September 24, 1776, private collector (Christies, 2017). Hawley's Russell broadside is not known to survive.

72. The ambiguity over what to do with the Russell broadsides has led to legal issues, as some towns only realized that their Russell broadside still existed after it was put up for auction by a collector. In 2009, the Virginia Supreme Court ruled that the Ezekiel Russell broadside that was sent to Wiscasset, Massachusetts, was the rightful property of a private collector. The skyrocketing costs to preserve and insure a rare copy of the Declaration have also challenged some Massachusetts towns. In 2022, the Southborough Historical Society decided to sell the town's Russell broadside and use the multi-million-dollar earnings to relocate the Southborough Historical Society Museum to a new building.

73. Ezekiel Russell broadside, Huntington Library, 21150.

74. Cambridge Selectman Minutes, City Clerk's Office, Cambridge, Massachusetts (emphasis in original).

75. Office of the Town Clerk, Natick, Massachusetts (emphasis in original).

76. Samuel Cooper to John Adams, August 14, 1776, *PJA*, vol. 4, 457–58.

77. Abigail [Smith] Adams to John Adams, August 14, 1776, *PJA*, vol. 2, 92–93.

78. Abigail [Smith] Adams to John Adams, July 29, 1776, *AFC*, vol. 2, 65–68.

79. Abigail [Smith] Adams to John Adams, ca. August 12, 1776, *AFC*, vol. 2, 86–88.

80. Abigail [Smith] Adams to John Adams, July 29, 1776, *AFC*, vol. 2, 65–68.

81. Abigail [Smith] Adams to John Adams, August 14, 1776, *AFC*, vol. 2, 93–95.

82. Ibid.

83. Abigail [Smith] Adams to John Adams, August 17, 1776, *AFC*, vol. 2, 98.

84. Abigail [Smith] Adams to John Adams, August [19], 1776, *AFC*, vol. 2, 101. Before John Adams received this letter, he visited Charles Willson Peale's gallery and saw a portrait of the child Peale had lost to smallpox. In the summer of 1776, Peale expanded the portrait to

include his wife, Rachel, weeping over the child. The image "struck" Adams "prodigiously." John Adams to Abigail [Smith] Adams, August 21, *AFC*, vol. 2, 103–105.

85. Abigail [Smith] Adams to John Adams, August 25, 1776, *AFC*, vol. 2, 106–108.

86. John Adams to Abigail [Smith] Adams, August 28, 1776, *AFC*, vol. 2, 111–12.

87. John Adams to Abigail [Smith] Adams, August 30, 1776, *AFC*, vol. 2, 114–15. John Adams was "glad" that his daughter would "have a few Pitts," and confident that if they affected her appearance, she would "learn to prize looks less, and Ingenuity more." Mercy Otis Warren made a similar comment in a letter to Abigail Adams. Smallpox as "a sad Enemy" to "soft Features," but "Miss Naby will be so Formed both by Example And Education, as to stand in Little Need of any External Accomplishments to Recommend her to the Esteem of the Worthy and Good." Mercy Otis Warren to Abigail [Smith] Adams, September 4, 1776, *AFC*, vol. 2, 118–19.

88. Abigail [Smith] Adams to John Adams, August 31–September 2, 1776, *AFC*, vol. 2, 115–17.

CHAPTER 6

1. *AA*, series 5, vol. 1, 844–47.

2. Ibid. In the minutes of the treaty proceedings, the secretary used "Micmack" and "St. John's" to describe the Mi'kmaw and Wolastoqiyik (also known as Maliseet) nations respectively.

3. On the relationship between white political leaders and Native Americans and First Nations people at the founding of the United States, see Ned Blackhawk, *The Rediscovery of America: Native Peoples and the Unmaking of U.S. History* (Yale University Press, 2023), chaps. 5–6; Colin G. Calloway, *The American Revolution in Indian Country: Crisis and Diversity in Native American Communities*, rev. ed. (Cambridge University Press, 2009); Alan Taylor, *The Divided Ground: Indians, Settlers, and the Northern Borderland of the American Revolution* (Knopf, 2006); John C. Winters, *"The Amazing Iroquois" and the Invention of the Empire State* (Oxford University Press, 2023).

4. *JCC*, vol. 5, 429–31.

5. Robert G. Parkinson, *The Common Cause: Creating Race and Nation in the American Revolution* (Omohundro Institute and University of North Carolina Press, 2016), 230–31, 241–43.

6. On the impact of the Battle of the Cedars on the Continental Congress's thinking about Native Americans, see Mark R. Anderson, *Down the Warpath to the Cedars: Indians' First Battles in the Revolution* (University of Oklahoma Press, 2021); Parkinson, *The Common Cause*, 235–41.

7. Speeches of the Caughnawaga, St. Johns, and Passamaquoddy Indians, January 31, 1776, *PGW*, vol. 3, 223–24.

8. *AA*, series 5, vol. 1, 838–41. The Massachusetts Council asked Colonel Arthur Lithgow, who understood "the Indian language," to assist John Prince.

9. *AA*, series 5, vol. 1, 838–41.

10. Ibid.

11. Ibid., 841–44.

12. James Bowdoin to George Washington, July 30, 1776, *PGW*, vol. 5, 510–14.

13. *AA*, series 5, vol. 1, 848–50.

14. Ibid. John Hazelton describes the presentation of the Declaration of Independence during the conference in Watertown as "perhaps the most striking incident" from 1776 "of all those which have come down to us." Hazelton, *The Declaration of Independence: Its History* (Dodd, Mead, 1906), 262.

15. *AA*, series 5, vol. 1, 848–50.

16. Ibid.

17. Ibid.

18. *JCC*, vol. 5, 525–28.

19. George Washington to the Massachusetts General Court, July 11, 1776, *PGW*, vol. 5, 270–71.

20. James Bowdoin to George Washington, July 30, 1776, *PGW*, vol. 5, 510–14.

21. George Washington to James Bowdoin, August 14, 1776, *PGW*, vol. 6, 18–19.

22. *JCC*, vol. 5, 574–90.

23. George Washington to John Hancock, August 13, 1776, *PGW*, vol. 6, 4–5.

24. George Washington to John Hancock, August 18, 1776, *PGW*, vol. 6, 61–63.

25. Philip Schuyler to George Washington, June 11–12, 1776, *PGW*, vol. 4, 504–506; Barbara Graymont, *The Iroquois in the American Revolution* (Syracuse University Press, 1972), 107–108.

26. *JCC*, vol. 2, 183.

27. Samuel Kirkland to Philip Schuyler, June 8, 1776, *AA*, series 4, vol. 6, 764.

28. Conference of Oneida Indians and Commissioners for Indian Affairs, June 19, 1776, *AA*, series 4, vol. 6, 977–79.

29. Samuel Kirkland to Philip Schuyler, June 8, 1776, *AA*, series 4, vol. 6, 764.

30. Philip Schuyler to George Washington, July 12–13, 1776, *PGW*, vol. 5, 286–90; Philip Schuyler to Jonathan Trumbull, July 17, 1776, *AA*, series 5, vol. 1, 395–96.

31. Philip Schuyler to John Hancock, July 17, 1776, *AA*, series 5, vol. 1, 394–95.

32. The Continental Congress asked the Commissioners for Indian Affairs in the middle department to thank Guyasuta for his "friendly conduct," and let him know that the Congress would welcome a visit from him. *JCC*, vol. 5, 621.

33. Philip Schuyler to John Hancock, July 17, 1776, *AA*, series 5, vol. 1, 394–95.

34. Philip Schuyler to Jonathan Trumbull, July 17, 1776, *AA*, series 5, vol. 1, 395–96.

35. Philip Schuyler to George Washington, August 2, 1776, *PGW*, vol. 5, 550–51. The spy was "an Indian Man, named Thomas Davis." After the end of the conference, Schuyler learned that the soldier who had given this intelligence had deserted to join the British.

36. George Washington to Philip Schuyler, July 11, 1776, *PGW*, vol. 5, 273–75; Philip Schuyler to George Washington, July 17, 1776, *PGW*, vol. 5, 367–68.

37. Philip Schuyler to George Washington, July 24, 1776, *PGW*, vol. 5, 445–53.

38. Philip Schuyler to George Washington, August 6, 1776, *PGW*, vol. 55, 583–87.

39. Philip Schuyler to Jonathan Trumbull, August 7, 1776, *AA*, series 5, vol. 1, 825.

40. Conference of the Commissioners for Indian Affairs with the Six Nations of Indians, August 8, 1776, *AA*, series 5, vol. 1, 1035–38.

41. Ibid. On the similarity between this large belt and the belt connected to the Treaty of Canandaigua in 1794, see Thomas S. Abler, *Cornplanter: Chief Warrior of the Allegany Senecas*, 38–39.

42. On Abraham, see Caitlin A. Fitz, " 'Suspected on Both Sides': Little Abraham, Iroquois Neutrality, and the American Revolution," *Journal of the Early Republic* 28, no. 3 (2008): 299–335.

43. Conference of the Commissioners for Indian Affairs with the Six Nations of Indians, August 9, 1776, *AA*, series 5, vol. 1, 1038–39.

44. Conference of the Commissioners for Indian Affairs with the Six Nations of Indians, August 12, 1776, *AA*, series 5, 1041–45.

45. Philip Schuyler to Jonathan Trumbull, August 30, 1776, *AA*, series 5, vol. 1, 1083–84.

46. Philip Schuyler to George Washington, August 16, 1776, *PGW*, vol. 6, 40–43.

47. Philip Schuyler to John Hancock, August 18, 1776, *AA*, series 5, vol. 1, 1030–31.

48. Philip Schuyler to George Washington, August 18, 1776, *PGW*, vol. 6, 66–70; George Washington to John Hancock, August 23, 1776, *PGW*, vol. 6, 111–12.

49. George Washington to Philip Schuyler, August 21, 1776, *PGW*, vol. 6, 101–102.

50. *JCC*, vol. 5, 700–701.

CHAPTER 7

1. Peter De La Roche to Richard Hind, August 26, 1776, Bodleian Library, SPG Letter Books, B Series, vol. 25, item 207.

2. James S. Leamon argues that the Declaration of Independence forced Anglican clergymen "to publicize their political positions once and for all and, in the process, to examine the nature and importance of their oaths to God, king and country." Leamon, *The Reverend Jacob Bailey, Maine Loyalist: For God, King, Country, and for Self* (University of Massachusetts Press, 2012), 116.

3. James B. Bell, *A War of Religion: Dissenters, Anglicans, and the American Revolution* (Palgrave Macmillan, 2008), 170. On Anglican clergymen in British North America and the United States before the establishment of the Episcopal Church in America, see James B. Bell, "The Making of an Eighteenth-Century American Anglican Clergyman," *Proceedings of the Massachusetts Historical Society* 106 (1994): 82–111; Katherine Carté, *Religion and the American Revolution: An Imperial History* (Omohundro Institute and University of North Carolina Press, 2021); David L. Holmes, "The Episcopal Church and the American Revolution," *Historical Magazine of the Protestant Episcopal Church* 47, no. 3 (1978): 261–91.

4. *The Book of Common Prayer, and Administration of the Sacraments, and other Rites and Ceremonies of the Church, According to the Use of the Church of England* (J. Baskerville, 1762).

5. Carté, *Religion and the American Revolution*, 196.

6. *AA*, series 4, vol. 5, 1597–98.

7. The Maryland Convention allowed for one exception, the second option for prayer during the Holy Communion service, because it was a prayer for the king's wisdom and not a prayer for the king's sovereignty or military victory.

8. *Book of Common Prayer*, Washington National Cathedral Rare Books Library.

9. *Virginia Gazette*, July 5, 1776, postscript, 1.

10. American Loyalist Claims, 1776–1835, 54. Evidence, Virginia, 1783–1786, 11–15.

11. On the SPG and slavery, see Travis Glasson, *Mastering Christianity: Missionary Anglicanism and Slavery in the Atlantic World* (Oxford University Press, 2011).

12. Jacob Duché to George Washington, October 8, 1777, *PGW*, vol. 11, 430–37.

13. Christ Church Philadelphia, Vestry Minutes.

14. *Book of Common Prayer*, Christ Church Philadelphia.

15. Christ Church Philadelphia, Vestry Minutes.

16. American Loyalist Claims, 1776–1835, Evidence, Pennsylvania, 1783–1786, 152. On Duché, see Bell, *A War of Religion*, 179–80; Carté, *Religion and the American Revolution*, 240–43; Spencer W. McBride, *Pulpit and Nation: Clergymen and the Politics of Revolutionary America* (University of Virginia Press, 2016), 54–66.

17. American Loyalist Claims, 1776–1835, Evidence, Pennsylvania, 1783–1786, 151–52.

18. John Hancock to Jacob Duché, July [9], 1776, *LDC*, vol. 4, 418.

19. Jacob Duché to George Washington, October 8, 1777, *PGW*, vol. 11, 430–37.

20. Copy of John Smith, John Jenkins, et al. to John Graves, July 8, 1776, Bodleian Library, SPG Letter Books, C Series, Box 9, item 159.

21. *Providence Gazette; and Country Journal*, July 13, 1776, 3.

22. Copy of John Graves to the Episcopal Church and Congregation in Providence, July 13, 1776, Bodleian Library, SPG Letter Books, C Series, Box 9, item 160.

23. Copy of John Graves to the Episcopal Church and Congregation in Providence, July 13, 1776 (emphasis in original).

24. John Graves to Richard Hind, September 19, 1776, Bodleian Library, SPG Letter Books, C Series, Box 9, item 161.

25. *AA*, series 5, vol. 1, 475.

26. *The Literary Diary of Ezra Stiles, D.D., LL.D.*, Vol. II: *March 14, 1776–December 1, 1781*, ed. Franklin Bowditch Dexter (Charles Scribner, 1901), 27–29.

27. Philip Reading to Richard Hind, August 25, 1776, Bodleian Library, SPG Letter Books, B Series, vol. 21, item 211.

28. Ibid.

29. Philip Reading to Richard Hind, September 30, 1778, Bodleian Library, SPG Letter Books, B Series, vol. 21, item 212.

30. C. E. Taylor to Richard Hind, October 13, 1783, Bodleian Library, SPG Letter Books, C Series, Box 8, item 118.

31. Andrew Oliver and James Bishop Peabody, eds., "The Records of Trinity Church, Boston, 1728–1830," *Publications of the Colonial Society of Massachusetts* 55 (1980), 170–71.

32. Daniel Dulany Addison, *The Life and Times of Edward Bass, First Bishop of Massachusetts* (Houghton Mifflin, 1897), 144–46.

33. Abigail [Smith] Adams to John Adams, September 29, 1776, *AFC*, vol. 2, 134–36.

34. Edward Winslow to Richard Hind, August 15, 1776, Bodleian Library, SPG Letter Books, B Series, vol. 23, item 408.

35. Abigail [Smith] Adams to John Adams, April 2, 1777, *AFC*, vol. 2, 193–95.

36. Ezekiel Russell broadside.

37. Bell, *A War of Religion*, 127–30; Carté, *Religion and the American Revolution*, 215; Leamon, *The Reverend Jacob Bailey, Maine Loyalist*.

38. Charles E. Allen, *Rev. Jacob Bailey: His Character and Works* (Lincoln County Historical Society, 1895), 9.

39. Leamon, *The Reverend Jacob Bailey, Maine Loyalist*, 116–22.

40. *Documentary History of the State of Maine*, ed. James Phinney Baxter (Portland, ME: Lefavor-Tower), vol. 14, 349.

41. Ibid., 389.

42. Ibid., 391.

43. Ibid., 393.

44. Leamon, *The Reverend Jacob Bailey, Maine Loyalist*, 156.

45. Addison, *The Life and Times of Edward Bass, First Bishop of Massachusetts*, 154.

46. Ibid., 198–99.

47. [Edward Bass], *A Brief Account of the Treatment Which Mr. Bass, Late Missionary from the Society for the Propagation of the Gospel in Foreign Parts, at Newbury-Port, New-England, Hath Received from Said Society* (London, 1786).

48. Tristram Dalton to Elbridge Gerry, July 19, 1776, *AA,* series 5, vol. 1, 461.

49. Addison, *The Life and Times of Edward Bass,* 157–58.

50. Charles Inglis to Richard Hind, October 31, 1776, Bodleian Library, SPG Letter Books, B Series, vol. 2, item 68; Bell, *A War of Religion,* 152–53.

51. Charles Inglis to Richard Hind, October 31, 1776, Bodleian Library, SPG Letter Books, B Series, vol. 2, item 68.

52. Ibid.

53. Ibid.

54. Benjamin L. Carp, *The Great New York Fire of 1776: A Lost Story of the American Revolution* (Yale University Press, 2023).

55. Joseph Hildreth to Richard Hind, October 6, 1776, Bodleian Library, SPG Letter Books, B Series, vol. 3, item 171.

56. *AA,* series 5, vol. 1, 1394–97.

57. Jacob Duché to George Washington, October 8, 1777, *PGW,* vol. 11, 430–37.

CHAPTER 8

1. *Pennsylvanischer Staatsbote,* July 9, 1776, 4.

2. Jonas Phillips to Gumpel Samson, July 28, 1776, CO 5/40 Part 2, 260–61; Adam Jortner, *A Promised Land: Jewish Patriots, the American Revolution, & the Birth of Religious Freedom* (Oxford University Press, 2024), 1, 94.

3. Rebecca [Machado] Phillips was sixteen when she married, and between 1763 and 1792 she gave birth to twenty-one children. As of 1776, she and Jonas had six living children (Zipporah, Phila, David, Rachel, Naphtali, and Benjamin).

4. *Pennsylvania Mercury; and the Universal Advertiser,* August 11, 1775, 4.

5. Samuel Curson subscribed the letter: "St. Eustatia 24 Sepr. 1776 Reced & forwarded by Your huml servt. Sam. Curson." CO 5/40, 260–61. It is unclear whether the letter took two months to reach Curson, or if he held onto it until he had an opportunity to forward it to Amsterdam. Another ship left Philadelphia around July 28 and arrived in the port of Christianstæd on the island of Saint Croix on August 14. The captain brought several newspapers, from which printer Daniel Thibou copied the Declaration of Independence in his biweekly English-language newspaper. *Royal Danish American Gazette,* August 17, 1776, 1.

6. CO EXT 9/93 (originally CO 5/40, 252). Joseph J. Felcone identified the broadside in 2008. In his frank review of Frederick Goff's *The John Dunlap Broadside,* Edwin Wolf complained that Goff included "very little information about provenance." He wished that Goff had noted that one of the Dunlap broadsides "in the Public Record Office (no. 16) was enclosed in a Yiddish letter written on 28 July 1776 to Gumpel Samson of Amsterdam by Jonas Phillips." Wolf was mistaken: no. 16 in Goff's book was the Dunlap broadside enclosed in Vice Admiral Richard Howe's August 11 letter to Lord George Germain. Wolf, Review of *The John Dunlap Broadside,* by Frederick Goff, *PBSA* 71, no. 2 (1977): 231–32.

7. Jonas Phillips's letter has been known to historians of Philadelphia's Jewish community for a long time. See Michael Hoberman, " 'How it Will End, the Blessed God Knows': A Reading of Jewish Correspondence During the Revolutionary War Era," *American Jewish History* 99, no. 4 (2015): 281–313; Jacob Rader Marcus, *Early American Jewry: The Jews of Pennsylvania and the South, 1655–1790,* vol. 2 (Jewish Publication Society of America, 1955), 62–63; Samuel Oppenheim, "Letter of Jonas Phillips, July 28, 1776, Mentioning the American Revolution and the Declaration of Independence," *Publications of the American Jewish Historical Society* 25 (1917): 128–31.

8. The Colonial Office Papers are stamped with black numbers in the upper corner of each page. Phillips's letter to Samson is numbered 260–61, the bill of exchange Phillips wanted to share with his mother is numbered 251, and the Dunlap broadside is numbered 252. At one point in the letter, Phillips said that he could explain what he meant better in English than Yiddish, indicating intentionality. Oppenheim, "Letter of Jonas Phillips, July 28, 1776, Mentioning the American Revolution and the Declaration of Independence," 130.

9. Oppenheim, "Letter of Jonas Phillips," 130.

10. Jacob Rader Marcus, *United States Jewry, 1776–1985*, vol. 1 (Wayne State University Press, 1989), chap. 2. Adam Jortner describes how "geography and the accidents of war gave Jewish patriots an unusual advantage," because the British occupation of towns with Jewish communities caused an exile that tripled the number of Jews in Philadelphia by the end of the war. This meant that "Philadelphia's synagogue, Mikveh Israel, inherited a Jewish community from across the new nation." Jortner, *A Promised Land*, 3–4.

11. For example, John Warder traveled to England to protect his family's interests during the war, and his correspondence reflects a transatlantic mercantile network of familial and Quaker connections. Warder also made several references to the news of independence. John Warder Letter Book, 1776–8, Historical Society of Pennsylvania, Am.179.

12. Oppenheim, "Letter of Jonas Phillips," 129–30.

13. Rachel [Phillips] Levy, Jonas and Rebecca's daughter and Uriah Phillips Levy's mother, moved to Monticello with her son and is buried along Mulberry Row.

14. As David Armitage argues, "the most efficient transmitters of the Declaration across the Atlantic were not the agents of Congress but British civilian and military officials in North America." Armitage, *The Declaration of Independence: A Global History* (Harvard University Press, 2007), 73–74.

15. Pauline Maier, *American Scripture: Making the Declaration of Independence* (Knopf, 1997), 130.

16. CSC to Peter Parker, July 10, 1776, *AA*, series 5, vol. 1, 156–57; CSC to Samuel and J. H. Delap, July 10, 1776, *AA*, series 5, vol. 1, 158.

17. CSC to Peter Parker, 156–57. After Captain Parker reached Bordeaux, he was supposed to recruit sailors—"especially American Seamen," but also "People of all Countrys or Nations that are willing to enter into the American Service"—before sailing back to North America.

18. Silas Deane to Charles-Guillaume-Frédéric Dumas, July 26, 1776, *AA*, series 5, vol. 1, 881.

19. J. H. Powell, "Speech of John Dickinson Opposing the Declaration of Independence, July 1, 1776," *Pennsylvania Magazine of History and Biography* 65, no. 4 (1941): 472.

20. CSC to Silas Deane, August 7, 1776, *PBF*, vol. 22, 553–55.

21. Molyneux Shuldham, 1st Baron Shuldham, to John Montagu, 4th Earl of Sandwich, July 10, 1776, National Maritime Museum, Montagu Family Papers, SAN/F/9/16. The letter is in Shuldham's handwriting. Note that there is an additional "of" in the quoted sentence which is partially crossed out in the manuscript.

22. Enclosure in Molyneux Shuldham, 1st Baron Shuldham to John Montagu, 4th Earl of Sandwich, July 10, 1776, National Maritime Museum, Montagu Family Papers, SAN/F/9/16. While copying the Declaration—presumably from a Dunlap broadside—the clerk made nine errors: two instances of overwriting, one missing word ("of" in "nature and of nature's God"), and six changed words ("and" instead of "that" in "that they are endowed" and "that whenever any form of Government," "or" instead of "and" in "Light and transient Causes," "to" instead of "his" in "He has refused his assent,"

"their" instead of "the" in "relinquish the Right of Representation," and "ever" instead of "every" in "In every Stage").

23. Hugh Gaine printed the Declaration of Independence in his newspaper as well, although he only printed a half-sheet that week, perhaps because his office was too busy with the broadsides. *New-York Gazette; and the Weekly Mercury*, July 15, 1776, 1.

24. National Archives (UK), EXT 9/26 (originally CO 5/1107). The name in the upper right corner of the verso appears to read "Elias Darling" or "Durling."

25. William Tryon to Lord George Germain, August 14, 1776, CO 5/1107 Part 2. The Gaine broadside, EXT 9/26, was docketed as an enclosure in Tryon's letter to Germain dated July 8. But it is unlikely that Gaine printed his broadsides in time for Tryon to enclose one in that letter, which traveled to England on HMS *Mercury*. It makes more sense to assume the broadside was enclosed in a later letter from Tryon to Germain. A note from the National Archives staff in the place where the broadside was extracted from CO 5/1107 concurs.

26. Richard Howe, 1st Earl Howe and William Howe to Lord George Germain, August 11, 1776, CO 5/177, 1–5.

27. National Archives (UK), EXT 9/76 (originally CO 5/177, 29). In a letter that Vice Admiral Howe wrote to Lord George Germain on the same day, he enclosed another document that "accidentally" came to his hands: a handbill of his declaration published by order of the Continental Congress. Richard Howe, 1st Earl Howe to Lord George Germain, August 11, 1776, CO 5/177, 14–15.

28. Richard Howe, 1st Earl Howe and William Howe to Lord George Germain, August 11, 1776, CO 5/177, 1–5.

29. James Corbett David, *Dunmore's New World: The Extraordinary Life of a Royal Governor in Revolutionary America—with Jacobites, Counterfeiters, Land Schemes, Shipwrecks, Scalping, Indian Politics, Runaway Slaves, and Two Illegal Royal Weddings* (University of Virginia Press, 2013), 121–26; Robert G. Parkinson, *The Common Cause: Creating Race and Nation in the American Revolution* (Omohundro Institute and University of North Carolina Press, 2016), 155–57, 245–47, 276–80.

30. John Murray, 4th Earl of Dunmore to Lord George Germain, June 26, 1776, CO 5/1353 Part 2, 385–88.

31. On rumors that Lord Dunmore engaged in germ warfare, see Andrew M. Wehrman, *The Contagion of Liberty: The Politics of Smallpox in the American Revolution* (Johns Hopkins University Press, 2022), 185–86.

32. *Virginia Gazette*, July 19, 1776, 2–3.

33. Ibid. This account also claimed that Lord Dunmore himself had been injured in the evacuation from Gwynn's Island, and had "roared out, *Good God, that ever I should come to this!*"

34. *Virginia Gazette*, July 20, 1776, 3.

35. Richard Henry Lee to Thomas Jefferson, July 21, 1776, *PTJ*, vol. 1, 471.

36. John Murray, 4th Earl of Dunmore to Lord George Germain, July 31, 1776, CO 5/177.

37. Ibid.

38. National Archives (UK), EXT 9/76 (originally CO 5/177, 29).

39. *Virginia Gazette*, July 12, 1776, supplement, 1–2 (emphasis in original); Parkinson, *The Common Cause*, 276.

40. *Virginia Gazette*, July 12, 1776, supplement, 1–2 (emphasis in original).

41. There are two manuscript copies of the Declaration of Independence in the Sackville Germain Papers at the Clements Library at the University of Michigan. One is part of a

set of manuscript fair copies, including the Olive Branch Petition and a document entitled "Remarks upon the Petition & Declaration of the Congress." The Clements Library designated the other manuscript as a "Gold Star" object, but there is no clear evidence to suggest that it has greater significance. The handwriting of the two copies of the Declaration is not exactly similar, so it can be assumed that they were handwritten by two different clerks within Germain's office, or at two different times.

42. Enclosure in Molyneux Shuldham, 1st Baron Shuldham to John Montagu, 4th Earl of Sandwich, July 10, 1776, National Maritime Museum, Montagu Family Papers, SAN/F/9/16; National Archives (UK), EXT 9/1 (originally ADM 1/487, 34).

43. *New-Lloyd's List*, August 13, 1776, 2. On coverage of the American Revolution in British newspapers, see Troy Bickham, *Making Headlines: The American Revolution as Seen Through the British Press* (Northern Illinois University Press, 2009); Solomon Lutnick, *The American Revolution and the British Press, 1775–1783* (University of Missouri Press, 1967), especially 75–76 on the Declaration of Independence.

44. William Knox, the under secretary for North America (not to be confused with William Knox, the brother of Continental Army officer Henry Knox), "chose the official items of war news Englishmen were permitted to read," and "knew more about America than did most of his contemporaries in the Government." Lutnick, *The American Revolution and the British Press, 1775–1783*, 20–22. Skepticism about the *London Gazette* can be found in newspapers across Great Britain and Ireland. A note to readers of a Dublin newspaper suggested that the British government had taken pains *"to keep the Public ignorant of all American affairs, but such, as by their mutilated Gazette accounts, may seem to favour their own wise measures, (by seizing and with holding the public Prints from that quarter)." Public Register; Or, Freeman's Journal*, July 27–30, 1776, 4 (emphasis in original).

45. *London Gazette*, August 6–10, 1776, 1. The first paragraph of Molyneux Shuldham's lengthy letter, dated July 8, was summarized. William Tryon had written two letters to Lord Germain on July 8, but only one was in the *London Gazette*. The excerpt excluded Tryon's frustration at being confined to a British ship for nine months and being passed over for a military promotion.

46. William Howe to Lord George Germain, July 8, 1776, *AA*, series 5, vol. 1, 121–22; *London Gazette*, August 6–10, 1776, 1. Howard Peckham remarks that it is "astonishing how casually the Declaration was first reported to official London." Peckham, "Independence: The View from Britain," in *The Declaration of Independence: Two Essays* (American Antiquarian Society, 1976), 389.

47. "Copy of a letter to one of the Ministry, received by the Mercury packet, dated New-York, July 7, 1776," *Morning Post, and Daily Advertiser*, August 16, 1776, 2.

48. Ibid.

49. "Extract of a letter from an officer in the 25th regiment, at Staten Island, dated July 9, 1776," Ibid.

50. Ibid.

51. Ibid. (emphasis in original).

52. *Gazetteer and New Daily Advertiser*, August 13, 1776, 2. Mary Say's husband, Charles Green Say, had died in 1775, and she had taken over his three newspapers: the *Gazetteer*, the *General Evening Post*, and the *Craftsman, or Say's Weekly Journal*. Robert L. Haig's book on the *Gazetteer* is a helpful case study of the business of newspapers in late-eighteenth-century London. Haig, *The Gazetteer, 1735–1797: A Study in the Eighteenth-Century English Newspaper* (Southern Illinois University Press, 1960).

53. "R. Figg" wrote that his "friend Senex says, the Devil took Mr. Adams, Mr. Hancock, &c. upon a high mountain, and shewed them the glories of the world, and said Europe and America will I give if you will worship me, and they did so." *Morning Chronicle, and London Advertiser*, August 17, 1776, 2.

54. Eliga H. Gould, *Among the Powers of the Earth: The American Revolution and the Making of a New World Empire* (Harvard University Press, 2010), chap. 4.

55. CSC to Silas Deane, March 3, 1776, *RDC*, vol. 2, 78–80.

56. Silas Deane to CSC, August 18, 1776, *RDC*, vol. 2, 112–22.

57. Thomas J. Schaeper, *Edward Bancroft: Scientist, Author, Spy* (Yale University Press, 2011), 52–55; Edward Bancroft to the Marquis of Carmarthen, September 17, 1784, quoted in Samuel Flagg Bemis, "British Secret Service and the French-American Alliance," *American Historical Review* 29, no. 3 (1924): 493.

58. Jonathan R. Dull, *A Diplomatic History of the American Revolution* (Yale University Press, 1985), 63; Schaeper, *Edward Bancroft*, 56–58. To the best of my knowledge, none of the existing scholarship on Bancroft acknowledges the coincidence of Bancroft's meeting with Weymouth and Suffolk and the arrival of the Declaration of Independence in London.

59. Copy of "A Narrative &c.," CO 5/43 Part 2, 254–60. This copy is in Suffolk's secretary's hand. It is written in third person, so Bancroft appears as "Dr. B." Thomas Schaeper argues that the original narrative was in Bancroft's hand and given from memory, rather than written while Bancroft was in Paris, because the dates he includes are off by a day or two. Schaeper treats this as evidence that Bancroft became a spy after—not before—his time with Deane. Schaeper, *Edward Bancroft*, 55–56.

60. Edward Bancroft to the Marquis of Carmarthen, September 17, 1784, quoted in Bemis, "British Service and the French-American Alliance," 493.

61. *Public Advertiser*, August 27, 1776, 2.

62. *Public Advertiser*, August 15, 1776, 2; August 16, 1776, 2.

63. *Public Advertiser*, August 15, 1776, 2.

CHAPTER 9

1. *Morning Post, and Daily Advertiser*, September 12, 1776, 2 (emphasis in original).

2. *Gazette d'Utrecht*, August 19, 1776, 3.

3. *Public Advertiser*, August 16, 1776, 1–2; *Lloyd's Evening Post*, August 14–16, 1776, 6. The increased digitization of newspapers has brought clarity to which London newspapers were the first to print the Declaration of Independence. In 1976, Howard Peckham incorrectly identified the *London Chronicle* as the first printing. Perhaps his source for this information was an 1898 article in *The Nation*, which cited the *"British Chronicle"* as the first printing. David Armitage says that the Declaration was printed in London in mid-August and cites the *Morning Chronicle, British [London] Chronicle, St. James's Chronicle*, and *General Evening Post*. The Declaration appeared in these newspapers on August 17. Peckham, "Independence: The View from Britain," in *The Declaration of Independence: Two Essays* (American Antiquarian Society, 1976), 390; D.D., "London Newspapers of 1776 and the Declaration of Independence," *The Nation*, February 17, 1898, 127–28; Armitage, *The Declaration of Independence*, 70, n. 12.

4. *Public Advertiser*, August 15, 1776, 2 (emphasis in original).

5. Thomas Jefferson originally wrote "pretended acts of legislation" in his rough draft and edited the phrase to "acts of pretended legislation." There is no evidence that the rough draft influenced the British printings. III. Jefferson's "original Rough draught" of the

Declaration of Independence, June 11–July 4, 1776, *PTJ*, vol. 1, 423–28. Another note-worthy change found in every British copy of the list of grievances is "Subsistence," rather than "Substance," in the tenth grievance. These changes do not have any correlation with the manuscript copy of the Declaration in the 4th Earl of Sandwich's papers at the National Maritime Museum.

6. John Laurens to James Laurens, August 19, 1776, South Caroliniana Library, University of South Carolina.

7. Henry Laurens to Jacob Read, August 16, 1776, South Caroliniana Library, University of South Carolina.

8. John Laurens to James Laurens, August 19, 1776, South Caroliniana Library, University of South Carolina.

9. *Public Advertiser*, August 16, 1776, 1–2; *Lloyd's Evening Post*, August 14–6, 1776, 6. By redacted, I mean that a dash was inserted for the entire word, or for all but its first and sometimes its last letter, so that the meaning was still somewhat legible.

10. According to the appendix of Solomon Lutnick's *The American Revolution and the British Press, 1775–1783*, the following newspapers were active in London in 1776: *Daily Advertiser* (no political affiliation), *Gazetteer and New Daily Advertiser* (anti-ministry), *General Advertiser and Morning Intelligencer* (anti-ministry), *General Evening Post* (pro-ministry), *Lloyd's Evening Post* (pro-ministry), *London Chronicle* (anti-ministry), *London Evening-Post* (anti-ministry), *London Gazette* (official), *London Packet; or, New Lloyd's Evening Post* (anti-ministry), *Middlesex Journal and Evening Advertiser* (anti-ministry), *Morning Chronicle and London Advertiser* (anti-ministry), *Morning Post and Daily Advertiser* (anti-ministry as of August 1776), *Public Advertiser* (anti-ministry), *Public Ledger; or Daily Register of Commerce and Intelligence* (anti-ministry), *St. James's Chronicle, or British Evening Post* (anti-ministry), *Westminster Journal; or New Weekly Miscellany* (anti-ministry), and *Whitehall Evening Post or London Intelligencer* (anti-ministry). I have not been able to locate copies of the *General Advertiser, Morning Post, London Packet, Public Ledger, Westminster Journal*, or *Whitehall Evening Post* for August 17 and cannot confirm whether the Declaration appeared in these newspapers or not.

11. *London Chronicle*, August 17, 1776, 4; *Middlesex Journal, and Evening Advertiser*, August 17, 1776, 2; *Morning Chronicle, and London Advertiser*, August 17, 1776, 2.

12. *General Evening Post*, August 15–17, 1776, 2.

13. Solomon Lutnick incorrectly suggests that "most newspapers published the document verbatim." Lutnick, *The American Revolution and the British Press*, 75.

14. *Daily Advertiser*, August 15–17, 1776, 2.

15. Lutnick, *The American Revolution and the British Press*, appendix.

16. *Gazetteer and New Daily Advertiser*, August 17, 1776, 2 (emphasis in original). It is not clear why Mary Say's newspapers treated the Declaration of Independence differently. Perhaps these two approaches to the text indicate a division of not only labor but editorial oversight between her publications. Still, it is worth noting that Mary Say and Mary Katharine Goddard are the only two women known to have printed the Declaration of Independence under their own names in 1776—though I imagine that Goddard would have been flummoxed by how the text was treated in Say's newspapers.

17. *St. James's Chronicle; Or, British Evening-Post*, August 15–17, 1776, 2.

18. "He has combined with others to subject us to a Jurisdiction foreign to our Constitution, and unacknowledged by our Laws; giving his Assent to their Acts of pretended Legislation:" was manipulated to read, "It has combined to subject us to a Jurisdiction

foreign to our Constitution, and unacknowledged by our Laws, giving its Assent to pretended Acts of Legislation." The grievance about foreign mercenaries was also a challenge to edit, and the "Head of a civilised Nation" was left unchanged.

19. *Public Advertiser*, August 21, 1776, 2.

20. Ibid. (emphasis in original).

21. *Morning Chronicle*, August 22, 1776, 1.

22. Ibid., August 26, 1776, 1.

23. *General Evening Post*, August 20–22, 1776, 1.

24. Ibid. (emphasis in original).

25. Lutnick, *The American Revolution and the British Press*, 36–40.

26. *Morning Post*, August 20, 1776, 1–2.

27. *Morning Post*, August 20, 1776, 1–2 (emphasis in original). This technique would be employed most famously seventy-two years later by Elizabeth Cady Stanton in the Declaration of Sentiments at the women's rights convention held in Seneca Falls, New York.

28. Lutnick, *The American Revolution and the British Press*, 67–68. Anti-ministry newspapers often lampooned Lord George Germain as the "hero of Minden." During the Seven Years' War, Germain had been court-martialed after the Battle of Minden and found guilty of disobeying orders by refusing to allow the troops under his command to advance. In this same battle, the Marquis de Lafayette died, and his title passed to his one-year-old son, who would later fight in the Continental Army.

29. On the 1770 case about the "Junius" letters, see Andrew Otis, "'Guilty of Publishing Only': Jury Nullification as a Legal Defense in the Eighteenth Century," *Journal of Interdisciplinary History* 53, no. 2 (2022): 267–88.

30. [Thomas Paine], *Common Sense* (J. Almon [London], 1776), 28; Lutnick, *The American Revolution and the British Press, 1775–1783*, 46.

31. *Gazetteer and New Daily Advertiser*, August 28, 1776, 1–2.

32. Neil L. York, "George III, Tyrant: *The Crisis* as Critic of Empire, 1775–1776," *History* 94, no. 4 (2009): 434–60.

33. *The Crisis*, no. LXXXIV, 527–31 (emphasis in original).

34. Neil York notes that, apart from this introduction to the text, "the once ardent authors [of *The Crisis*] did not use the news of the Declaration to reinvigorate themselves, to stoke their dying rhetorical fire; instead, it marked an effective end to their efforts." York, "George III, Tyrant," 458.

35. John Carter Brown Library, BDB.U58 1776 DW17. In 1977, the John Carter Brown Library acquired this copy, tipped into a volume of *The Crisis* after the first flyleaf. The margins of the broadside had been cut down to make it fit in the bound volume, and the right margin was significantly reduced when it was later cut out of the binding. There is another copy of this broadside at the Library Company of Philadelphia, but the top of the broadside with the portrait of John Hancock was cut off. Michael Walsh treated these two broadsides as separate imprints, numbered 17 and 18 in his survey. He also speculated that these broadsides were printed in London, possibly in connection with *The Crisis*. Walsh, "Contemporary Broadside Printings of the Declaration of Independence," *Harvard Library Bulletin* 3, no. 1 (1949), 40–41.

36. The engraving was copied from a mezzotint produced in London in 1775.

37. On support for the colonists in London, see John Sainsbury, *Disaffected Patriots: London Supporters of Revolutionary America, 1769–1782* (McGill–Queen's University, 1987).

38. *Bath Journal*, August 19, 1776, 4.

39. *Bath Chronicle*, August 22, 1776, 1 (emphasis in original).

40. *Hampshire Chronicle*, August 19, 1776, 3.

41. *Aris's Birmingham Gazette*, August 19, 1776, 3.

42. For the Irish perspective on the American Revolution, especially the grievances in the Declaration of Independence, see Samuel K. Fisher, *The Gaelic and Indian Origins of the American Revolution: Diversity and Empire in the British Atlantic, 1688–1783* (Oxford University Press, 2022), introduction.

43. *Hibernian Journal; or, Chronicle of Liberty*, August 21–23, 1776, 2; August 23–26, 1776, 3.

44. Ibid., August 26–28, 1776, 1.

45. *Haerlemse Courant*, August 20, 1776, 1.

46. Ibid., August 22, 1776, 1.

47. Ibid. (emphasis in original).

48. *Nouvelles Extraordinaires de Divers Endroits*, August 20, 1776, supplement, 4. Unlike most American and British newspapers, which were formatted in folio, European gazettes tended to be in quarto or octavo. In many European newspapers, including the Leiden gazette, the four main pages of the newspaper, called the *ordinaire*, were printed before the four-page *supplement*, but both parts were issued on the same day. The *supplement* tended to include timelier news. In a note on the last page of the *supplement*, dated August 19, Luzac apologized that the news from Poland and England took up so much space and explained that the usual suite of news from France, plus the news from northern Europe, the German states, and Rome would have to wait for the next issue. For more on European newspapers in the late eighteenth century, see Hannah Barker and Simon Burrows, eds., *Press, Politics, and the Public Sphere in Europe and North America, 1760–1820* (Cambridge University Press, 2002); Jack R. Censer, *The French Press in the Age of Enlightenment* (Routledge, 1994); Jeremy D. Popkin, *News and Politics in the Age of Revolution: Jean Luzac's "Gazette de Leyde"* (Cornell University Press, 1989).

49. In the late eighteenth century, the Leiden gazette held an "almost unquestioned position as Europe's newspaper of record." As of 1772, the gazette was edited by Jean Luzac, the nephew of the former editor, Etienne Luzac. Jeremy Popkin argues that, although Etienne Luzac lived until 1787, "the paper was fortunate to be in younger, more vigorous hands when the drama of the age of revolutions opened," and Jean Luzac "benefited from the reputation his uncle had earned for the paper." Popkin, *News and Politics in the Age of Revolution*, quotations, 9, 15.

50. *Morning Chronicle*, August 14, 1776, 2.

51. Original, in French: "Dans les Copies, qu'on voit ici de la Déclaration de Guerre du Congrès & de celle d'Indépendance, il est dit, 'qu'aïent maintenant tire l'Epée pour la défense de tout ce qui leur est cher, les Américains ne la remettront jamais dans le fourreau, qu'il ne leur soit fait une ample compensation, pour les actes cruëls d'oppression qu'on leur a fait essuyer.'" *Nouvelles Extraordinires de Divers Endroits*, August 20, 1776, supplement, 4.

52. *JCC*, vol. 2, 127–57.

53. The most explicit grievance in the Declaration of Independence on this point is: "He has abdicated Government here, by declaring us out of his Protection and waging War against us." The rough draft of the Declaration also argued that the king had "waged cruel war" and engaged in "piratical warfare" through the transatlantic slave trade. III. Jefferson's "original Rough draught" of the Declaration of Independence, June 11–July 4, 1776, *PTJ*, vol. 1, 423–28.

54. Emer de Vattel, *Law of Nations* (G. G. and J. Robinson, 1797), chap. 4; Armitage, *The Declaration of Independence*, 38–41; William Ossipow and Dominik Gerber, "The Reception of Vattel's *Law of Nations* in the American Colonies," *American Journal of Legal History* 57, no. 4 (December 2017): 521–55.

55. On the Declaration of Independence in the *Nouvelles Extraordinaires de Divers Endroits*, see Popkin, *News and Politics in the Age of Revolution*, 150–51. Popkin writes that, "surprisingly, the paper made no editorial comment on this document," but I would argue that the composition of this paragraph is in itself an editorial comment on the Declaration.

56. *Courier du Bas-Rhin* (Cleves), August 24, 1776, 547; *Augspurgische Ordinari Postzeitung* (Augsburg), August 28, 1776, 2; *Munsterisches Intelligenzblat* (Münster), August 30, 1776, 3–4; *Stockholms Post-Tidningar* (Stockholm), September 2, 1776, 2–3; *Gazzette Bolognesi* (Bologna), September 3, 1776, 3.

57. *Munsterisches Intelligenzblatt*, August 30, 1776, 4; *Stockholms Post-Tidningar*, September 2, 1776, 2–3; *Gazzetta Universale* (Florence), September 3, 1776, 562.

58. *Nouvelles Extraordinaires de Divers Endroits*, August 30, 1776, 3–4.

59. Ibid.

60. Ibid.

61. *Notizie del Mondo* (Florence), September 14, 1776, 567–69.

62. *Nouvelles Extraordinaires de Divers Endroits*, August 30, 1776, 4 (emphasis in original); *Notizie del Mondo*, September 14, 1776, 567–69.

63. *Reichspostreuter* (Altona), August 26, 1776, 2–3.

64. *Münsterisches Intelligenzblatt*, August 30, 1776, 3–4.

CHAPTER 10

1. CSC to Arthur Lee, December 12, 1775, *RDC*, vol. 2, 63–64.

2. CSC to Silas Deane, March 3, 1776, *RDC*, vol. 2, 78–80.

3. Arthur Lee wrote a letter on August 13 from London that made no mention of the Declaration of Independence, though he noted that "we expect every day some decisive news from New York." Arthur Lee to Charles-Guillaume-Frédéric Dumas, August 13, 1776, *RDC*, vol. 2, 110–11.

4. Silas Deane to Charles Gravier, Comte de Vergennes, August 22, 1776, *RDC*, vol. 2, 132–33.

5. Silas Deane to Charles-Guillaume-Frédéric Dumas, August 18, 1776, *RDC*, vol. 2, 128–29.

6. Silas Deane to Charles-Guillaume-Frédéric Dumas, August 18, 1776, *AA*, series 5, vol. 1, 1021.

7. Benjamin Franklin to Charles-Guillaume-Frédéric Dumas, December 9, 1775, *PBF*, vol. 22, 287–91.

8. *Archives ou Correspondance Inédite de la Maison d'Orange-Nassau*, 5th series, vol. I (1776–1779) (A. W. Sijthof, 1910), 448; David Armitage, *The Declaration of Independence: A Global History* (Harvard University Press, 2007), 43. My thanks to Jen Motter for her help with this translation.

9. Silas Deane to Charles-Guillaume-Frédéric Dumas, July 26, 1776, *AA*, series 5, vol. 1, 881.

10. Silas Deane to Charles-Guillaume-Frédéric Dumas, August 18, 1776, *AA*, series 5, vol. 1, 1021.

11. William Lee to Charles-Guillaume-Frédéric Dumas, September 10, 1776, *AA*, series 5, vol. 2, 270–71.

12. Arthur Lee to Charles-Guillaume-Frédéric Dumas, September 23, 1776, *AA*, series 5, vol. 2, 455–56.

13. David Murray, 2nd Earl of Mansfield and Viscount Stormont to Thomas Thynne, 3rd Viscount Weymouth, September 25, 1776, SP 78/299, 536–38. This letter appears to be in Stormont's handwriting, rather than the hand of a clerk.

14. David Murray, 2nd Earl of Mansfield and Viscount Stormont to Thomas Thynne, 3rd Viscount Weymouth, October 10, 1776, SP 78/300, 66–67.

15. David Murray, 2nd Earl of Mansfield and Viscount Stormont to Thomas Thynne, 3rd Viscount Weymouth, October 10, 1776, 66–67 (emphasis in original).

16. Silas Deane to the CSC, October 1, 1776, *RDC*, vol. 2, 157–61.

17. Silas Deane to Charles-Guillaume-Frédéric Dumas, October 6, 1776, *AA*, series 5, vol. 2, 916–17.

18. Silas Deane to the CSC, October 8, 1776, *RDC*, vol. 2, 167–69.

19. Silas Deane to Charles-Guillaume-Frédéric Dumas, October 13, 1776, *AA*, series 5, vol. 2, 1020.

20. Silas Deane to CSC, October 17, 1776, *RDC*, vol. 2, 173–75.

21. Ibid.

22. Silas Deane to CSC, October 25, 1776, *RDC*, vol. 2, 183–84.

23. Silas Deane to CSC, November 6, 1776, *RDC*, vol. 2, 190–92.

24. CSC to Silas Deane, August 7, 1776, *PBF*, vol. 22, 553–55; Silas Deane to CSC, November 28, 1776, *RDC*, vol. 2, 196–200. On Deane's receipt of the Declaration of Independence, see Armitage, *The Declaration of Independence*, 81–82; Carl Becker, *The Declaration of Independence: A Study on the History of Political Ideas* (Harcourt, Brace, 1922), 229–30; Benjamin H. Irvin, *Clothed in Robes of Sovereignty: The Continental Congress and the People Out of Doors* (Oxford University Press, 2011), 131–32; Pauline Maier, *American Scripture: Making the Declaration of Independence* (Knopf, 1997), 130.

25. Silas Deane to CSC, November 28, 1776, *RDC*, vol. 2, 196–200.

26. Archives Diplomatiques, États-Unis, vol. 1, 109–16.

27. Silas Deane to Charles Gravier, Comte de Vergennes, November 18, 1776, Archives Diplomatiques, États-Unis, vol. 1, 282, 284.

28. Silas Deane to CSC, November 28, 1776, *RDC*, vol. 2, 196–200.

29. Silas Deane to John Jay, December 3, 1776, *PJJ*, vol. 1, 249–50.

30. Silas Deane to CSC, November 28, 1776, *RDC*, vol. 2, 196–200.

31. Silas Deane to John Jay, December 3, 1776, *PJJ*, vol. 1, 249–50.

32. Silas Deane to CSC, October 8, 1776, *RDC*, vol. 2, 167–69.

33. Silas Deane to John Jay, December 3, 1776, *PJJ*, vol. 1, 249–50.

34. Nicholas Rogers, *Blood Waters: War, Disease and Race in the Eighteenth Century British Caribbean* (Boydell Press, 2021), chap. 5.

35. Silas Deane to John Jay, December 3, 1776, *PJJ*, vol. 1, 249–50.

36. Silas Deane to CSC, November 28, 1776, *RDC*, vol. 2, 196–200.

37. Benjamin Franklin to Jacques Barbeu-Dubourg, December 4, 1776, *PBF*, vol. 23, 23–25.

38. CSC to Silas Deane, October 2, 1776, *RDC*, vol. 2, 162–63.

39. Memorandum Books, 1776, *PTJ*, vol. 1, 412–37.

40. Martha Jefferson's letters to her husband, which had given him so many concerns for her health during the weeks when he was working on the Declaration of Independence, unfortunately do not survive. On July 3, Francis Eppes wrote to Thomas Jefferson that he had visited Martha, who was "perfectly recover'd from her late indisposition, and except being a little weak, is as well as ever she was." Francis Eppes to Thomas Jefferson, July 3, 1776, *Founders Online*.

41. John Hancock to Thomas Jefferson, September 30, 1776, *PTJ*, vol. 1, 523–24.

42. Thomas Jefferson to John Hancock, October 11, 1776, *PTJ*, vol. 1, 524. Hancock sent his letter with an express rider who was supposed to return with Jefferson's answer. Jefferson apologized for taking three days to answer, "during which I could not determine to dismiss your messenger." Martha gave birth to an unnamed son on May 28, 1777. If Martha carried this child to full term, then he would have been conceived after Jefferson returned to his Monticello plantation in September 1776. In any event, Thomas and Martha may not have known that she was pregnant when he declined his commission to France in mid-October.

43. Silas Deane to CSC, December 12, 1776, *RDC*, vol. 2, 224.

44. Benjamin Franklin to Silas Deane, December 4, 1776, *RDC*, vol. 2, 216–18.

45. Silas Deane to Charles Gravier, Comte de Vergennes, December 8, 1776, *RDC*, vol. 2, 223.

46. Silas Deane to Charles-Guillaume-Frédéric Dumas, December 13, 1776, *AA*, series 5, vol. 3, 1196–97.

47. Arthur Lee to William Petty, 2nd Earl of Shelburne, December 23, 1776, *RDC*, vol. 2, 239–40.

CONCLUSION

1. Oliver Wolcott to Laura Wolcott, June 1, 1776, *LDC*, vol. 4, 114.

2. Roger Sherman had been absent in March and April and Samuel Huntington left Philadelphia in May. Although Sherman wanted another break, Oliver Wolcott thought that he had "a prior and better Right." Oliver Wolcott to Laura Wolcott, June 25, 1776, *LDC*, vol. 4, 322–23.

3. Oliver Wolcott to Matthew Griswold, July 1, 1776, *LDC*, vol. 4, 367–68.

4. There is no record of exactly when or how the Wolcott family learned about the Declaration of Independence. The Connecticut Council of Safety did not order any public readings of the Declaration. Litchfield was some distance from Hartford, New Haven, and New London, the three Connecticut towns with active newspapers at this time, but it is possible that Wolcott read the Declaration in one of those newspapers.

5. Wendy Bellion, *Iconoclasm in New York: Revolution to Reenactment* (Penn State University Press, 2019), 1. New York Historical has several larger fragments of the statue, including part of the tail.

6. Connecticut Digital Archive. The eldest living child, sixteen-year-old Oliver Wolcott, Jr., was at school at this time.

7. Jonathan Trumbull to George Washington, August 13, 1776, *PGW*, vol. 6, 12–13; Oliver Wolcott to Jonathan Trumbull, August 15, 1776, *AA*, series 5, vol. 1, 970.

8. General Orders, September 24, 1777, *PGW*, vol. 6, 385–86; George Washington to Jonathan Trumbull, September 26, 1776, *PGW*, vol. 6, 410. As soon as Oliver Wolcott returned to Philadelphia, Roger Sherman took his leave.

9. Oliver Wolcott to Laura Wolcott, October 8, 1776, *LDC*, vol. 4, 322–23.

10. Oliver Wolcott read about his reappointment in a Philadelphia newspaper, which copied the news from New Haven. Oliver Wolcott to Samuel Adams, November 16, 1776, *LDC*, vol. 5, 507–508; *JCC*, vol. 7, 11–13.

11. Seven delegates are known to have signed after August 2: Elbridge Gerry, Richard Henry Lee, Thomas McKean, Lewis Morris, Matthew Thornton, Oliver Wolcott, and George Wythe.

12. Previous documents signed by the Continental Congress, including the Olive Branch Petition, were signed in state order from north to south, from left to right on the page.

The parchment copy of the Declaration of Independence set a precedent of signing from right to left that was followed for the Articles of Confederation and the United States Constitution.

13. John Adams to Abigail [Smith] Adams, July 15, 1776, *AFC*, vol. 2, 49–50.

14. Elbridge Gerry to Samuel Adams and John Adams, July 21–22, 1776, *PJA*, vol. 4, 398–404.

15. Pennsylvania's new pro-independence delegation included Benjamin Rush, George Clymer, James Smith, George Taylor, and George Ross.

16. Thomas McKean's belated signing was a political albatross, so much so that he personally examined the Continental Congress's papers—then in the custody of the State Department—to confirm that his signature was on the parchment. Thomas McKean to John Adams, January 7, 1814, *Founders Online*. The movie *National Treasure* cites fifty-five signers of the Declaration of Independence, which could be an oversight, or could instead be evidence that the clues for the movie's treasure predated McKean signing the parchment.

17. The United States Constitution was signed on September 17, 1787, and George Read signed John Dickinson's name by proxy because Dickinson was ill.

18. To the best of my knowledge, this detail has not been noted in any histories of the engrossed and signed parchment that predate my research. Jefferson historian Dumas Malone, for example, writes that "the order of signatures within a delegation has no particular significance and need not be heeded." Malone, *The Story of the Declaration of Independence* (Oxford University Press, 1954), 96.

19. Thomas Jefferson, Design for Tombstone and Inscription, before July 4, 1826, *Founders Online*; Pauline Maier, *American Scripture: Making the Declaration of Independence* (Knopf, 1997), 186.

20. Robert R. Livingston to John Jay, July 6, 1776, *LDC*, vol. 4, 398–99.

21. Oliver Wolcott to Laura Wolcott, December 11, 1776, *LDC*, vol. 5, 599–600.

22. Oliver Wolcott to Laura Wolcott, December 13, 1776, *LDC*, vol. 5, 605–607.

23. Maryland delegate Samuel Chase cautioned that he did not know of "any House in Baltimore Town in which the Congress can sit," and that Baltimore was "a most disagreeable place in Winter." He was in Annapolis at the time and thought it would be a better meeting place. Samuel Chase to [William Paca], December 18, 1776, *LDC*, vol. 5, 613–14.

24. Oliver Wolcott to Laura Wolcott, January 1, 1776, *LDC*, vol. 6, 14–15.

25. Oliver Wolcott to Laura Wolcott, January 22, 1777, *LDC*, vol. 6, 129–30. Wolcott estimated that the prices for goods in Baltimore were fifty percent higher than in Philadelphia.

26. Robert Morris to Silas Deane, December 20, 1776, *LDC*, vol. 5, 620–27.

27. *Dunlap's Pennsylvania Packet or the General Advertiser*, December 27, 1776, 1.

28. Robert Morris to Silas Deane, January 8, 1777, *LDC*, vol. 6, 58–62.

29. Robert Morris to Silas Deane, January 29, 1777, *LDC*, vol. 6, 160–61.

30. *JCC*, vol. 7, 45–49.

31. *Maryland Journal and the Baltimore Advertiser*, July 10, 1776, 1.

32. Mary Katharine Goddard broadside (emphasis in original).

33. Mary Katharine Goddard broadside (emphasis in original). Danielle Allen, *Our Declaration: A Reading of the Declaration of Independence in Defense of Equality* (Liveright, 2014), 76.

34. Mary Katharine Goddard broadside (emphasis in original).

35. Thomas Starr argues that the Goddard broadside was "the publication that Dunlap's might have been" if the Congress had privileged calligraphy over typography on July 4. Starr, "Separated at Birth: Text and Context of the Declaration of Independence," *Proceedings of the American Antiquarian Society* 110, no. 2 (2000): 175–76.

36. John Hancock to the States, January 31, 1776, *LDC*, vol. 6, 171.

37. The broadsides sent to Maryland, Massachusetts, and Rhode Island are still in their respective state archives.

38. Ward L. Miner, *William Goddard, Newspaperman* (Duke University Press, 1962), 18–47, 56–58.

39. My thanks to Ken Carlson at the Rhode Island State Archives for showing me images from before the conservation of the document, which was done by the Northeast Document Conservation Center.

40. John Hancock to the States, January 31, 1777, *LDC*, vol. 6, 171.

Bibliography

ARCHIVES AND DATABASES

Albert H. Small Library, University of Virginia
American Antiquarian Society
American Loyalist Claims, 1776–1835
Archives Diplomatiques, Paris
Archives of Maryland Online
Arquivo Nacional da Torre do Tombo, Lisbon
Beinecke Rare Book and Manuscript Library, Yale University
Bodleian Library, Oxford University
Boston Public Library
Brooklyn Museum
Burney Newspaper Collection, British Library
Chapin Library Special Collections, Williams College
Christ Church Philadelphia
City Clerk's Office, Cambridge, Massachusetts
Clements Library, University of Michigan
Connecticut Digital Archive
Evans Early American Imprints
Evans Early American Newspapers
Fort Ticonderoga Museum
Founders Online
Gilder Lehrman Institute of American History, New York
Historical Society of Pennsylvania
Houghton Library, Harvard University
John Carter Brown Library, Brown University
Library of Congress
Maine Historical Society
Massachusetts Archives
Massachusetts Historical Society
National Archives (UK)
National Archives and Records Administration (USA)
National Cathedral Rare Books Library, Washington, DC
National Maritime Museum, Greenwich, London
New England Historic Genealogical Society
New Jersey State Archives
New York Historical
New York Public Library
Office of the Town Clerk, Natick, Massachusetts

Rhode Island State Archives
South Caroliniana Library, University of South Carolina

NEWSPAPERS AND PERIODICALS

American Gazette: or, the Constitutional Journal (Salem: J. Rogers).
Aris's Birmingham Gazette (Birmingham: J. Pearson and Co.).
Augspurgische Ordinari Postzeitung (Augsburg: Johann Anton Moy).
Bath Chronicle (Bath: R. Cruttwell).
Bath Journal (Bath: John Keene).
Connecticut Journal (New Haven: Thomas and Samuel Green).
Constitutional Gazette (New York: John Anderson).
Courier du Bas-Rhin (Cleves).
Daily Advertiser (London: J. Jenour).
Dunlap's Maryland Gazette; or, the Baltimore General Advertiser (Baltimore: John Dunlap).
Dunlap's Pennsylvania Packet or the General Advertiser (Philadelphia: John Dunlap).
Essex Journal and New-Hampshire Packet (Newburyport, Massachusetts: John Mycall).
Freeman's Journal, or New-Hampshire Gazette (Portsmouth: Benjamin Dearborn).
Gazzetta Universale (Florence).
Gazzette Bolognesi (Bologna).
Gazette d'Utrecht (Utrecht: Claude-Isaac Peuch).
Gazetteer and New Daily Advertiser (London: M. Say).
General Evening Post (London: M. Say).
Haerlemse Courant (Haarlem: Johannes Enschedé).
Hampshire Chronicle (Southampton: Linden, Wise).
Hibernian Journal; or, Chronicle of Liberty (Dublin: M. Mills).
Lloyd's Evening Post (London: W. Nicoll).
London Chronicle (London: J. Wilkie).
London Gazette (London: Thomas Harrison).
Maryland Gazette (Annapolis: Frederick Green).
Maryland Journal and the Baltimore Advertiser (Baltimore: M. K. Goddard).
Massachusetts Spy Or, American Oracle of Liberty (Worcester: W. Stearns and D. Bigelow).
Middlesex Journal, and Evening Advertiser (London: R. Ayre and G. Moore).
Morning Chronicle, and London Advertiser (London: William Woodfall).
Morning Post, and Daily Advertiser (London: R. Haswell).
Münsterisches Intelligenzblat (Münster).
New-England Chronicle (Boston: Samuel Hall [to June 1776], Powars and Willis [from June 1776]).
New Hampshire Gazette, or, Exeter Morning Chronicle (Exeter: [Robert Luist Fowle]).
New-Lloyd's List (London: James Phillips).
New-York Gazette; and the Weekly Mercury (New York: Hugh Gaine).
New-York Journal; or, the General Advertiser (New York: John Holt).
Newport Mercury (Newport, Rhode Island: Solomon Southwick).
Notizie del Mondo (Florence).
Nouvelles Extraordinaires de Divers Endroits (Leiden: Etienne Luzac [Jean Luzac]).
Pennsylvania Evening Post (Philadelphia: Benjamin Towne).
Pennsylvania Journal; and the Weekly Advertiser (Philadelphia: William and Thomas Bradford).

Pennsylvania Ledger Or the Virginia, Maryland, Pennsylvania, and New-Jersey Weekly Advertiser (Philadelphia: James Humphreys, Jr.).

Pennsylvania Mercury; and the Universal Advertiser (Philadelphia: Story and Humphreys).

Pennsylvanischer Staatsbote (Philadelphia: Henry Miller).

Providence Gazette; and Country Journal (Providence: John Carter).

Public Advertiser (London: H. S. Woodfall)

Public Register; Or, Freeman's Journal (Dublin: Samuel Leathley).

Reichspostreuter (Altona, Germany).

Royal Danish American Gazette (Christianstæd, Saint Croix: Daniel Thibou).

St. James's Chronicle; Or, British Evening-Post (London: H. Baldwin).

Stockholms Post–Tidningar (Stockholm: Johan Georg Lange).

The Crisis (London: T. W. Shaw).

Virginia Gazette (Williamsburg: Alexander Purdie).

Virginia Gazette (Williamsburg: Dixon & Hunter).

PRINTED PRIMARY SOURCES AND EDITED
CORRESPONDENCE

Archives ou Correspondance Inédite de la Maison d'Orange-Nassau, 5th Series. Vol. I: *1776–1779.* A. W. Sijthof, 1910.

[Bass, Edward]. *A Brief Account of the Treatment Which Mr. Bass, Late Missionary from the Society for the Propagation of the Gospel in Foreign Parts, at Newbury-Port, New-England, Hath Received from Said Society.* [London], 1786.

Baxter, James Phinney, ed. *Documentary History of the State of Maine.* Vol. 14. Lefavor-Tower, 1902.

The Book of Common Prayer, and Administration of the Sacraments, and other Rites and Ceremonies of the Church, According to the Use of the Church of England. John Baskerville [Cambridge], 1762.

Boyd, Julian P., ed. *The Papers of Thomas Jefferson.* Vol. I: *1760–1776.* Princeton University Press, 1950.

Butterfield, L. H., ed. *Adams Family Correspondence.* Vol. 1: *December 1761–May 1776.* Belknap Press of Harvard University Press, 1963.

Butterfield, L. H., ed. *Adams Family Correspondence.* Vol. 2: *June 1776–March 1778.* Belknap Press of Harvard University Press, 1963.

Butterfield, L. H., ed. *Diary and Autobiography of John Adams.* Vol. 2: *Diary 1771–1781.* Belknap Press of Harvard University Press, 1961.

Butterfield, L. H., ed. *Diary and Autobiography of John Adams.* Vol. 3: *Diary 1782–1804, Autobiography Part One to October 1776.* Belknap Press of Harvard University Press, 1962.

"By the King, A Proclamation For Suppressing Rebellion and Sedition." Charles Eyre and William Strahan [London], 1775.

Chase, Philander D., ed. *The Papers of George Washington, Revolutionary War Series.* Vol. 1: *16 June 1775–15 September 1775.* University Press of Virginia, 1985.

Chase, Philander D., ed. *The Papers of George Washington, Revolutionary War Series.* Vol. 3: *1 January 1776–31 March 1776.* University Press of Virginia, 1988.

Chase, Philander D., ed. *The Papers of George Washington, Revolutionary War Series.* Vol. 4: *1 April 1776–15 June 1776.* University Press of Virginia, 1991.

Chase, Philander D., ed. *The Papers of George Washington, Revolutionary War Series*. Vol. 5: *16 June 1776–12 August 1776*. University Press of Virginia, 1993.

Chase, Philander D. and Frank E. Grizzard, Jr., eds. *The Papers of George Washington, Revolutionary War Series*. Vol. 6: *13 August 1776–20 October 1776*. University Press of Virginia, 1994.

Chase, Philander D. and Edward G. Lengel, eds. *The Papers of George Washington, Revolutionary War Series*. Vol. 11: *19 August 1777–25 October 1777*. University Press of Virginia, 2001.

[Coghlan, Margaret]. *Memoirs of Mrs. Coghlan, (Daughter of the late Major Moncrieffe), Written By Herself and Dedicated to the British Nation*. Vol. 1. Printed for the Author and Sold by C. and G. Kearsley [London], [1794].

[Demophilus]. *The Genuine Principles of the Ancient Saxon, or English Constitution*. Robert Bell [Philadelphia], 1776.

de Vattel, Emer. *Law of Nations*. G. G. and J. Robinson [London], 1797.

Dexter, Franklin Bowditch, ed. *The Literary Diary of Ezra Stiles, D.D., LL.D*. Vol. II: *March 14, 1776–December 1, 1781*. Charles Scribner's Sons, 1901.

"Diary of Col. Landon Carter," *William and Mary Quarterly* 18, no. 1 (1909), 37–44.

Documents and Records Relating to the State of New-Hampshire During the Period of the American Revolution, from 1776 to 1783. Vol. 8. Edward A. Jenks, 1874.

"Dom José por graça de Deos rey de Portugal, e dos Algarves, daquém, e dalém mar, . . . não só se declaráram inteiramente apartadas de sujeição á Coroa da Grão Bretanha." Printed by Authority [Lisbon], ca. July 5, 1776.

Force, Peter, ed. *American Archives: Fifth Series*. Vol. 1. M. St. Clair Clarke and Peter Force, 1848.

Force, Peter, ed. *American Archives: Fifth Series*. Vol. 3. M. St. Clair Clarke and Peter Force, 1853.

Force, Peter, ed. *American Archives: Fourth Series*. Vol. 5. M. St. Clair Clarke and Peter Force, 1844.

Force, Peter, ed. *American Archives: Fourth Series*. Vol. 6. M. St. Clair Clarke and Peter Force, 1846.

Ford, Worthington Chauncey, ed. *Correspondence and Journals of Samuel Blachley Webb*. Vol. 1. 1893.

Ford, Worthington Chauncey, ed. *Journals of the Continental Congress, 1774–1789*. Vol. II: *1775, May 10–September 20*. Government Printing Office, 1905.

Ford, Worthington Chauncey, ed. *Journals of the Continental Congress, 1774–1789*. Vol. III: *1775, September 21–December 30*. Government Printing Office, 1905.

Ford, Worthington Chauncey, ed. *Journals of the Continental Congress, 1774–1789*. Vol. IV: *1776, January 1–June 4*. Government Printing Office, 1906.

Ford, Worthington Chauncey, ed. *Journals of the Continental Congress, 1774–1789*. Vol. V: *1776, June 5–October 8*. Government Printing Office, 1906.

Ford, Worthington Chauncey, ed. *Journals of the Continental Congress, 1774–1789*. Vol. VII: *1777, January 1–May 21*. Government Printing Office, 1907.

Georgini, Sara, et al., eds. *Papers of John Adams*. Vol. 20: *June 1789–February 1791*. Belknap Press of Harvard University Press, 2020.

Hogan, Margaret A., et al., eds. *Adams Family Correspondence*. Vol. 9: *January 1790–December 1793*. Belknap Press of Harvard University Press, 2009.

Journals of the House of Representatives of Massachusetts, 1776. Vol. 52. Massachusetts Historical Society, 1985.

Journals of the Provincial Congress, Provincial Convention, Committee of Safety and Council of Safety of the State of New York, 1775–1776. Vol. 1. Thurlow Weed [Albany], 1842.

Koenig, W. J. and S. L. Mayer, eds. *European Manuscript Sources of the American Revolution.* Bowker, 1974.

Lint, Gregg and Richard Alan Ryerson, eds. *Papers of John Adams.* Vol. 9: *March 1780–July 1780.* Belknap Press of Harvard University Press, 1996.

Mattern, David B. et al., eds. *The Papers of James Madison. Retirement Series.* Vol. 2: *1 March 1823–24 February 1826.* University of Virginia Press, 2016.

Miller, Lillian B., ed. *The Selected Papers of Charles Willson Peale and His Family.* Vol. I: *Charles Willson Peale: Artist in Revolutionary America, 1735–1791.* Published for the National Portrait Gallery, Smithsonian Institution, by Yale University Press, 1983.

Minutes of the Provincial Congress and the Council of Safety of the State of New Jersey. Naar, Day & Naar, 1879.

Minutes of the Provincial Council of Pennsylvania, From the Organization to the Termination of the Proprietary Government. Vol. 10. Theo. Fenn [Harrisburg], 1852.

Morgan, William James, ed. *Naval Documents of the American Revolution.* Vol. 5: *American Theatre: May 9, 1776–July 31, 1776.* Government Printing Office, 1970.

Moultrie, William. *Memoirs of the American Revolution, So Far as It Related to the States of North and South Carolina, and Georgia.* Vol. 1. David Longworth [New York], 1802.

Nuxoll, Elizabeth M., ed. *The Selected Papers of John Jay.* Vol. 1: *1760–1779.* University of Virginia Press, 2010.

Oliver, Andrew and James Bishop Peabody, eds. The Records of Trinity Church, Boston, 1728–1830. Colonial Society of Massachusetts, 1980.

Oppenheim, Samuel. "Letter of Jonas Phillips, July 28, 1776, Mentioning the American Revolution and the Declaration of Independence." *Publications of the American Jewish Historical Society* 25 (1917): 128–31. https://www.jstor.org/stable/43058066.

[Paine, Thomas]. *Common Sense.* J. Almon [London], 1776.

[Paine, Thomas]. *Common Sense.* R. Bell [Philadelphia], 1776.

[Pickering, Timothy]. *Col. Pickering's Observations Introductory to Reading the Declaration of Independence, at Salem, July 4, 1823.* Warwick Palfray, Jr. [Salem], 1823.

Powell, J. H. "Speech of John Dickinson Opposing the Declaration of Independence, 1 July 1776." *Pennsylvania Magazine of History and Biography* 65, no. 4 (October 1941): 458–81.

Ryerson, Richard Alan, et al., eds. *Adams Family Correspondence.* Vol. 6: *December 1784–December 1785.* Belknap Press of Harvard University Press, 1993.

Smith, Paul H., et al. *Letters of Delegates to Congress, 1774–1789.* Library of Congress, 1976–2000.

Tatum, Jr., Edward H., ed. *The American Journal of Ambrose Serle, Secretary to Lord Howe, 1776–1778.* Huntington Library, 1940.

Taylor, Robert J., ed. *Papers of John Adams.* Vol. 4: *February–August 1776.* Belknap Press of Harvard University Press, 1979.

Thomas, Isaiah. *The History of Printing in America, With a Biography of Printers, and an Account of Newspapers.* Vol. 1. Isaac Sturtevant [Worcester], 1810.

Wharton, Francis, ed. *The Revolutionary Diplomatic Correspondence of the United States.* Vol. 2. Government Printing Office, 1889.

Willcox, William B., ed. *The Papers of Benjamin Franklin.* Vol. 22: *March 23, 1775, through October 27, 1776.* Yale University Press, 1982.

Willcox, William B., ed. *The Papers of Benjamin Franklin.* Vol. 23: *October 27, 1776, Through April 30, 1777.* Yale University Press, 1983.

SECONDARY SOURCES

Abler, Thomas S. *Cornplanter: Chief Warrior of the Allegany Senecas*. Syracuse University Press, 2007.

Adams, Thomas R. and Nicolas Barker, "A New Model for the Study of the Book." In *A Potencie of Life*, ed. Nicolas Barker. British Library, 1993.

Adams, Willi Paul. *The First American Constitutions: Republican Ideology and the Making of the State Constitutions in the Revolutionary Era*. Translated by Rita Kimber and Robert Kimber. Rev. ed. Rowman & Littlefield, 2001.

Adams, Willi Paul. "German Translations of the American Declaration of Independence." *Journal of American History* 85, no. 4 (March 1999): 1325–49. doi:10.2307/2568255.

Addison, Daniel Dulany. *The Life and Times of Edward Bass, First Bishop of Massachusetts*. Houghton, Mifflin, 1897.

Adelman, Joseph M. *Revolutionary Networks: The Business and Politics of Printing the News, 1763–1789*. Johns Hopkins University Press, 2019.

Aggarwala, Rohit T. "'I want a Packet to arrive': Making New York City the Headquarters of British America, 1696–1783." *New York History* 98, no. 1 (Winter 2017): 7–39. https://www.jstor.org/stable/90018770.

Alden, Dauril. "The Marquis of Pombal and the American Revolution." *The Americas* 17, no. 4 (April 1961), 369–76. doi:10.2307/979303.

Allen, Charles E. *Rev. Jacob Bailey: His Character and Works*. Lincoln County Historical Society, 1895.

Allen, Danielle. *Our Declaration: A Reading of the Declaration of Independence in Defense of Equality*. Liveright, 2014.

Anderson, Benedict. *Imagined Communities: Reflections on the Origin and Spread of Nationalism*. Rev. ed. Verso, 2006.

Anderson, Mark R. *Down the Warpath to the Cedars: Indians' First Battles in the Revolution*. University of Oklahoma Press, 2021.

Armitage, David. *Civil Wars: A History in Ideas*. Yale University Press, 2017.

Armitage, David. *The Declaration of Independence: A Global History*. Harvard University Press, 2007.

Armitage, David. "Three Concepts of Atlantic History." In *The British Atlantic World, 1500–1800*, edited by David Armitage and Michael J. Braddick. Macmillan, 2002.

Arndt, Karl J. R. "The First Translation and Printing in German of the American Declaration of Independence." *Monatshefte* 77, no. 2 (1985): 138–42. https://www.jstor.org/stable/30161566.

Baer, Friederike. *Hessians: German Soldiers in the American Revolutionary War*. Oxford University Press, 2022.

Bailyn, Bernard and John B. Hench, eds. *The Press & the American Revolution*. American Antiquarian Society, 1980.

Bancroft, George. *History of the United States, From the Discovery of the American Continent*. 3rd ed. Vol. 9. Little, Brown, 1873.

Barker, Hannah and Simon Burrows, eds. *Press, Politics and the Public Sphere in Europe and North America, 1760–1820*. Cambridge University Press, 2002.

Becker, Ann M. *Smallpox in Washington's Army: Disease, War, and Society During the Revolutionary War*. Lexington, 2023.

Becker, Carl. *The Declaration of Independence: A Study in the History of Political Ideas*. Harcourt, Brace, 1922.

Beeman, Richard R. *Our Lives, Our Fortunes and Our Sacred Honor: The Forging of American Independence, 1774–1776*. Basic, 2013.

Bell, J. L. "Sheriff Greenleaf and Col. Crafts Read the Declaration." Boston 1775, July 2007. https://boston1775.blogspot.com/2007/07/sheriff-greenleaf-and-col-crafts-read.html.

Bell, James B. "The Making of an Eighteenth-Century American Anglican Clergyman." *Proceedings of the Massachusetts Historical Society* 106 (1994): 82–111. https://www.jstor.org/stable/25081085.

Bell, James B. *A War of Religion: Dissenters, Anglicans, and the American Revolution*. Palgrave Macmillan, 2008.

Bell, Jr., Whitfield J. *The Declaration of Independence: Four 1776 Versions*. American Philosophical Society, 1976.

Bellion, Wendy. *Iconoclasm in New York: Revolution to Reenactment*. Penn State University Press, 2019.

Bemis, Samuel Flagg. "British Secret Service and the French-American Alliance." *American Historical Review* 29, no. 3 (April 1924): 474–95. doi:10.2307/1836521.

Bemis, Samuel Flagg. *The Diplomacy of the American Revolution*. American Historical Association, 1935.

Berger, Carl. *Broadsides and Bayonets: The Propaganda War of the American Revolution*. Rev. ed. Presidio Press, 1976.

Bickham, Troy. *Making Headlines: The American Revolution as Seen Through the British Press*. Northern Illinois University Press, 2008.

Bidwell, John. *The Declaration in Script and Print: A Visual History of America's Founding Document*. Pennsylvania State University Press, 2024.

Blackhawk, Ned. *The Rediscovery of America: Native Peoples and the Unmaking of U.S. History*. Yale University Press, 2023.

Boulton, Alexander. "The Declaration of Independence and the Language of Slavery." *Journal of the Early Republic* 44, no. 1 (Spring 2024): 1–26. doi:10.1353/jer.2024.a922049.

Boyd, Julian P. *The Declaration of Independence: The Evolution of the Text as Shown in Facsimiles of Various Drafts by Its Author, Thomas Jefferson*. Library of Congress, 1943.

Boyd, Julian P. "The Declaration of Independence: The Mystery of the Lost Original." *Pennsylvania Magazine of History and Biography* 100, no. 4 (1976): 438–67. https://www.jstor.org/stable/20091099.

Bragg, C. L. *Crescent Moon over Carolina: William Moultrie & American Liberty*. University of South Carolina Press, 2013.

Browning, Morgan. "Preserving the Dunlap Broadside of the Declaration of Independence." Pieces of History: A Blog of the U.S. National Archives, July 2021. https://prologue.blogs.archives.gov/2021/07/02/preserving-the-dunlap-broadside-of-the-declaration-of-independence/.

Calloway, Colin G. *The American Revolution in Indian Country: Crisis and Diversity in Native American Communities*. Rev. ed. Cambridge University Press, 2009.

Calvert, Jane E. *Penman of the Founding: A Biography of John Dickinson*. Oxford University Press, 2024.

Carp, Benjamin L. *The Great New York Fire of 1776: A Lost Story of the American Revolution*. Yale University Press, 2023.

Carté, Katherine. *Religion and the American Revolution: An Imperial History*. Omohundro Institute and University of North Carolina Press, 2021.

Castronovo, Russ. *Propaganda 1776: Secrets, Leaks, and Revolutionary Communications in Early America*. Oxford University Press, 2014.

Censer, Jack R. *The French Press in the Age of Enlightenment.* Routledge, 1994.

Chamberlain, Mellen. "The Alleged Signing of the Declaration of Independence, July 4, 1776." *Proceedings of the Massachusetts Historical Society* 1 (1884–5): 272–98.

Cushing, John D. "Ezekiel Russell's Edition of Jonathan Mitchell Sewall's 'War and Washington': A Bibliographical Note." *Proceedings of the Massachusetts Historical Society* 93 (1981), 109–14. https://www.jstor.org/stable/25080891.

Darnton, Robert. "What is the History of Books?" *Daedalus* 111, no. 3 (1982): 65–83. https://www.jstor.org/stable/20024803.

David, James Corbett. *Dunmore's New World: The Extraordinary Life of a Royal Governor in Revolutionary America—with Jacobites, Counterfeiters, Land Schemes, Shipwrecks, Scalping, Indian Politics, Runaway Slaves, and Two Illegal Royal Weddings.* University of Virginia Press, 2013.

Deshler, Charles D. "How the Declaration Was Received in the Old Thirteen." *Harper's New Monthly Magazine* 85, no. 506 (July 1892): 165–87.

Detweiler, Philip F. "The Changing Reputation of the Declaration of Independence: The First Fifty Years." *William and Mary Quarterly* 19, no. 4 (October 1962): 557–74. doi:10.2307/1920163.

D.D. "London Newspapers of 1776 and the Declaration of Independence." *The Nation* (1898): 127–28.

Dippel, Horst, *Germany and the American Revolution, 1770–1800: A Sociohistorical Investigation of Late Eighteenth-Century Political Thinking.* Translated by Bernhard A. Uhlendorf. University of North Carolina Press, 1977.

Dull, Jonathan R. *A Diplomatic History of the American Revolution.* Yale University Press, 1985.

Eisenstein, Elizabeth L. *The Printing Revolution in Early Modern Europe.* 2nd ed. Cambridge University Press, 2005.

Ellis, Joseph J. *Revolutionary Summer: The Birth of American Independence.* Knopf, 2013.

Fenn, Elizabeth A. *Pox Americana: The Great Smallpox Epidemic of 1775–82.* Hill and Wang, 2001.

Ferreiro, Larrie D. *Brothers at Arms: American Independence and the Men of France & Spain Who Saved It.* Knopf, 2016.

Fisher, Samuel K. *The Gaelic and Indian Origins of the American Revolution: Diversity and Empire in the British Atlantic, 1688–1783.* Oxford University Press, 2022.

Fisher, Sydney George. "The Twenty-Eight Charges Against the King in the Declaration of Independence." *Pennsylvania Magazine of History and Biography* 31, no. 3 (1907): 257–303. https://www.jstor.org/stable/20085387.

Fitz, Caitlin A. " 'Suspected on Both Sides': Little Abraham, Iroquois Neutrality, and the American Revolution." *Journal of the Early Republic* 28, no. 3 (2008): 299–335. https://www.jstor.org/stable/40208153.

Fliegelman, Jay. *Declaring Independence: Jefferson, Natural Language & the Culture of Performance.* Stanford University Press, 1993.

Fox, Francis S. *Sweet Land of Liberty: The Ordeal of the American Revolution in Northampton County, Pennsylvania.* Pennsylvania State University Press, 2000.

Friedenwald, Herbert. *The Declaration of Independence: An Interpretation and an Analysis.* Macmillan, 1904.

Glasson, Travis. *Mastering Christianity: Missionary Anglicanism and Slavery in the Atlantic World.* Oxford University Press, 2011.

Goff, Frederick R. *The John Dunlap Broadside: The First Printing of the Declaration of Independence*. Library of Congress, 1976.

Gould, Eliga H. *Among the Powers of the Earth: The American Revolution and the Making of a New World Empire*. Harvard University Press, 2012.

Graymont, Barbara. *The Iroquois in the American Revolution*. Syracuse University Press, 1972.

Haig, Robert L. *The Gazetteer, 1735–1797: A Study in the Eighteenth-Century English Newspaper*. Southern Illinois University Press, 1960.

Harris, Leslie M. *In the Shadow of Slavery: African Americans in New York City, 1626–1863*. University of Chicago Press, 2003.

Hawke, David Freeman. *In the Midst of a Revolution*. University of Pennsylvania Press, 1961.

Hays, I. Minis. "A Note on the History of the Jefferson Manuscript Draught of the Declaration of Independence in the Library of the American Philosophical Society." *Proceedings of the American Philosophical Society* 157 (July 1898). https://www.jstor.org/stable/983698.

Hazelton, John H. *The Declaration of Independence: Its History*. Dodd, Mead, 1906.

Hoberman, Michael. "'How it Will End, the Blessed God Knows': A Reading of Jewish Correspondence During the Revolutionary War Era." *American Jewish History* 99, no. 4 (October 2015): 281–313. https://www.jstor.org/stable/24805490.

Hogeland, William. *Declaration: The Nine Tumultuous Weeks When America Became Independent, May 1–July 4, 1776*. Simon & Schuster, 2010.

Holmes, David L. "The Episcopal Church and the American Revolution." *Historical Magazine of the Protestant Episcopal Church* 47, no. 3 (September 1978): 261–91. https://www.jstor.org/stable/42973625.

Howell, Wilbur Samuel. "The Declaration of Independence and Eighteenth-Century Logic." *William and Mary Quarterly* 18, no. 4 (October 1961): 463–84. doi:10.2307/1921097.

Humphrey, Carol Sue. *The American Revolution and the Press: The Promise of Independence*. Northwestern University Press, 2013.

Hutson, James H. "The Partition Treaty and the Declaration of American Independence." *Journal of American History* 58, no. 4 (March 1972): 877–96. doi:10.2307/1917849.

Irvin, Benjamin H. *Clothed in Robes of Sovereignty: The Continental Congress and the People Out of Doors*. Oxford University Press, 2011.

Jayne, Allen. *Jefferson's Declaration of Independence: Origins, Philosophy, and Theology*. University Press of Kentucky, 1998.

Jortner, Adam. *A Promised Land: Jewish Patriots, the American Revolution, & the Birth of Religious Freedom*. Oxford University Press, 2024.

Larson, Carlton F. W. *The Trials of Allegiance: Treason, Juries, and the American Revolution*. Oxford University Press, 2019.

Leamon, James S. *The Reverend Jacob Bailey, Maine Loyalist: For God, King, Country, and for Self*. University of Massachusetts Press, 2012.

Loughran, Trish. *The Republic in Print: Print Culture in the Age of U.S. Nation Building, 1770–1870*. Columbia University Press, 2007.

Lucas, Stephen E. "The Rhetorical Ancestry of the Declaration of Independence." *Rhetoric and Public Affairs* 1, no. 2 (Summer 1998): 143–84. https://www.jstor.org/stable/41939441.

Lurie, Maxine N. *Taking Sides in Revolutionary New Jersey: Caught in the Crossfire*. Rutgers University Press, 2022.

Lutnick, Solomon. *The American Revolution and the British Press, 1775–1783*. University of Missouri Press, 1967.

Lutz, Donald S. "The Declaration of Independence as Part of an American National Compact." *Publius* 19, no. 1 (Winter 1989): 41–58. https://www.jstor.org/stable/3330564.

Kammen, Michael G. *A Rope of Sand: The Colonial Agents, British Politics, and the American Revolution.* Cornell University Press, 1968.

Kaplan, Sidney. "The 'Domestic Insurrections' of the Declaration of Independence." *Journal of Negro History* 61, no. 3 (1976): 243–55. doi:10.2307/2717252.

Maier, Pauline. *American Scripture: Making the Declaration of Independence.* Knopf, 1997.

Malone, Dumas. *The Story of the Declaration of Independence.* Oxford University Press, 1954.

Marcus, Jacob Rader. *Early American Jewry.* Vol. 2: *The Jews of Pennsylvania and the South, 1655–1790.* Jewish Publication Society of America, 1955.

Marcus, Jacob Rader. *United States Jewry, 1776–1985.* Vol. 1. Wayne State University Press, 1989.

Marks, Arthur S. "The Statue of King George III in New York and the Iconology of Regicide." *American Art Journal* 13, no. 3 (1981): 61–82. doi:10.2307/1594285.

Marston, Jerrilyn Greene. *King and Congress: The Transfer of Political Legitimacy, 1774–1776.* Princeton University Press, 1987.

McBride, Spencer W. *Pulpit and Nation: Clergymen and the Politics of Revolutionary America.* University of Virginia Press, 2016.

McConville, Brendan. *The King's Three Faces: The Rise and Fall of Royal America, 1688–1776.* Omohundro Institute and University of North Carolina Press, 2006.

McDonald, Robert M. S. "Thomas Jefferson's Changing Reputation as Author of the Declaration of Independence: The First Fifty Years." *Journal of the Early Republic* 19, no. 2 (Summer 1999): 169–95. doi:10.2307/3124951.

Merritt, Eli. *Disunion Among Ourselves: The Perilous Politics of the American Revolution.* University of Missouri Press, 2023.

Miner, Ward L. *William Goddard, Newspaperman.* Duke University Press, 1962.

Mires, Charlene. *Independence Hall in American Memory.* University of Pennsylvania Press, 2002.

Morgan, David T. and William J. Schmidt. "From Economic Sanctions to Political Separation: The North Carolina Delegation to the Continental Congress, 1774–1776." *North Carolina Historical Review* 52, no. 3 (July 1975): 215–34. https://www.jstor.org/stable/23529692.

Nettels, Curtis P. "A Link in the Chain of Events Leading to American Independence." *William and Mary Quarterly* 3, no. 1 (January 1946): 36–47. doi:10.2307/1922894.

O'Keefe, Kieran J. "Mass Incarceration as Revolutionary Policy: The Imprisonment of the Hudson Valley Loyalists." *Early American Studies* 19, no. 3 (2021): 495–527. doi:10.1353/eam.2021.0016.

O'Shaughnessy, Andrew Jackson. *The Men Who Lost America: British Leadership, the American Revolution, and the Fate of the Empire.* Yale University Press, 2013.

Onuf, Peter S. "A Declaration of Independence for Diplomatic Historians." *Diplomatic History* 22, no. 1 (Winter 1998): 71–83. https://www.jstor.org/stable/24913722.

Ossipow, William, and Dominik Gerber. "The Reception of Vattel's *Law of Nations* in the American Colonies." *American Journal of Legal History* 57, no. 4 (December 2017): 521–55. https://www.jstor.org/stable/48545068.

Otis, Andrew. "'Guilty of Publishing Only': Jury Nullification as a Legal Defense in the Eighteenth Century." *Journal of Interdisciplinary History* 53, no. 2 (2022): 267–88. https://muse.jhu.edu/article/865298/.

Papas, Phillip. *That Ever Loyal Island: Staten Island and the American Revolution*. New York University Press, 2007.

Parkinson, Robert G. *The Common Cause: Creating Race and Nation in the American Revolution*. Omohundro Institute and University of North Carolina Press, 2016.

Peckham, Howard H. "Independence: The View from Britain." In Howard Mumford Jones and Howard H. Peckham, *The Declaration of Independence: Two Essays*. American Antiquarian Society, 1976.

Pencak, William. "The Declaration of Independence: Changing Interpretations and a New Hypothesis." *Pennsylvania History* 57, no. 3 (July 1990): 225–35. https://www.jstor.org/stable/27773386.

Pincus, Steve. *The Heart of the Declaration: The Founders' Case for an Activist Government*. Yale University Press, 2016.

Popkin, Jeremy D. *News and Politics in the Age of Revolution: Jean Luzac's* Gazette de Leyde. Cornell University Press, 1989.

Prado, Fabrício. "Anglo-Portuguese Cooperation in Eighteenth-Century Atlantic South America." In *The Río de la Plata from Colony to Nations: Commerce, Society, and Politics*, ed. Fabrício Prado, Viviana L. Grieco, and Alex Borucki. Palgrave Macmillan, 2022.

Preston, David L. *Braddock's Defeat: The Battle of the Monongahela and the Road to Revolution*. Oxford University Press, 2015.

Rakove, Jack N. *The Annotated U.S. Constitution and Declaration of Independence*. Belknap Press of Harvard University Press, 2009.

Rakove, Jack N. *The Beginnings of National Politics: An Interpretive History of the Continental Congress*. Rev. ed. Johns Hopkins University Press, 2019.

Ritz, Wilfred J. "From the *Here* of Jefferson's Handwritten Rough Draft of the Declaration of Independence to the *There* of the Printed Dunlap Broadside." *Pennsylvania Magazine of History and Biography* 116, no. 4 (1992): 499–512. https://www.jstor.org/stable/20092759.

Rogers, Nicholas. *Blood Waters: War, Disease and Race in the Eighteenth-Century British Caribbean*. Boydell Press, 2021.

Ruddiman, John A. " 'A record in the hands of thousands': Power and Negotiation in the Orderly Books of the Continental Army." *William and Mary Quarterly* 67, no. 4 (October 2010): 747–74. doi:10.5309/willmaryquar.67.4.0747.

Ryerson, Richard Alan. *The Revolution Is Now Begun: The Radical Committees of Philadelphia, 1765–1776*. University of Pennsylvania Press, 1978.

Sadosky, Leonard J. *Revolutionary Negotiations: Indians, Empires, and Diplomats in the Founding of America*. University of Virginia Press, 2009.

Sainsbury, John. *Disaffected Patriots: London Supporters of Revolutionary America, 1769–1782*. McGill–Queen's University, 1987.

Sarson, Steven. *The Course of Human Events: The Declaration of Independence and the Historical Origins of the United States*. University of Virginia Press, 2025.

Schaeper, Thomas J. *Edward Bancroft: Scientist, Author, Spy*. Yale University Press, 2011.

Schuetze, Sarah. "Carrying Home the Enemy: Smallpox and Revolution in American Love and Letters, 1775–76." *Early American Literature* 53, no. 1 (2018): 97–125. https://www.jstor.org/stable/90019133.

Singerton, Jonathan. *The American Revolution and the Habsburg Monarchy*. University of Virginia Press, 2022.

Slauter, Eric. "The Declaration of Independence and the New Nation." In *The Cambridge Companion to Thomas Jefferson*, edited by Frank Shuffelton. Cambridge University Press, 2009.

Slauter, Will. "News and Diplomacy in the Age of the American Revolution." Ph.D. diss., Princeton University, 2007.

Starr, Thomas. "Separated at Birth: Text and Context of the Declaration of Independence." *Proceedings of the American Antiquarian Society* 110, no. 1 (April 2000): 153–99.

Stuckey, Mary E., ed. *Used, Abused, and Sidelined: Debating the Declaration*. The Pennsylvania State University Press, 2025.

Taylor, Alan. *The Divided Ground: Indians, Settlers, and the Northern Borderland of the American Revolution*. Knopf, 2006.

Taylor, Jordan E. "Enquire of the Printer: Newspaper Advertising and the Moral Economy of the North American Slave Trade, 1704–1807." *Early American Studies* 18, no. 3 (Summer 2020): 287–323. https://www.jstor.org/stable/27077808.

Taylor, Jordan E. *Misinformation Nation: Foreign News and the Politics of Truth in Revolutionary America*. Johns Hopkins University Press, 2022.

Tsesis, Alexander. *For Liberty and Equality: The Life and Times of the Declaration of Independence*. Oxford University Press, 2012.

Tupper, Frederick and Helen Tyler Brown, eds. *Grandmother Tyler's Book: The Recollections of Mary Palmer Tyler (Mrs. Royall Tyler) 1775–1866*. G. P. Putnam's Sons, 1925.

Tyler, Moses Coit. "The Declaration of Independence in the Light of Modern Criticism." *North American Review* 163, no. 4 (July 1896): 1–16.

Waldstreicher, David. *In the Midst of Perpetual Fetes: The Making of American Nationalism, 1776–1820*. Omohundro Institute and University of North Carolina Press, 1997.

Walsh, Michael J. "Contemporary Broadside Editions of the Declaration of Independence." *Harvard Library Bulletin* 3, no. 1 (Winter 1949): 31–43.

Warner, Michael. *The Letters of the Republic: Publication and the Public Sphere in Eighteenth-Century America*. Harvard University Press, 1990.

Warner, William B. *Protocols of Liberty: Communication Innovation and the American Revolution*. University of Chicago Press, 2013.

Warren, Charles. "Fourth of July Myths." *William and Mary Quarterly* 2, no. 3 (July 1945): 237–72. doi:10.2307/1921451.

Wehrman, Andrew M. *The Contagion of Liberty: The Politics of Smallpox in the American Revolution*. Johns Hopkins University Press, 2022.

Wendorf, Richard. "Declaring, Drafting, and Composing American Independence." *Papers of the Bibliographical Society of America* 108, no. 3 (September 2014): 307–24. doi:10.1086/680864.

Wills, Garry. *Inventing America: Jefferson's Declaration of Independence*. Rev. ed. Houghton Mifflin Company, 2002.

Wilson, Lisa. *A History of Stepfamilies in Early America*. University of North Carolina Press, 2014.

Winch, Julie. *A Gentleman of Color: The Life of James Forten*. Oxford University Press, 2002.

Winters, John C. *"The Amazing Iroquois" and the Invention of the Empire State*. Oxford University Press, 2023.

Wood, Gordon S. *The Creation of the American Republic, 1776–1787*. Rev. ed. Omohundro Institute and University of North Carolina Press, 1998.

Wolf, 2nd, Edwin. Review of *The John Dunlap Broadside*, by Frederick Goff. *Papers of the Bibliographical Society of America* 71, no. 2 (1977): 231–2. https://www.jstor.org/stable/24302084.

Wunder, John R. "'Merciless Indian Savages' and the Declaration of Independence: Native Americans Translate the Ecunnaunuxulgee Document." *American Indian Law Review* 25, no. 1 (2000/1): 65–92. doi:10.2307/20070651.

York, Neil. "George III, Tyrant: *The Crisis* as Critic of Empire, 1775–1776." *History* 94, no. 4 (October 2009): 434–60. https://www.jstor.org/stable/24429092.

Zuckert, Michael P. "Self-Evident Truth and the Declaration of Independence." *Review of Politics* 49, no. 3 (1987): 319–39. https://www.jstor.org/stable/1407839.

Index

For the benefit of digital users, indexed terms that span two pages (e.g., 52–53) may, on occasion, appear on only one of those pages.